*Semiotics and
the Philosophy
of Language*

# Semiotics and the Philosophy of Language

## UMBERTO ECO

MACMILLAN

First published in the UK 1984 by
THE MACMILLAN PRESS LTD
Houndmills, Basingstoke, Hampshire RG21 2XS
and London
Companies and representatives
throughout the world

Reprinted 1984, 1985

Printed in Hong Kong

ISBN 0–333–36354–X (hardcover)
ISBN 0–333–36355–8 (paperback)

# CONTENTS

# *Note*

Early versions of Chapters 1, 3, 4, and 5 of this book were written in Italian as entries of the *Enciclopedia Einaudi*; however, these have been reworked and rewritten for the purposes of this book. Slightly different versions of the following chapters have already been published in English: "Signs" (Chapter 1), as "The Sign Revisited," translated by Lucia Re, *Philosophy and Social Criticism* 7 (1980); "Metaphor" (Chapter 3), as "The Scandal of Metaphor," translated by Christopher Paci, *Poetics Today* 3 (1982); "Isotopy" (Chapter 6), as part of the article "Two Problems in Textual Interpretation," *Poetics Today* 1a (1980). An earlier version of "Mirrors" (Chapter 7) was written for a volume in honor of Thomas A. Sebeok for his sixty-fifth birthday. The translators mentioned above are not responsible for the changes in the final versions.

Figure 3.5 of this book is adapted from Groupe $\mu$, *Rhétorique générale* (Paris: Larousse, 1970), p. 109. Figure 6.1 of this book is reprinted from Umberto Eco, *The Role of the Reader* (Bloomington: Indiana University Press, 1979), p. 14.

In the course of this book, I use (as I did in *A Theory of Semiotics*) single slashes to indicate expressions; guillemets indicate the corresponding content. Thus /x/ means, or is an expression for, «x». However, when it is not strictly necessary to stress such a distinction (that is, when words or sentences are used as expressions whose corresponding content is taken as intuitively understood), I simply use italics.

All the subjects dealt with in this book have been widely discussed during the last four years in my courses at the University of Bologna and during my visiting terms at Yale University and Columbia University; many of the topics were also elaborated in the course of various congresses, symposia, seminars — in so many circumstances that it would be difficult to be honest and exhaustive in expressing my gratitude to all those students and colleagues who have contributed to the original draft with their objections and suggestions. I am, however, particularly indebted to Barbara Spackman and John Deely, who have kindly revised part of the chapters.

*Semiotics and
the Philosophy
of Language*

# [0]

# INTRODUCTION

## 0.1.

The empirical reader of this book could have the impression that its various chapters deal with two theoretical objects, mutually incompatible, each being focused on as *the* object of a general semiotic approach: the sign, or the sign-function, and semiosis. The sign is usually considered as a correlation between a signifier and a signified (or between expression and content) and therefore as an action between pairs. Semiosis is, according to Peirce, "an action, or influence, which is, or involves, an operation of *three* subjects, such as a sign, its object, and its interpretant, this tri-relative influence not being in any way resolvable into an action between pairs" (*C. P.* 5.484).

The Model Reader should (as I hope) understand that the aim of this book is to show that these two notions are not incompatible. If one thinks of the more trivial and current notion of linguistic sign, one cannot match a theory of semiosis as indefinite interpretation with a 'doctrine of signs'; in this case, one has to choose either a theory of the sign or a theory of semiosis (or of the significant practice, of the communicative processes, of textual and discursive activity). However, the main purpose of this book is to show that such an alternative is a misleading one: the sign is the origin of the semiosic processes, and there is no opposition between the 'nomadism' of semiosis (and of interpretive activity) and the alleged stiffness and immobility of the sign. The concept of sign must be disentangled from its trivial identification with the idea of coded equivalence and identity; the semiosic process of interpretation is present at the very core of the concept of sign.

Chapter I ("Signs") shows that this idea was clearly spelled out by the

[1]

classical doctrines where the *sēmeîon* was not considered as an equivalence but as an inference.

Chapter 7 ("Mirrors") tackles the question of a threshold between semiotic and presemiotic phenomena. The phenomenology of our experience with mirror images represents the *experimentum crucis* for testing the role played by two fundamental characteristics of any semiosic experience: a sign is an $x$ standing for a $y$ which is absent, and the process which leads the interpreter from $x$ to $y$ is of an inferential nature.

Definition is the subject matter of Chapter 2 ("Dictionary vs. Encyclopedia"), from the allegedly Aristotelian model called the Porphyrian Tree to the contemporary discussions on the possibility of an encyclopedia-like representation of our semantic competence. In this chapter, the current opposition 'dictionary/encyclopedia' is traced back to the classical models of the tree and the labyrinth. /Tree/ and /laby·inth/ are not metaphors. They are topological and logical models, and as such they were and are studied in their proper domain. However, I have no difficulties in admitting that, as labels or emblems for the overall discussion developed in the various chapters of this book, they can be taken as metaphors. As such, they stand for the nonmetaphoric Peircean notion of *unlimited semiosis* and for the Model Q outlined in *A Theory of Semiotics* (Eco 1976).

If texts can be produced and interpreted as I suggested in *The Role of the Reader* (Eco 1979), it is because the universe of semiosis can be postulated in the format of a labyrinth. The regulative hypothesis of a semiosic universe structured as a labyrinth governs the approach to other classical issues such as metaphor, symbol, and code.

Metaphors can be read according to multiple interpretations; yet these interpretations can be more or less legitimated on the grounds of an underlying encyclopedic competence. In this sense, Chapter 3 ("Metaphor") aims at improving some of the proposals of my essay "The Semantics of Metaphor" (Eco 1979, ch. 2), where the image of the Swedish stall-bars required a more rigorous explanation in terms of a representable encyclopedic network.

The notion of symbolic mode outlined in Chapter 4 ("Symbol") accounts for all these cases of textual production that do not rely on a preestablished portion of encyclopedia but invent and propose for the first time a new interpretive connection.

### 0.2.

The principle of interpretation says that "a sign is something by knowing which we know something more" (Peirce). The Peircean idea of semiosis is the idea of an infinite process of interpretation. It seems that the symbolic mode is the paramount example of this possibility.

However, interpretation is not reducible to the responses elicited by the textual strategies accorded to the symbolic mode. The interpretation of metaphors shifts from the univocality of catachreses to the open possibilities offered by inventive metaphors. Many texts have undoubtedly many possible senses, but it is still possible to decide *which one* has to be selected if one approaches the text in the light of a given topic, as well as it is possible to tell of certain texts *how many* isotopies they display. (See Chapter 6, "Isotopy," where I discuss the many senses of the concept of isotopy.) Besides, we are implementing inferences (and we are facing a certain interpretive freedom) even when we understand an isolated word, a sentence, a visual sign.

All this amounts to saying that the principle of interpretation (in its Peircean sense) has not to be identified with the farfetched assumption that — as Valéry said — *il n'y a pas de vrai sens d'un texte.*

When considering contemporary theories of interpretation (especially in the literary domain), we can conceive of a range with two extremes $x$ and $y$. (I refuse to represent it spatially as a line going from left to right, so as not to suggest unfair and misleading ideological connotations.) Let us say that at the extreme $x$ stand those who assume that every text (be it a conversational utterance or a poem) can be interpreted in one, and only one, way, according to the intention of its author. At the extreme $y$ stand those who assume that a text supports every interpretation — albeit I suppose that nobody would *literally* endorse such a claim, except perhaps a visionary devotee of the Kabalistic *temura.*

I do not think that the Peircean notion of semiosis should privilege one of these extremes. At most, it provides a theoretical tool for identifying, according to different semiosic processes, a continuum of intermediate positions. If I ask someone what time it is and if he answers /6:15/, my interpretation of this expression can conclude that (provided there are no other co-textual clues and provided the speaker is not a notorious liar or a psychotic subject) the speaker positively said that it is forty-five minutes to seven and that he intended to say so.

On the other hand, the notion of interpretation can explain both in which sense a given text displays two and no more possibilities of disambiguation and why an instance of the symbolic mode requests an indefinite series of alternative or complementary interpretations. In any case, between $x$ and $y$ stands a recorded thesaurus of encyclopedic competence, a social storage of world knowledge, and on these grounds, and only on these grounds, any interpretation can be both implemented and legitimated — even in the case of the most 'open' instances of the option $y$.

## 0.3.

In order to discuss these points, all the chapters of this book, while examining a series of fundamental concepts traditionally related to the one of sign, revisit each of them from a historical point of view, looking backward at the moment they were posited for the first time and were endowed with a theoretical fecundity that sometimes they have lost in the course of a millenary debate.

It is clear from the index that most of my authors are not linguists or full-time semioticians, but philosophers who have speculated about signs. This is not solely due to the fact that I started my academic career as a philosopher, particularly interested in the Middle Ages, and that since the Second Congress of the IASS (Vienna, 1979) I have advocated a revisitation of the whole history of philosophy (as well as of other disciplines) to take back the origins of semiotic concepts. This is not (or not only) a book in which a semiotician pays a visit, *extra moenia*, to the alien territory of philosophy. This is a book on philosophy of language for the very simple reason that a general semiotics is nothing else but *a* philosophy of language and that the 'good' philosophies of language, from *Cratylus* to *Philosophical Investigations*, are concerned with all the semiotic questions.

It is rather difficult to provide a 'catholic' definition of philosophy of language. In a nondogmatic overview, one should list under this heading Plato's discussions on *nomos* and *phusis*, Aristotle's assumption that /Being/ is used in various senses, Russell's theory of denotation, as well as Heidegger, Cassirer, and Merleau-Ponty. I am not sure that a general semiotics can answer all the questions raised during the last two thousand years by the various philosophies of language; but I am sure that all the questions a general semiotics deals with have been posited in the framework of some philosophy of language.

## 0.4.

In order to make this point clear, one must distinguish between *specific semiotics* and *general* semiotics. I understand that this is a very crude distinction as compared with more subtle classifications. I am thinking of Hjelmslev's proposal according to which there are a *scientific semiotic* and a *nonscientific semiotic*, both studied by a *metasemiotic;* a *semiology* as a *metasemiotic* studying a *nonscientific semiotic*, whose terminology is studied by a *metasemiology*. Since semiotics can be either denotative or connotative, there is also a *meta (connotative) semiotic*. Pelc (1981) has outlined a far more analytical classification of the many levels of a semiotic study. At the present state of the art, I am inclined to take these and other distinctions as fruitfully descriptive, while I am not sure that they can be taken as normative. In any case, for the purposes of the present discourse, I think it will be sufficient to work upon the distinction between general and specific.

A specific semiotics is, or aims at being, the 'grammar' of a particular sign system, and proves to be successful insofar as it describes a given field of communicative phenomena as ruled by a system of signification. Thus there are 'grammars' of the American Sign Language, of traffic signals, of a playing-card 'matrix' for different games or of a particular game (for instance, poker). These systems can be studied from a syntactic, a semantic, or a pragmatic point of view. Sometimes a specific semiotics only focuses on a particular subsystem (or s-code, as defined in Eco 1976) that works within a more complex system of systems: such is the case of the theory of phonemic distinctive features or of the description of the phonemic oppositions holding for a given verbal language.

Every specific semiotics (as every science) is concerned with general epistemological problems. It has to posit its own theoretical object, according to criteria of pertinence, in order to account for an otherwise disordered field of empirical data; and the researcher must be aware of the underlying philosophical assumptions that influence its choice and its criteria for relevance. Like every science, even a specific semiotics ought to take into account a sort of 'uncertainty principle' (as anthropologists must be aware of the fact that their presence as observers can disturb the normal course of the behavioral phenomena they observe). Notwithstanding, a specific semiotics can aspire to a 'scientific' status. Specific semiotics study phenomena that are reasonably independent of their observations. Their objects are usually 'stable' — even though the duration of a code for traffic signals has a shorter range than the duration of a phonological system, whereas lexical systems are in a continuous process of transformation. Being scientific, a specific semiotics can have a predictive power: it can tell which expressions, produced according to the rules of a given system of signification, are acceptable or 'grammatical' and which ones a user of the system would presumably produce in a given situation.

Obviously, there are different degrees of scientificity, according to the rigidity or the flexibility of the sign system in question. The 'grammar' of traffic lights and the structure of a phonological system seem to be more 'objective' (more 'scientific') than the description of the narrative function in Russian fairy tales; and the narrative function of the Russian fairy tales seems to be less questionable than, let us say, a possible system of narrative function in the novels of French Romanticism. Not every specific semiotics can claim to be like a natural science. In fact, every specific semiotics is at most a human science, and everybody knows how controversial such a notion still is. However, when cultural anthropology studies the kinship system in a certain society, it works upon a rather stable field of phenomena, can produce a theoretical object, and can make some prediction about the behavior of the members of this society. The same happens with a lexical analysis of the system of terms expressing kinship in the same society.

In this sense, a specific semiotics (as any other science) can also have effects in terms of social engineering. When the anthropologist increases our knowledge of a given society, his or her descriptions can be used for 'missionary' purposes in order to improve, to preserve, or to destroy a given culture, or to exploit its members. It goes without saying that the natural sciences have engineering purposes, not only in the strict technological sense; a good knowledge of human anatomy also can help one to improve one's physical fitness. In the same way, the description of the internal logic of road signals can suggest to some public agency how to improve the practice of road signaling. Such an engineering power is the result of a free decision, not an automatic side effect of the scientific research.

All around this area of more or less established and rigorous 'grammatical' knowledge is a hardly definable 'twilight zone' of semiotically oriented practices, such as the application of semiotic notions to literary criticism, the analysis of political discourses, perhaps a great part of the so-called linguistic philosophy when it attempts "to solve philosophical problems by analyzing the meanings of words, and by analyzing logical relations between words in natural languages" (Searle 1971:1). Frequently, these semiotic practices rely on the set of knowledge provided by specific semiotics, sometimes they contribute to enriching them, and, in many other cases, they borrow their fundamental ideas from a general semiotics.

0.5.

The task and the nature of a general semiotics are different. To outline a project for a general semiotics, it is not sufficient to assert, as Saussure did, that language is a system comparable to writing, symbolic rites, deaf-mute alphabets, military signals, and so on, and that one should conceive of a science able to study the life of signs within the framework of social and general psychology. In order to conceive of such a science, one must say in which sense these different systems are mutually comparable: if they are all systems in the same sense of the word system; if, by consequence, the mutual comparison of these systems can reveal common systematic laws able to explain, from a unified point of view, their way of functioning. Saussure said that such a science did not exist as yet, even though it had a right to exist. Many semioticians assume (and I rank among them) that Peirce in fact outlined such a discipline; but others maintain (and I still rank among them) that such a discipline cannot be a science in the sense of physics or electronics.

Thus the basic problem of a general semiotics splits into three different questions: (a) Can one approach many, and apparently different, phenomena as if they were all phenomena of signification and/or of communication? (b) Is there a unified approach able to account for all these semiotic phenomena as if they were based on the same system of rules (the notion of system not being a mere analogical one)? (c) Is this approach a 'scientific' one?

If there is something which deserves the name of general semiotics, this something is a discourse dealing with the questions above, and this discourse is a philosophical one. In any case, it encounters the problem raised by philosophy of language because, in order to answer the questions above, it is obliged to reconsider, from a general (not merely 'linguistic') point of view, classical issues such as meaning, reference, truth, context, communicational acts (be they vocal or else), as well as many logical problems as analytic vs. synthetic, necessity, implication, entailment, inference, hypothesis, and so on.

Naturally, many problems that originally were simply philosophical now belong to the province of some science. Perhaps in the future some of the problems raised today by a general semiotics will find a 'scientific' answer — for instance, the debated and still speculative problem of the universals of language, today tackled by the catastrophe theory. Some others will remain purely philosophical.

General semiotics was first of all concerned with the concept of sign. This concept is better discussed in Chapter 1, where I give the reasons why I think it is still tenable, despite the various criticisms it has undergone. It must be clear that one can decide that the theoretical object of semiotics can be a different and more fruitful one, let us say, text, semiosis, significant practice, communication, discourse, language, effability, and so on — but the real problem is not so much *which* object has to be appointed as the central one; the problem is to decide whether there is a unified object or not. Now, this object (let it be the concept of sign) can become the central object of a general semiotics insofar as one decides that such a category can explain a series of human (and maybe animal) behaviors, be they vocal, visual, termic, gestural, or other. In this sense, the first question of a general semiotics is close to the capital question of any philosophy of language: what does it mean for human beings to say, to express meanings, to convey ideas, or to mention states of the world? By which means do people perform this task? Only by words? And, if not, what do verbal activity and other signifying or communicative activities have in common?

A general semiotics at most improves some of the traditional approaches of philosophy of language. It assumes that it is impossible to speak about verbal language without comparing it to other forms of signification and/or communication. In this sense, a general semiotics is fundamentally comparative in its approach. But it is enough to think — for instance — of Wittgenstein, Husserl, or Cassirer to realize that a *good* philosophy of language necessarily takes up this issue.

A general semiotics is influenced, more than any philosophy of language, by the experiences of specific semiotics. But the history of philosophy displays other examples of speculations about signification and communication that have attempted to elaborate a systematic approach to every sort of 'language' — starting from the results and from the technicalities of some specific semiotics. Thus a general semiotics is simply a philosophy of language which stresses the comparative and systematic approach to languages (and not only to verbal language) by exploiting the result of different, more local inquiries.

### 0.6.

Not all philosophers of language would agree with such a project. Many of them assume that the categories provided in order to explain verbal language — including 'signification', 'meaning', and 'code' — cannot hold when applied to other systems of signification. In Chapter 1 of this book, I discuss a strong objection formulated in this line of thought, according to which semiotics unduly fuses three different problems concerning three different and mutually irreducible phenomena, studied by three different theoretical approaches — namely, *intended meaning, inference from evidences,* and *pictorial representation.* It goes without saying that, on the contrary, I assume that these three problems concern a unique theoretical object. Elsewhere (Eco 1976) I discussed in which sense verbal signification and pictorial representation (as well as other phenomena) can be subsumed under the general model of the sign-function. Here I shall maintain that inferential processes (mainly under the form of Peircean *abduction*) stand at the basis of every semiotic phenomenon.

It has been suggested (see, for instance, Scruton 1980) that the word *sign* means too many things and points to many functions; thus semiotics would play on mere — and weak — analogies when it asserts that a cloud *means* rain in the same sense in which the French sentence 'je m'ennuie' *means* that I am bored. What these two phenomena have in common is "only a small feature on the surface of each" and "if there is a common essence of 'signs' it is sure to be very shallow; semiology pretends that it is deep" (Scruton 1980). I suspect that no semiotician would say that *on the surface* a cloud and a sentence have something in common. As I recall in Chapter 1 of this book, Greek philosophers took a long time to recognize that there was some relation between 'natural signs' and words, and even the Stoics, who decidedly approached the problem, found some difficulty in settling it definitively. This means that, if a cloud and a sentence have something in common, this something is not shallow but deep.

On the other hand, there is something 'intuitively' common to the red light of a traffic signal and the verbal order /stop/. One does not need to have a semiotic mind to understand this. The semiotic problem is not so much to recognize that both physical vehicles convey more or less the same command; it begins when one wonders about the cultural or cognitive mechanisms that allow any trained addressee to react to both sign-vehicles in the same way. To realize that /stop/ and the red light convey the same order is as intuitive as to decide that, to convince people to refrain from drinking a certain liquid, one can either write /poison/ or draw a skull on the bottle. Now, the basic problem of a semiotic inquiry on different kinds of signs is exactly this one: why does one understand something *intuitively?*

As posited this way, the question is more than semiotic. It starts as a philosophical question (even though it can have a scientific answer, too). Frequently, one uses the adjective 'intuitive' as an empiricist shibboleth and gets rid of a lot of interesting questions by recurring to 'intuitive truths'. To say that some truth is intuitive usually means that one does not want to challenge it for the sake of economy — that is, because its explanation belongs to some other science. However, one (if not the most important) of the semiotic endeavors is to explain why something looks intuitive, in order to discover under the felicity of the so-called intuition a complex cognitive process.

It is intuitive that I can seduce a lady, a potential partner in an important business, or a corrupt politician, either by saying that I am rich and generous or by offering her or him a titillating dinner in the most luxurious restaurant of the city, with a menu that would have syntagmatically delighted Roland Barthes. It is equally intuitive that probably the dinner would be more convincing than a crude verbal statement. It is not intuitive why all this is intuitive. Perhaps it is by virtue of a 'shallow' similarity in their effect that one intuitively understands that both behaviors produce ideas and emotions in the mind of the potential victim. But, in order to explain how both behaviors produce the same effect, one should look for something 'deeper'. To look for such a deeper common structure, for the cognitive and cultural laws that rule both phenomena — such is the endeavor of a general semiotics. Once having addressed this problem, one probably would be in the position of deciding whether the same cultural or cognitive mechanisms also hold in the case of the cloud and the sentence.

Notice that semiotics is not strictly obliged to answer positively to all the questions raised above; it can also decide, for instance (as many semioticians did), that the way in which a cloud signifies rain is different from the way in which a French sentence signifies — or is equivalent to — an allegedly corresponding English sentence. Semiotics is characterized by its interest in these problems, not by a prerecorded set of answers.

To be interested in these problems requires a philosophical curiosity; according to Aristotle, it is by an act of *wonder* that men began, and begin, to philosophize; and, according to Peirce, all new discoveries start when "we find some very curious circumstances which will be explained by the supposition that it was the case of a general rule and thereupon adopt that supposition" (*C. P.* 2.624). The concept of sign — or every other concept a general semiotics decides to *posit* as its own theoretical object — is nothing but the result of a supposition of this sort. Signs are not empirical objects. Empirical objects become signs (or they are looked at as signs) only from the point of view of a philosophical decision.

### 0.7.

When semiotics posits such concepts as 'sign', it does not act like a science; it acts like philosophy when it posits such abstractions as subject, good and evil, truth or revolution. Now, a philosophy is not a science, because its assertions cannot be empirically tested, and this impossibility is due to the fact that philosophical concepts are not 'emic' definitions of previously recognizable 'etic' data that display even minimal resemblance in shape or function. Philosophical entities exist only insofar as they have been philosophically *posited*. Outside their philosophical framework, the empirical data that a philosophy organizes lose every possible unity and cohesion.

To walk, to make love, to sleep, to refrain from doing something, to give food to someone else, to eat roast beef on Friday — each is either a physical event or the absence of a physical event, or a relation between two or more physical events. However, each becomes an instance of good, bad, or neutral behavior *within a given philosophical framework*. Outside such a framework, to eat roast beef is radically different from making love, and making love is always the same sort of activity independent of the legal status of the partners. From a given philosophical point of view, both to eat roast beef on Friday and to make love to $x$ can become instances of 'sin', whereas both to give food to someone and to make love to $y$ can become instances of virtuous action.

Good or bad are theoretical stipulations according to which, by a philosophical decision, many scattered instances of the most different facts or acts become *the same thing*. It is interesting to remark that also the notions of 'object', 'phenomenon', or 'natural kind', as used by the natural sciences, share the same philosophical nature. This is certainly not the case of specific semiotics or of a human science such as cultural anthropology. Anthropologists elaborate the notion of brother-in-law to define emically a series of etic occurrences, where different persons play the same social function — and they would play this function etically even though no science had previously defined their emic role. A brother-in-law exists independently as a male human being who, like other male human beings, has a sister who has married another male human being; like other male human beings in the same position, a brother-in-law performs (during certain ceremonies) certain ritual acts, allegedly because of his relationship with a given woman and a given man. Anthropologists can fail in detecting the true reason he performs these ritual acts or in selecting certain features of his behavior as relevant, disregarding other phenomena (or can overdo in asserting that the opposition brother-in-law/sister-in-law is analogous to the phonetic opposition voiced/unvoiced . . .). But the anthropologists start from the unquestionable fact that there are nuclei of three persons each, forming both a couple of siblings of the same parents and a couple of persons of different sex living and having sex together.

In philosophy things go differently. What is 'true' for Hegel is radically different from what is 'true' for Tarski, and, when the Schoolmen said that truth is the *adaequatio rei et intellectus*, they did not describe entities that were recognizable as such before that definition. The definition decides what a thing is, what understanding is, and what *adaequatio* is.

This does not mean that a philosophy cannot explain phenomena. It has a great *explanatory power*, since it provides a way to consider as a whole many otherwise disconnected data — so that, when a scientific approach starts with defining an observable datum and a correct (or true) observation, it starts by positing philosophical categories. A philosophy cannot, however, be true in the sense in which a scientific description (even though depending on previous philosophical assumptions) is said to be true. A philosophy is true insofar as it satisfies a need to provide a coherent form to the world, so as to allow its followers to deal coherently with it.

In this sense, a philosophy has a *practical power:* it contributes to the changing of the world. This practical power has nothing to do with the engineering power that in the discussion above I attributed to sciences, including specific semiotics. A science can study either an animal species or the logic of road signals, without necessarily determining their transformation. There is a certain 'distance' between the descriptive stage and the decision, let us say, to improve a species through genetic engineering or to improve a signaling system by reducing or increasing the number of its pertinent elements.

On the contrary, it was the philosophical position of the modern notion of thinking subject that led Western culture to think and to behave in terms of subjectivity. It was the position of notions such as class struggle and revolution that led people to behave in terms of class, and not only to make revolutions but also to decide, on the grounds of this philosophical concept, which social turmoils or riots of the past were or were not a revolution. Since a philosophy has this practical power, it *cannot* have a *predictive power*. It cannot predict what would happen if the world were as it described it. Its power is not the direct result of an act of engineering performed on the basis of a more or less neutral description of independent data. A philosophy can know what it has produced only *après coup*. Marxism as a philosophy displays a reasonable explanatory power and has had, indeed, a consistent practical power: it contributed to the transformation, in the long run, of many ideas and some states of the world. It failed when, assuming to be a science, it claimed to have a predictive power: it transformed ideas and states of the world in a direction it could not exactly foresee. Applying to globality, a philosophy does not play its role as an actor during a recital; it interacts with other philosophies and with other facts, and it cannot know the results of the interaction between itself and other world visions. World visions can conceive of everything, except alternative world visions, if not in order to criticize them and to show their inconsistency. Affected as they are by a constitutive solipsism, philosophies can say everything about the world they design and very little about the world they help to construct.

## o.8.

A general semiotics is philosophical in this very sense. It cannot work on concrete evidence, if not as already filtered by other specific semiotics (which depends on a general semiotics to be justified in their procedures). A general semiotics studies the whole of the human signifying activity — languages — and languages are what constitutes human beings as such, that is, as semiotic animals. It studies and describes languages through languages. By studying the human signifying activity it influences its course. A general semiotics transforms, for the very fact of its theoretical claim, its own object.

I do not know, as yet, whether a pragmatic theory of speech acts is a chapter of general semiotics or a chapter of a philosophy of language. It should be clear, from the whole of this introduction, that such a question is, to me, devoid of any interest. Undoubtedly, a theory of speech acts starts from the observation (although never innocent) of certain empirical behaviors. In this sense, many of its discoveries could be ranked as items of a specific semiotics. However, I doubt whether a notion such as the one of performative sentence is a neutral one. One says /I promise you/ and bets one's shirt on this promise; in other cases, one utters the same expression without being aware of the fact that one is 'doing things with words'. But a theory of speech acts provides us with such an organized knowledge of our linguistic interaction that the future of our linguistic behavior cannot but be profoundly influenced by the sort of awareness it provides. So a theory of speech acts is explanatory, practically powerful, and not fully predictive. It is an instance of philosophy of language, perhaps a chapter of a general semiotics, not a case of specific semiotics.

I am not saying that philosophies, since they are speculative, speak of the nonexistent. When they say 'subject' or 'class struggle' or 'dialectics', they always point to something that should have been defined and posited in some way. Philosophies can be judged, at most, on the grounds of the perspicacity with which they decide that something is worthy of becoming the starting point for a global explanatory hypothesis. Thus I do not think that the sign (or any other suitable object for a general semiotics) is a mere figment. Notwithstanding, signs exist only for a philosophical glance which decides to see them where other minds see only the fictive result of an analogical 'musement'.

Certainly, the categories posited by a general semiotics can prove their power insofar as they provide a satisfactory working hypothesis to specific semiotics. However, they can also allow one to look at the whole of human activity from a coherent point of view. To see human beings as signifying animals — even outside the practice of verbal language — and to see that their ability to produce and to interpret signs, as well as their ability to draw inferences, is rooted in the same cognitive structures, represent a way to give form to our experience. There are obviously other philosophical approaches, but I think that this one deserves some effort.

# [1]

# SIGNS

## 1.1. Crisis of a concept

Current handbooks of semiotics provide us with different definitions of the concept of sign which are often complementary rather than contradictory. According to Peirce, a sign is "something which stands to somebody for something in some respect or capacity" (*C. P.* 2.228). This definition is a more articulate version of the classical definition *aliquid stat pro aliquo*. When dealing with the inner structure of the sign, Saussure speaks of a twofold entity (signifier and signified). Hjelmslev's definition, which assumes the sign-function as a mutual correlation between two functives (expression-plane and content-plane), can be taken as a more rigorous development of the Saussurean concept.

However, in the same period at the turn of the century in which semiotics asserted itself as a discipline, a series of theoretical propositions concerning the death, or at least the crisis of the concept, of sign was developed. Throughout the history of Western thought, the idea of a semiotic theory — however differently defined — was always labeled as a doctrine of signs (see Jakobson 1974; Rey 1973; Sebeok 1976; Todorov 1977). The disparity of meanings attributed each time to the notion of sign calls for a rigorous critique (at least in the Kantian sense of the word 'critique'). We shall see, however, that the notion of sign had been seriously questioned in this sense since the very beginning.

In the last few years, this reasonable critical attitude seems to have generated its own mannerism. Since it is rhetorically effective to begin a course in philosophy by announcing the death of philosophy, as Freud is pronounced dead at the opening of debates on psychoanalysis, many people have deemed useful to start out in semiotics by announcing the death of the sign. This announcement is rarely prefaced by a philosophical analysis of the concept of sign or by its reexamination in terms of historical semantics. The death sentence is therefore pronounced upon an entity which, being without its identity papers, is likely to be resuscitated under a different name.

## 1.2. The signs of an obstinacy

Everyday language and the dictionaries which record its usages disregard theoretical discussions and insist on using the notion of sign in the most varied ways. Even too varied. A phenomenon of this kind deserves attention.

### 1.2.1.
First of all, we find a cluster of linguistic usages according to which the sign is a manifest indication from which inferences can be made about something latent. This includes the usage of sign for medical symptoms, criminal evidence, weather forecast, premonitory signs, presages, the signs of the coming of the Antichrist. . . . A sample of urine for analysis was called *signum* by the ancients, which leads us to think in terms of a synecdochic relationship, as if the sign were a part, an aspect, a peripheral manifestation of something which does not appear in its entirety. But the relationship appears to be a metonymic one as well, since the dictionaries speak of sign also for any trace or visible imprint left by an imprinter on a surface. Therefore, the sign is also revelatory of a contact, in a way which tells us something about the shape of the imprinter. These signs, besides revealing the nature of the imprinter, may become marks of the imprinted objects — for instance, bruises, scratches, scars (identifying marks). Ruins belong to the same category: they are the signs of ancient grandeur, of human settlement, or of the flourishing trades of the past.

In all these cases, the fact that the sign is produced intentionally or by a human sender is not relevant. Any natural event can be a sign. Morris asserted that "something is a sign only because it is interpreted as a sign of something by some interpreter. Semiotics, then, is not concerned with the study of a particular kind of object, but with ordinary objects insofar (and only insofar) as they participate in semiosis" (1938:20). However, this first category of signs seems to be characterized by the fact that the 'standing for' relationship is based on an inferential mechanism: *if* red sky at night, *then* sailor's delight. It is the Philonian mechanism of implication: $p \supset q$. The Stoics were thinking about this sign category when they asserted that a sign is "a proposition constituted by a valid and revealing connection to its consequent" (Sextus Empiricus,

*Adv. Math.* 7.245). The same sign category was the object of Hobbes'
and Wolff's definitions. According to Hobbes, a sign is the evident
antecedent of a consequent or the consequent of an antecedent when
similar consequences have previously been observed (*Leviathan* 1.3). For
Wolff, a sign is "an entity from which the present or future or past existence of another being is inferred" (*Ontology*, p. 952).

### 1.2.2.

Common language, though, points to a second category of signs. The
sign is a *gesture* produced with the *intention of communicating*, that is, in
order to transmit one's representation or inner state to another being.
The existence of a certain rule (a code) enabling both the sender and the
addressee to understand the manifestation in the same way must, of
course, be presupposed if the transmission is to be successful; in this
sense, navy flags, street signs, signboards, trademarks, labels, emblems,
coats of arms, and letters are taken to be signs. Dictionaries and culti-
vated language must at this point agree and take as signs also words, that
is, the elements of verbal language. In all the cases examined here, the
relationship between the *aliquid* and that for which it stands seems to be
less adventurous than for the first category. These signs appear to be
expressed by a relation of equivalence rather than by one of inference: $p$
$\equiv q$. /Woman/ $\equiv$ *«femme* or *donna»;* or /woman/ $\equiv$ «animal, human,
feminine, adult». Furthermore, these signs seem to depend on arbitrary
decisions.

### 1.2.3.

The clear opposition between the two categories mentioned above is
upset by the use of the word *sign* in relation to those so-called symbols
which represent abstract objects and relationships, such as logical, chemical, algebraic formulas, and diagrams. They appear as arbitrary as the
signs of the second category; yet, through a structural formula or a diagram, the operations which I perform on the expression modify the content. If these operations are performed following certain rules, the result
provides me with new information about the content. By altering the
lines of a topographical chart, I can predict the possible order of the
corresponding territory; by inscribing triangles within a circle, I discover
new properties of the circle. This happens because in these sign there
are one-to-one correspondences between expression and content. Therefore, they are usually arbitrary and yet contain elements of *motivation*. As
a consequence, the signs of the third category, even though emitted by
human beings with the intention of communicating, seem to follow the
same model as the signs of the first category: $p \supset q$, even though they
are not natural. They are called iconic or analogical.

**1.2.4.**

In a similar way, any visual procedure reproducing concrete objects, such as the drawing of an animal in order to communicate the corresponding object and concept, is considered to be an iconic sigh. What do drawings and diagrams have in common? The fact that I can perform on them certain operations: if I draw a moustache on my portrait, I know what I will look like if I wear a moustache. What makes them different? The (apparent) fact that the diagram responds to highly codified and precise rules of production, whereas the drawing appears more spontaneous. Also, the diagram reproduces an abstract object, whereas the drawing reproduces a concrete object. But this is not always true: the unicorns of the British royal coat of arms stand for an abstraction, a fictitious object; they stand at most for a (an imaginary) class of animals. On the other hand, Goodman (1968) discusses at length the problematic difference between a person's image and the image of a person. What makes the difference between the two? Is it related to the intensional properties of the content reproduced by the drawing or to the extensional use that we decide to make of the drawing? The problem was present already (and not entirely resolved) in Plato's *Cratylus*.

**1.2.5.**

However, common usage also considers as signs those drawings which reproduce something, but in a stylized form, so that recognizing the object represented is less important that recognizing a content 'other' for which the represented object stands. The Cross, the Crescent, the Hammer and Sickle stand for Christianity, Islam, and Communism, respectively. These signs are iconic because — like diagrams and drawings — they can be subjected to manipulations of the expressions which affect the content. They are also arbitrary because by now they are in a state of catachresis. They are commonly called symbols, but in a sense opposite to that adopted for formulas and diagrams. Whereas the latter are quite empty, open to any meaning, the former are quite full, filled with multiple but definite meanings.

**1.2.6.**

Finally, certain languages — for instance, Italian — adopt expressions such as *colpire nel segno* (to hit the target, to touch the sore spot), *mettere a segno* (to score, as in to score an uppercut), *fare un segno dove si deve tagliare* (to draw a dressmaker's pattern for where the cloth is to be cut), *passare il segno* (to overstep the mark): signs as targets, *termina ad quae*, to be used as markings in order to proceed in a thorough way (*per filo e per segno*). The *aliquid* in this case, rather than *standing for*, stands *where* a certain operation is to be addressed. It is an *instruction* rather than a substitution. In this sense, the North Star is a sign for the sailor. The structure of the link is inferential, but with some complications: *if p* now, and if therefore you will do *z*, *then* you will obtain *q*.

## 1.3.   Intension and extension

Too many things are signs, and too different from each other. This turmoil of homonymies is complicated by a further equivocation. Is the sign *"res, praeter speciem quam ingerit sensibus, aliud aliquid ex se faciens in cognitationem venire"* (Augustine, *De Doctrina Christiana* 2.1.1), or, as in elsewhere suggested by the same Augustine, is the sign something by which we indicate objects or states of the world? Is the sign an intensional or an extensional device? Let us attempt an analysis of a typical semiotic maze. A red flag with a Hammer and Sickle is equivalent to Communism ($p \equiv q$). But if someone carries a red flag with a Hammer and Sickle, then that person is probably a Communist ($p \supset q$). If we take a statement such as *at home I have ten cats*, what is the sign? Is it the word *cats* (domestic felines), the global content of the sentence (in my house I keep ten domestic felines), the reference to the fact that it just so happens that within the world of our actual experience there is a specific house where there are ten specific cats? Or is it the fact that, *if* I have ten cats at home, *then* I must have enough space for them, *then* I probably cannot keep a dog, and *then* I am an animal lover? Furthermore, in all these cases, what constitutes the sign? Is it the concrete occurrence or the abstract type? Is is the phonetic utterance [kat], or the phonological and lexical model /cat/? Is it the fact that *hic et nunc* I have ten cats at home (with all the possible inferences), or the class of all the facts of this nature, so that anyone who somehow happens to have ten cats at home will show himself or herself to be an animal lover who cannot possibly keep a dog?

## 1.4.   Elusive solutions

Some people claim that the word *sign* can be applied only to linguistic entities. Malmberg, for instance, decides to call a symbol any element representing something else, and to keep the term 'sign' to indicate "those units which, like the signs of language, have a double articulation and owe their existence to an act of signification" (where signification means intentional communication) (1977:21). Every sign is a symbol, but not every symbol is a sign. This decision, in itself moderate, does not determine, however, (a) to what extent signs are relatable to symbols and (b) which science should study symbols and which categories should be employed. Furthermore, the difference between extension and intension is not clarified, even though the study of signs is presumed to be intensionally oriented.

This distinction between areas is suggested at times on the basis of more radical epistemological intentions. Harman, for instance, argues as follows:

> Smoke means fire and the word *combustion* means fire, but not in the same sense of *means*. The word *means* is ambiguous. To say that smoke means fire is to say that smoke is a symptom, sign, indication, or evidence for fire. To say that the word *combustion* means fire is to say that people use the word to mean fire. Furthermore, there is no ordinary sense of the word *mean* in which a picture of a man means a man or means that man. This suggests that Peirce's theory of signs would comprise at least three rather different subjects: a theory of the intended meaning, a theory of evidence, and a theory of pictorial depiction. There is no reason to think that these theories must contain common principles. (1977:23)

Harman's argument clashes, first of all, with the linguistic usage. Why have people used the word *sign* for more than two thousand years to define phenomena which should be divided into three different categories? Second, Harman's objection goes against the *consensus gentium* of the philosophical tradition. From the Stoics to the Middle Ages, from Locke to Peirce, from Husserl to Wittgenstein, there has been a constant attempt to find a common basis for the theory of linguistic meaning and for the theory of pictorial representation, and also for the theory of meaning and the theory of inference.

Finally, the objection goes against a philosophical instinct, very adequately summarized by Aristotle in terms of the 'wonder' which induces persons to philosophize. What is the 'meaning' of the expression *at home I have ten cats?* Is it its propositional content or what can be inferred from the fact that I have ten cats? One could answer that the second phenomenon has nothing to do with linguistic meaning, since it belongs to the universe of proofs which can be articulated by using the facts represented by the propositions. Yet, is the antecedent evoked by language so easily separable from the language which represented it? When we examine the problem of the Stoic *sēmeîon* (σημεῖον), we shall see how ambiguous and inextricable is the relationship among a fact, the proposition which represents it, and the sentence which expresses that proposition. In any event, what makes the two problems difficult to separate is precisely the fact that in both cases *aliquid stat pro aliquo*. The manner of standing for may vary, yet we still face a peculiar dialectic of presence and absence in both cases. Is this not a good enough reason to ask whether a common mechanism, however deep, might govern both phenomena?

A man wears a badge with a Hammer and Sickle at his buttonhole. Are we facing a case of 'intended meaning' (the man wants to say that he is a Communist), of pictorial representation (the badge represents 'symbolically' the union of workers and peasants), or of inferential proof (if he wears the badge, then he must be a Communist)? The same event falls within the scope of what Harman sees as three different categories. It is true that the same phenomenon can be the object of quite different theories: the badge can be studied by inorganic chemistry in terms of the material of which it is made, by physics in terms of its being subjected to gravitational laws, by economics in terms of its being an industrial product which is bought and sold. But, in our case, the badge is the object of the three (presumed) theories of meaning, of representation and of evidence only inasmuch as *it does not stand for itself*. It does not stand for its molecular composition, its tendency to fall down, its capability of being packaged and transported. It stands for something which is outside itself. In this sense it gives rise to wonder, and it becomes the same abstract object of the same theoretical question.

### 1.5.  The deconstruction of the linguistic sign

The following critiques have characteristics in common: first, when they speak of sign in general and consider other kinds of signs, they point to the structure of the *linguistic* sign. Second, they tend to dissolve the sign into entities of greater or lesser purport.

### 1.5.1.  Sign vs. *figura*

As an entity, the sign is too large. Phonology's work on linguistic signifiers, seen as the result of the articulation of lesser phonological units, starts out with the Stoic's discovery of the *stoicheîa* (στοιχεῖα), it reaches maturity with Hjelmslev's postulating the existence of *figurae*, and is crowned by Jakobson's theory of distinctive features. This theoretical achievement does not in itself question the notion of linguistic sign, but with Hjelmslev there arises the possibility of identifying *figurae* at the content level as well:

> If, for example, a mechanical inventory at a given stage of the procedure leads to a registration of the entities of content 'ram', 'ewe', 'man', 'woman', 'boy', 'girl', 'stallion', 'mare', 'sheep', 'human being', 'child', 'horse', 'he', and 'she' — then 'ram', 'ewe', 'man', 'woman', 'boy', 'girl', 'stallion', and 'mare' must be eliminated from the inventory of elements if they can be explained univocally as relational units that include only 'he' or 'she' on the one hand, and 'sheep', 'human being', 'child', 'horse', on the other. (1943:70)

The discovery of a content articulation leads Hjelmslev to argue that languages cannot be described as pure sign systems:

> By the aims usually attributed to them they are first and foremost sign systems; but by their internal structure they are first and foremost something different, namely, systems of *figurae* that can be used to construct signs. The definition of a language as a sign system has thus shown itself, on closer analysis, to be unsatisfactory. It concerns only the external functions of a language, its relation to the nonlinguistic factors that surround it, but not its proper, internal functions. (Ibid., p. 47)

The sign (or the sign-function) appears, therefore, as the manifest and recognizable end of a net of aggregations and disintegrations constantly open to further combinations. The linguistic sign is not a unit of the system of signification; it is, rather, a detectable unit in the process of communication.

Despite being invaluable for the whole development of structural semantics, Hjelmslev's proposal does not account for other kinds of signs in which it appears that the two functives are not analyzable further into *figurae*. If the cloud which announces the storm and the portrait of the Mona Lisa are to be taken as signs, there must be signs without expression *figurae*, and perhaps without content *figurae* as well. Prieto (1966) has decidely widened the field of sign analysis by showing the existence of systems without articulation, and systems which have only a first articulation. The white stick of the blind — a positive presence which constitutes itself as pertinent against the absence of the stick, as a signifier without articulations — represents blindness in general, requesting the right of way, postulating understanding on the part of bystanders. In short, it conveys a *content nebula*. As a system the stick is quite simple (presence vs. absence), but its communicational use is very complex. If the stick is not a sign, what is it, and what should it be called?

### 1.5.2. Signs vs. sentences

In the same years which saw Hjelmslev's critique of the sign format as too broad, Buyssens maintained that the format of the sign was too minute. The semantic unit is not the sign, but something corresponding to the sentence, which Buyssens calls *sème*. The example given by Buyssens concerns street signs as well as linguistic signs. He maintains that an arrow, isolated from the context of the street sign, does not allow for the concretization of a "state of consciousness." In order to perform this function it will have to have a certain color, a certain orientation, and it will have to appear on a specific street sign, placed in a specific location. "The same thing happens with the isolated word, for instance, the word *table*. This word appeared as the potential member of different sentences in which different things are talked about" (Buyssens 1943:38).

Strange opposition: Hjelmslev is uninterested in the sign because he is interested in language as an abstract system; Buyssens is uninterested in the sign because he is interested in communication as a concrete act. Obviously, the opposition extension vs. intension is in the background of this debate. Unpleasant homonymy: componential semantics will call Hjelmslev's content *figurae* (smaller than the sign) 'semes', while the tradition which developed from Buyssens (Prieto, De Mauro) will use the term 'sème' for utterances larger than the sign.

In any case, Buyssens' seme is what others will call sentence or a performed speech act. What is surprising is the initial statement by Buyssens, according to which a sign does not have meaning. If it is true that *nominantur singularia sed universalia significantur*, one should rather say that the word *table* by itself does not name (it does not refer to) anything, but has a meaning, which Hjelmslev could have subdivided into *figurae*. Buyssens admits that this word (like the arrow) can be a potential member of different phrases. What is there, then, in the content of *table* which allows it to enter expressions such as *dinner is on the table* or *the table is made of wood*, and not in expressions such as *the table eats the fish* or *he washed his face with the dinner table?* It must be agreed, then, that precisely because of its susceptibility to analysis by content *figurae*, the word *table* must include both atomic units of content and contextual instructions ruling over the word's capacity to enter linguistic segments larger than the sign.

Prieto (1975:27) clarified this apparent disagreement between Hjelmslev and Buyssens by stating that the seme (for Buyssens) is a *functional unit*, whereas the *figura* is an *economic unit*. Hjelmslev postulated the sign as a functional unit and the *figura* as an economic unit. The problem is to identify, not two, but three or more levels, where the lower level is always constituted as the economic unit of the upper level's functional unit.

Buyssens' distinction certainly anticipates, with its concreteness and complexity, all the theories opposing to the sign the speech act. However, Plato and Aristotle, the Stoics and the Sophists had already talked about the differences existing between the meaning of words and the pragmatic nature of the question, the prayer, and the order. Those who oppose a *pragmatics of discourse* to a *semantics of sign units* shift the attention from the systems of signification to the process of communication (Eco 1976); but the two perspectives are actually complementary. One cannot think of the sign without seeing it in some way characterized by its contextual destiny, but at the same time it is difficult to explain why a certain speech act is understood unless the nature of the signs which it contextualizes is explained.

### 1.5.3. The sign as difference

The elements of the signifier are set into a system of oppositions in which, as Saussure explained, there are only differences. The same thing happens with the signified. In the famous example given by Hjelmslev (1943:39), the difference in the content of two apparently synonymous terms, /Holz/ and /bois/, is given by the different segmentation of the continuum. The German /Holz/ encompasses everything which is not /Baum/ and is not /Wald/. The correlation between expression-plane and content-plane is also given by a difference: the sign-function exists by a dialectic of presence and absence, as a mutual exchange between two heterogeneities. Starting from this structural premise, one can dissolve the entire sign system into a net of fractures. The nature of the sign is to be found in the 'wound' or 'opening' or 'divarication' which constitutes it and annuls it at the same time.

This idea, although vigorously developed by poststructuralist thought, that of Derrida in particular, was actually developed much earlier. In the short text *De organo sive arte cogitandi*, Leibniz, searching for a restricted number of thoughts from whose combination all the others could be derived (as is the case with numbers), locates the essential combinational matrix in the opposition between God and nothing, presence and absence. The binary system of calculation is the wondrous likeness of this dialectics.

From a metaphysical perspective, it may be fascinating to see every oppositional structure as based on a constitutive difference which dissolves the different terms. Still, in order to conceptualize an oppositional system where something is perceived as absent, something else must be postulated as present, at least potentially. *The presence of one element is necessary for the absence of the other.* All observations concerning the importance of the absent element hold symmetrically for the present element as well. All observations concerning the constitutive function of difference hold for the poles from whose opposition the difference is generated. The argument is, therefore, an autophagous one. A phoneme is no doubt an abstract position within a system, and it acquires its value only because of the other phonemes to which it is opposed. Yet, for an 'emic' unit to be recognized, it must be formulated somehow as 'etic'. In other words, phonology builds up a system of oppositions in order to explain the functioning of a number of phonetic presences which, if they do not exist prior to the system, nonetheless are associated with its ghost. Without people uttering sounds, phonology could not exist, but without the system postulated by phonology, people could not distinguish between sounds. *Types* are recognized through their realizations into concrete *tokens*. One cannot speak of a form (of the expression or of the content) without presupposing a matter and linking it immediately (neither before nor after) to a substance.

### 1.5.4.  The predominance of the signifier

The answer given to the preceding question could confirm a further critique of the notion of sign. If the sign can be known only through the signifier and if the signified emerges only through an act of perpetual substitution of the signfer, the semiotic chain appears to be just a 'chain of signifiers'. As such, it could be manipulated even by the unconscious (if we take the unconscious as being linguistically constituted). By the 'drift' of signifiers, other signifiers are produced. As a more or less direct consequence of these conclusions, the universe of signs and even of sentences would dissolve into discourse as an activity. This line of thought, derived from Lacan, has generated a number of varied, but essentially related, positions.

The basis for this critique is actually a misunderstanding, a wordplay. Only by substituting 'signified' every time 'signifier' appears, does the discourse of these theoreticians become comprehensible. The misunderstanding derives from the fact that every signifier can only be translated into another signifier and that only by this process of *interpretation* can one grasp the 'corresponding signified'. It must be clear, though, that in none of various displacement and condensation processes described by Freud — however multiplied and almost automatic the generative and drifting mechanisms might appear — does the interplay (even if based on assonances, alliterations, likeness of expression) fail to reverberate immediately on the aggregation of the content units, actually determining the content. In the Freudian passage from /Herr-signore/ to /Signorelli/, a series of expression differences is at work, based on identities and progressive slidings of the content. The Freudian example can, in fact, be understood only by someone who knows both German and Italian, seeing words as complete sign-functions (expression + content). A person who does not know Chinese cannot produce Freudian slips interpretable in Chinese, unless a psychoanalyst who knows Chinese demonstrates that his or her patient had displaced linguistic remembrances and that he or she unconsciously played with Chinese expressions. A Freudian slip, in order to make sense, plays on *content figurae;* if it plays only with *expression figurae* it amounts to a mechanical error (typographical or phonetic). This kind of mechanical error is likely to involve content elements only in the eye of the interpreter. But in this case it is the interpreter who must be psychoanalyzed.

### 1.5.5.  Sign vs. text

The so-called signifying chain produces texts which carry with them the recollection of the intertextuality which nourishes them. Texts generate, or are capable of generating, multiple (and ultimately infinite) readings and interpretations. It was argued, for instance, by the later Barthes, by the recent Derrida, and by Kristeva, that signification is to be located exclusively in the text. The text is the locus where meaning is produced and becomes productive (signifying practice). Within its texture, the signs of the dictionary (as codifying equivalences) can emerge only by a rigidification and death of all sense. This critical line takes up Buyssens' argument (communication is given only at the level of sentence), but it goes deeper. A text is not simply a communicational apparatus. It is a device which questions the previous signifying systems, often renews them, and sometimes destroys them. *Finnegans Wake* — a textual machine made to liquidate grammars and dictionaries — is exemplary in this sense, but even rhetorical figures are produced and become alive only at the textual level. The textual machine empties the terms which the literal dictionary deemed univocal and well defined, and fills them with new content figures. Yet, the production of a metaphor such as *the king of the forest* (where a figure of humanity is added to lions and an animal property reverberates on the class of kings) implies the existence of both /king/ and /lion/ as functives of two previously codified sign-functions. If signs (expressions and content) did not preexist the text, every metaphor would be equivalent simply to saying that something is something. But a metaphor says that *that* (linguistic) thing is at the same time *something else*.

The ability of the textual manifestations to empty, destroy, or reconstruct pre-existing sign-functions depends on the presence within the sign-function (that is, in the network of content figures) of a set of instructions oriented toward the (potential) production of different texts. (This concept will be further developed in 1.9.) It is in this sense that the thematization of textuality has been particularly suggestive.

### 1.5.6  The sign as identity

The sign is supposed to be based on the categories of 'similitude' or 'identity'. This presumed fallacy renders the sign coherent with the ideological notion of the subject. The subject as a presupposed transcendental unity which opens itself to the world (or to which the world opens) through the act of representation, as well as the subject that transfers its representations onto other subjects in the process of communication, is supposedly a philosophical fiction dominating all of the history of philosophy. Let us postpone the discussion of this objection and see now in what sense the notion of sign is seen to be coherent with the (no longer viable) notion of subject:

> Under the mask of socialization or of mechanistic realism, ideological linguistics, absorbed by the science of signs, turns the sign-subject into a center. The sign-subject becomes the beginning and the end of all translin-

guistic activity; it becomes closed up in itself, located in its own word, which is conceived of by positivism as a kind of 'psychism' residing in the brain. (Kristeva 1969:69)

The statement above *implies the identification of the sign with the linguistic sign*, where the linguistic sign is based on the equivalence model: $p \equiv q$. In point of fact, Kristeva defines the sign as "resemblance":

The sign brings separate instances (subject-object on one hand, subject-interlocutor on the other) back to a unified whole (a unity which presents itself as a sentence-message), replacing praxis with a single meaning, and difference with *resemblance*. . . . The relationship instituted by the sign will therefore be a *reconciliation of discrepancies*, and *identification of differences*. (Ibid., pp. 70, 84)

It seems, however, that such a criticism can apply only to a degenerate notion of linguistic sign, rooted on the equivalence model. The problem is to see whether and to what extent this notion has ever been supported by the most mature theories of signs. For instance, the notion of sign as resemblance and identity does not appear in Peirce: "A sign is something by knowing which we know something more" (*C. P.* 8.332). The sign is an instruction for interpretation, a mechanism which starts from an initial stimulus and leads to all its illative consequences. Starting from the sign, one goes through the whole semiotic process and arrives at the point where the sign becomes capable of contradicting itself (otherwise, those textual mechanisms called 'literature' would not be possible). For Peirce, the sign is a potential proposition (as even Kristeva [1974:43] notes). In order to comprehend this notion of sign, we need to reconsider the initial phase of its historical development. Such reconsideration requires the elimination of an embarrassing notion, that of linguistic sign. Since this notion is after all a late cultural product, we shall postpone its treatment until later.

## 1.6.  Signs vs. words

The term which the Western philosophical tradition has translated as *signum* was originally the Greek *sēmeîon* (σημεῖον). It appeared as a technical-philosophical term in the fifth century, with Parmenides and Hippocrates. It is often found as a synonym of *tekmérion* (τεκμήριον: proof, clue, symptom). A first distinction between the two terms appears only with Aristotle's *Rhetoric*.

Hippocrates took the notion of clue from the physicians who came before him. Alcmeon said that "the Gods have immediate knowledge of invisible and mortal things, but men must 'proceed by clues' (τεκμαίρεϑαι)" (D. K., B1). The Cnidarian physicians knew the value of symptoms. Apparently, they codified them in the form of equivalences. Hippocrates maintained that the symptom is equivocal if it is not analyzed contextually, taking into account the air, the water, the environment, the general state of the body, and the regimen which is likely to modify the situation. Such a model functions as if to say: if $p$ then $q$, but only with the concurrence of factors $y$ and $z$. A code exists, but it is not a univocal one.

Hippocrates was not interested in linguistic signs. In any event, it appears that at the time the term 'sign' was not applied to words. A word was a *name* (*ónoma*, 'όνομα). Parmenides made use of this difference when he opposed the truth of the thought concerning Being to the illusory nature of opinions and the fallacy of sensations. Now, if representations are deceptive, names are nothing but equally deceptive levels superimposed on the objects that we think we know. *Onomázein* ('Ονομάζειν) is always used by Parmenides in order to give an arbitrary name, which is deemed to be true but does not actually correspond to the truth. The name establishes a pseudoequivalence with reality, and in doing so it conceals it. On the other hand, Parmenides uses the term 'signs' (*sēmata*: σήματα) When he speaks of *evidence*, of an inferential principle: "That Being exists, there are signs" (D. K., B8.2).

With Plato and Aristotle words are analyzed from a double point of view: (a) the difference between signifier and signified and (b) the difference between *signification* and *reference*. Signification (that is, meaning) says *what* a thing is, and in this sense it is a function performed also by single terms; in the act of reference one says, on the contrary, *that* a thing is, and in this sense reference is a function performed only by complete sentences. Throughout his whole work on logic and language, Aristotle is reluctant to use the term *sign* (*sēmeîon*) for words.

At first glance, contrary evidence is provided by the well-known page of *De Interpretatione*, 16a, where it seems that it is said that words are signs. But this page requires some careful interpretation. First, Aristotle says that both spoken and written words are *symbols* (σύμβολα) of the affections of the soul. Then he says that spoken and written words are not the same for all human beings, since (as it is restated in 16a20–30) they are posited by convention. In this sense, words are different from the sounds emitted by animals. Words are conventional and arbitrary, whereas other kinds of sounds are natural and motivated. It is evident that Aristotle reserves the term *symbol* for spoken and written words (see also Di Cesare 1981 and Lieb 1981).

It must be noticed that *symbol* was at that time, as a philosophical term, more neutral than *sign*. The notion of sign was already introduced and discussed by the Hippocratic tradition as a precise category, whereas *symbol* was generally used as «token» or «identification mark» (see Chapter 4 of this book).

On the same page (16a.5), Aristotle says that the affections of the soul are likenesses, or images, or copies of things, and as such they cannot be studied in a logical (linguistic) framework. Therefore they will be dealt with in *De Anima*. In stressing this difference between mental images and words, he states, incidentally, that spoken and written words are signs (*sēmeîa*) of the affections of the soul. Thus *prima facie* he equates signs with symbols.

One could object that in this context *sign* is used in a metaphorical way. But one should make a more radical remark. If Aristotle was following the terminological criterion he also follows in *Rhetoric*, /signs/ still means «proof», «clue», «symptom». If this is true, he is thus saying that words (spoken or written) are the *proof* that one has something in one's mind to express; at the same time he is stating that, even though words are symptoms of mental affections, this does not mean that they have the same semiotic and psychological status of these affections.

This interpretive hypothesis is reinforced by the way in which Aristotle (16b.19*ff*) wonders whether verbs as *to be* or *not to be* are signs of the existence of the thing. His line of thought is the following: (a) outside the sentence, no verb can state that something really exists or actually does something; (b) verbs can perform this function only in a complete assertive sentence; (c) not even *to be* or *not to be*, uttered in isolation, assert the existence of something; (d) however, when they are inserted into a sentence, they are signs (or, as some translators interpret, "they are indicative of the fact") that the existence of something is asserted. Such an interpretation is confirmed by what Aristotle has previously said (16b.5*ff*), namely, that a verb is always the sign (or that it is indicative of the fact) that something is said or asserted of something. Aquinas, in his commentary on *De Interpretatione*, lucidly analyzes this passage. He excludes, however, a reading that could sound very attractive to a contemporary mind, that is, that the verb is the signifier of which a predication is the signified, or that the sentence that contains the verb is the vehicle of an assertive proposition. On the contrary, Aquinas chooses a more commonsensical reading: the presence of the verb within a sentence is the *proof*, the symptom that this sentence asserts the existence of something by actually predicating something of something.

Thus we are entitled to understand that, when Aristotle incidentally uses the term *sign* for words, he is simply stressing that even words can be taken as symptoms. He is not equating linguistic symbols with natural signs. He is only saying that *sometimes* symbols can be taken as proofs. But symbols are different from other natural signs because, when they function primarily as symbols (independently of their possible use as proofs), they are not based on the model of inference but on the model of equivalence. Aristotle was in fact the first to insist that linguistic terms are equivalent to their definitions and that word and definition are fully reciprocable (as we shall see in Chapter 2 of this book).

The sign makes its appearance in the *Rhetoric*, where the enthymemes are said to be derived from verisimilitudes (*eikóta:* εἰκότα) and from signs (*sēmeîa*). But the signs are divided into two logically well-differential categories. The first type of sign has a specific name, *tekmérion*, in the sense of 'evidence'. We can translate it as *necessary sign;* if one has a fever, then one is ill; if a woman has milk, then she has given birth. The necessary sign can be translated into the universal statement 'all those who have a fever are ill'. It must be noted that this statement does not establish a relation of equivalence (biconditional). One can be ill (for instance, with an ulcer) without having a fever.

The second type of sign, says Aristotle, does not have a specific name. We could call it a *weak sign:* if one has difficulty in breathing, then one has a fever. The conclusion is obviously only probable, because the difficulty in breathing could be caused by excessive physical exercise. Transformed into a premise, the sign would only give a particular affirmative: 'some people have difficulty in breathing and they have a fever' (the logical form is one of conjunction rather than implication). The weak sign is such just because the necessary sign does not establish an equivalence. A weak sign can be produced by converting the universal affirmative — into which the necessary sign has been turned — into a particular affirmative. The subordinate of 'all those who have a fever are ill' yields in terms of a logical square, 'there are some people who are ill and who have a fever', which in fact is a weak sign and permits — at most — an *induction*.

Actually, Aristotle is uneasy with these different types of signs. He knows the apodictic syllogism, but he does not know, at least not with theoretical clarity, the hypothetical syllogism, that is, the $p \supset q$ form which will be the glory of the Stoics. For this reason Aristotle traces argumentative schemes, but he does not dwell on their logical form.

## 1.7. The Stoics

The Stoics also (from what can be gathered of their quite complex semiotics) do not seem to integrate clearly their theory of language and their theory of signs. In verbal language, they distinguish clearly between *sēmaînon* (σημαῖνον: expression), *sēmainómenon* (σημαινόμενον: content), and *tynchánon* (τυγχάνον: referent). They seem to reproduce the triad suggested by Plato and Aristotle, but they rework it with a theoretical subtlety lacking in many of those who have today reinvented such a semantic triangle.

The Stoics analyze the multiple articulation of the expression and distinguish the simple *sound* emitted by the larynx and the articulatory muscles (an as-yet-inarticulate sound) from the *articulate linguistic element* and from the actual *word* which exists only insofar as it is related or relatable to a content. Such a model functions as if to say, with Saussure, that the linguistic sign is a twofold entity. Augustine, in the wake of the Stoics, will call *dictio* that *verbum vocis* which *foris sonat*, being at the same time perceived and recognized because it is related to a *verbum mentis* or *cordis*. The Stoics thought that the barbarians were able to perceive the physical sound, but unable to recognize it as a word. This happened, not because the barbarians lacked the corresponding mental image, but because they did not know the correlational rule. In this respect, the Stoics go much further than their predecessors and discover the provisional and unstable nature of the sign-function (the same content can make up a word with an expression of a different language).

With Stoics, the content ceases to be, as it was with their predecessors, an affection of the soul, a mental image, a perception, a thought or an idea. It is neither an idea in the Platonic sense, since the Stoics have a materialistic metaphysics, nor an idea in the psychological sense, since even in this case the content would be a body, a physical fact, an alteration of the soul (which is also a body), a seal impressed upon the mind. Instead, the Stoics suggest that the content is an 'incorporeal'.

The void, location, and time are incorporeals, as well as spatial relations, chronological sequences, actions, and events. The incorporeals are not things, they are states, modes of being. Geometric surfaces and the thinnest section of the cone are incorporeals. Incorporeals are *entia rationis* insofar as every *ens rationis* is a relationship, a way of looking at things. Among the incorporeals the Stoics put the *lektón* (λεκτόν), which has been translated as 'expressible', *dictum*, or *dicible*. The *lektón* is a semiotic category. The fact of Dion walking is, in the moment of its expression, a *lektón*.

The first problem is the relationship between the *sēmainómenon* and the *lektón*. If 'Dion walks' is a proposition (and, therefore, an incorporeal), are 'Dion' and 'walks' also incorporeals? Sextus Empiricus identifies *sēmainómenon* and *lektón* as synonyms (*Adv. Math.* 8.12); however, the solution appears to be more complex. The Stoics talk of complete and incomplete *lektá*. The complete *lektón* is a proposition, whereas the incomplete *lektá* are parts, pieces of propositions which are combined into the proposition through a series of syntactical links. The subject and the predicate are listed among the incomplete *lektá*. They appear to be grammatical and lexical categories and, therefore, categories of the expression, but in point of fact they are categories of the content. The *subject* (which is the usual translation of the word *ptósis*, πτωσις) represents the uppermost example of case, because the attention devoted to assertive propositions caused the subject to be seen as the case par excellence. But the case is not the inflection form (a grammatical category that *expresses* the case). Rather, it is the expressed or expressible content. Today we would say that it is a pure *actantial position*. In this sense, the subject, principal example of incomplete *lektón*, is an incorporeal. The Stoics, therefore, had already de-psychologized semantics, so that we can translate *sēmainómenon* as "content" in Hjelmslev's sense, that is, as a position within a system, the result of an abstract segmentation of the noetic field, a cultural unit (rather than a mental image, a thought, or an engram).

When the Stoics speak of the signs (*sēmeîa*), they seem to refer to something immediately evident which leads to some conclusions about the existence of something not immediately evident. The sign can be *commemorative:* in this case it derives from an association, confirmed by preceding experience, between two events. On the basis of past experience I know that, if there is smoke, then there must be fire. But the sign can also be *indicative.* In this case it points to something which has never been evident and probably will never be, such as the motions of the body which signify the motions of the soul, or the bodily humors which by passing through the skin indicate that there must be perceptible (but unperceived) pores. In all these cases, the signs seem to be physical events: the smoke, the presence of milk revealing birth, the light revealing the day, and so on. Yet, the fact that the events, the transitory state of the bodies, are called incorporeals should give us pause. Sextus Empiricus, in fact, does acknowledge that the sign from which the inference is derived is not the physical event, but the proposition which expresses it. The sign is the "antecedent proposition within a valid and larger hypothetical premise which serves the purpose of revealing its consequent" (*Adv. Math.* 7.245) or "a true antecedent proposition within a true condition, serving the purpose of revealing its consequent" (*Hyp. Pyrrh.* 2.104).

The Stoic model of sign assumes, therefore, the form of the inference $(p \supset q)$, where the variables are neither physical realities nor events, but the propositions that express the events. A column of smoke is not a sign unless the interpreter sees the event as the true antecedent of a hypothetical reasoning (*if* there is smoke . . .) which is related by inference (more or less necessary) to its consequent (. . . *then* there is fire). This is why the Stoics can say, and they do, that the sign is a *lektón* and, therefore, an incorporeal. The sign is not concerned with *that* smoke and *that* fire, but with the possibility of a relationship between antecedent and consequent regulating of *any* occurrence of the smoke (and of the fire). The sign is *type*, not *occurrence*.

By now it is clear how, in the Stoics' semiotics, the theory of language becomes rightfully associated with the theory of signs. In order to have signs, propositions must be formulated, and the propositions must be organized according to a logical syntax which is reflected and made possible by the linguistic syntax (see Frede 1978). Signs emerge only insofar as they are rationally expressible through the elements of language. Language is articulated inasmuch as it expresses meaningful events. It must be stressed that the Stoics do not still say that words are signs (at most they say that words serve as vehicles for *types* of signs). The lexical difference between the couple *sēmaînon/sēmainómenon* and the *sēmeîon* remains. But the common and obvious etymological root is an indication of their relatedness. We could have the Stoics say, as Lotman does, that language is a primary modeling system, through which the other systems are expressed.

Referring once again to contemporary theories (see also Todorov 1977), we could then say that the linguistic term and the natural sign are constituted by a double relation of signification, a double elevation translatable into the Hjelmslevian model of connotation (in the diagram form popularized by Barthes; see Figure 1.1).

The word /smoke/ refers to a portion of content segmentation which we will conventionally designate as «smoke». At this point, we have three alternatives, whether intensional or extensional: (a) «smoke» connotes «fire» on the basis of an encyclopedia-like representation which takes into account metonymic relationships of effect-to-cause (a case grammar accounting for 'actants' like Cause or Agent can represent rather well this sort of meaning postulate); (b) the sentence /there is smoke/ expresses as its content the proposition «there is smoke» which, always by virtue of an underlying encyclopedic representation including frames or scripts (see 3.2 of this book), suggests as a reasonable inference «there is fire» (notice that we are still at an intensional level, since the possibility of the inference is coded among the properties of smoke, independently of any actual world experience); (c) in a process of reference to states of the actual world the proposition «there is smoke», on the grounds of the aforementioned meaning postulates, leads to the indexical proposition «therefore *here* there is fire», to be evaluated in terms of truth values.

When I perceive a cloud or a column of smoke as mere physical events, they do not differ from any sound which I can perceive without attributing a semantic relevance to it (as the barbarian does). But if, on the basis of a preexisting rule, I know that smoke in general refers to fire, then I make the event pertinent as a single expression of a more general content, and the smoke I perceived becomes the perceptive content «smoke». This first movement, from the sensation to the perception invested with meaning, is so immediate that we tend to consider it as semiotically irrelevant. Gnoseology has always questioned precisely this presumed immediacy of sensation and perception.

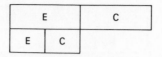

FIGURE I.I

Even according to the medieval perspective, *simplex apprehensio*, that is, the first operation of the intellect, allows one to grasp the thing in its essence through the phantasm, but it is only by the act of *judgment*, that is, the second operation of the intellect, that the thing is recognized and viewed as relevant for the purpose of further predications. It is not by chance that gnoseology talks of the perceptive meaning where the term 'meaning' seems at once a semantic category and a category of the phenomenology of perception. Actually, in order to grasp, from a series of sensory data, the form 'smoke', I must already be directed by the belief that smoke is relevant to the making of further inferences. Otherwise, the smoke provided for me by the sensation remains a potential perception which I have not yet make pertinent as smoke, but as mist, miasma, or as any exhalation which is not caused by combustion. Only if I already know the general rule which makes for 'if smoke, then fire' am I able to render the sensory datum *meaningful*, by seeing it as that smoke which can reveal fire.

## 1.8. Unification of the theories and predominance of linguistics

Some centuries later, in *De Magistro*, Augustine will definitely bring together the theory of signs and the theory of language. Fifteen centuries before Saussure, he will be the one to recognize the *genus* of signs, of which linguistic signs are a *species*, such as insignias, gestures, ostensive signs. But in so doing Augustine delivers to the tradition that follows him a problem that not even the Stoics had clearly solved. Augustine had actually provided a solution, but he had failed to stress it sufficiently to make it indisputable. The Stoics had left unresolved the problem of the difference between the relation of linguistics expression to content on the one hand (what Hjelmslev will call denotation) and the relation of sign-proposition to consequent meaning on the other. One suspects that the first level may still be based on equivalence, while the second is doubtlessly based on inference (Figure 1.2).

However, we must ask whether or not this difference is based on a curious 'optical illusion'. From the moment in which Augustine introduces verbal language among signs, language starts to appear in an awkward position. Being too strong, too finely articulated and therefore sci-

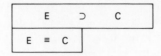

FIGURE 1.2

entifically analyzable (and the work of the Hellenistic grammarians must be kept in mind in this respect), language could hardly be the object of a theory of signs born in order to describe the relationship between natural events, so elusive and generic (and we will see how much the Stoics' inference was epistemologically open to a continuum of relationships of necessity and weakness). Since language was increasingly believed to be the semiotic system which could be analyzed with the most profit (a careful study of this aspect of the history of semiotics would be very worth vhile) and the system which could serve as a model for all other systems (translating every other semiotic onto the plane of its content), the model of the linguistic sign gradually came to be seen as the semiotic model par excellence.

By the time this conclusion was reached (the definitive sanction took place with Saussure), the linguistic model was crystallized into its 'flattest' form, the one encouraged by the dictionaries and, unfortunately, by a lot of formal logic which had to fill its empty symbols only for the sake of exemplification as well. As a consequence, the notion of *meaning as synonymy* and as essential definition began to develop.

/Man/ is equivalent to «rational animal» in certain contexts, but certainly not in the expression /mom, there is a man with a package to deliver/, where the content «man» can be analyzed according to many properties (male, unknown, human being, person of a low social extraction, even foreign presence or threat), but certainly not as a rational animal. Aristotle delivered to us the principle of (biconditional) equivalence between term and definition by genus and species because he worked only on *categorematic* terms to be inserted within assertive propositions. The Stoics, on the other hand (see Frede 1978; Graeser 1978), thought that *every syntactic category had its semantic counterpart*, including *syncategorematic* terms. If the complete *lektá* derived from the combination of incomplete ones, they had also to include conjunctions, articles, and pronouns. Augustine later shows that even prepositions have meaning.

## 1.9. The 'instructional' model

In *De Magistro* 2, Augustine analyzes with Adeodatus the verse by Virgil "*Si nihil ex tanta superis placet urbi relinqui,*" and defines the eight words as "*octo signa.*" He then proceeds to analyze the meaning of /si/ and to point out that this term conveys a meaning of «doubt». And since he knows that *non esse signum nisi aliquid significet,* he is forced to define the meaning (certainly not the referent!) of /*nihil*/. Granting that it is impossible to produce signs which do not say anything, and since the meaning of /nothing/ does not seem to be either an object or a state of the world, Augustine concludes that this term expresses an *affection of the soul,* that is, the state of mind which, although not recognizing something, recognizes at least its absence.

Augustine then goes on to ask what /*ex*/ means. He refuses to accept the synonymical answer, according to which /*ex*/ would mean «*de*». This synonym is an interpretation that must in turn be interpreted. The conclusion is that /*ex*/ means a kind of separation (*secretionem quandam*) from that in which something was included. Augustine adds a further instruction for contextual decoding: the word can express separation from something which has ceased to exist, as when the city cited in the line by Virgil disappeared, or it can express separation from something which still exists, as when one says that some merchants are coming from (*ex*) Rome.

The meaning of a syncategorematic term is, therefore, a set (a series, a system) of instructions for its possible contextual insertions and for its different semantic outputs in different contexts (all registered by the code).

Can this solution apply to categorematic terms as well? This is, in point of fact, the solution increasingly preferred by context-oriented componential semantics. The forerunners of this type of instructional semantics were Peirce's logic of relatives (*C. P.* 2.379, 3.66; see also Eco 1979), the various case grammars (Fillmore 1968; Bierwisch 1970, 1971), the semantic models based on contextual and circumstantial selections (Eco 1976, 2.11), and their reformulation for the disambiguation of the metaphor (see Chapters 2 and 3 of this book). *The semantic type is the description of the contexts in which the term can be expected to occur.*

If this is the case, then the connoted meaning is possible because, at the first level of signification (where the linguistic sign is primarily at work), inference, rather than mere equivalence, is already present. A linguistic term appears to be based on pure equivalence simply because we do not recognize in it a 'sleeping' inference.

The process of recognition of natural events which generates sign-proposition takes place in the same manner. Perception is always interrogative and conditional and is invariably based (even if we do not realize it) on a bet. If certain perceptual data are present, then (there is) perhaps smoke, as long as other contextual elements authorize me to think that the perceptual interpretation is appropriate. Peirce was aware of the fact that perception is always presumptive evidence, a source of potential semiosis. The fact that perception takes place without effort does not invalidate its inferential mechanism (see *C. P.* 5.266–68).

We are left with the problem of the so-called substitutional tables, that is, minimal ciphers where the content-plane is given by the expression-plane of another semiotic system. In Morse code, for instance, $/. - /  \equiv$ «a», and vice versa, with complete reciprocity. A substitutional table could be viewed as a degraded semiotic system, but in point of fact equivalence appears to be a 'sleeping' inference here as well (see Chapter 7 of this book).

Therefore, there is no difference in the semiotic structure of first- and second-level signification (we use this distinction because the couple denotation/connotation is equivocal, since 'denotation' is used by extensional semantic theories in order to refer to truth-values). The fluctuating object, which is commonly called 'sign' in so many different cases, exists as a scientifically unified object, *constructed* by the discipline which studies it, subsuming different phenomena under the same formal scheme $p \supset q$.

What varies according to the phenomena is the cogency of the inference. If (there is) the first, then (there is) the second. But what is the epistemological value of *if* and *then*?

## 1.10.   Strong codes and weak codes

The Stoics' inference was the Philonian one, the material inference of modern logic. As such, it did not deal with the epistemological value of the link between antecedent and consequent. The Stoics gave various examples: 'if there is daytime, then there is light' is an equivalence (biconditional). 'If it is daytime, then Dion walks' is an example of material inference devoid of epistemological value. 'If she gives milk, then she has given birth' is an inference from effect to cause based on previous inductions. 'If a torch is seen, then the enemy is coming' seems to be a very vague supposition, because the torch could be carried by friends as well. Sextus interprets this sign as a conventional one, supposing that it is recognized on the basis of a previous agreement. At this point, the epistemological value would depend on social laws rather than on natural laws. By introducing, along with the example, all the commemorative signs among those founded on an arbitrary correlation, Sextus acknowledges the inferential nature of conventional signs. In this case, the epistemological value of *if-then* assumes the legalistic nature of the norms sanctioned by juridical codes.

Aristotle, who was interested in finding arguments capable of explaining the necessary links between facts, posited a number of epistemological distinctions between necessary signs and weak signs. The Stoics, who were only interested in the formal mechanisms of inference, avoided the problem. Only Quintilian (*Institutio oratoria* 5.9), who was interested in the reactions of a forensic audience, tried to account for every type of persuasive sign according to an epistemological hierarchy.

Quintilian does not disagree with Aristotle's classification in the *Rhetoric,* but he warns that necessary signs can deal with the past (if she has given birth she must have been with a man), with the present (if there is a strong wind on the sea, there must necessarily be waves) and with the future (if one has been stabbed in the heart, one will necessarily die).

Clearly, though, these presumed temporal links are in truth different combinations of cause-effect links. The link between giving birth and sexual intercourse (*diagnostic* sign) goes back from the effect to the cause, while the link between wound and death (*prognostic* sign) goes from the cause to its possible effects. However, this distinction is not homologous to the distinction between necessary signs and weak signs. Every cause does not necessarily refer us forward to all its possible effects (weak prognostic sign), and not all effects necessarily refer us back to the same cause (weak diagnostic sign). Who carries the torch, the enemy or the allies? A distinction should also be made between *necessary causes* and *sufficient causes.* Oxygen is a necessary cause for combustion (so that if there is combustion, then there is oxygen), but the striking of a match is only a sufficient cause for combustion (in occurrence with other possible causes). One could then say that Aristotle's weak sign goes from effect to sufficient cause (if one has a hard time breathing, then one has a fever); but, when better examined, the weak sign also exhibits a degree of 'necessity' — except that this sign refers to a class of causes, rather than to one cause; if there is a torch, then *someone* must have lit it and must be carrying it. If there is difficulty in breathing, then necessarily there is an alteration of the cardiac rhythm (a class of events which includes *also* fever). These types of signs should have a necessary consequent, but the consequent is still too wide and it must be narrowed (passage from the class to a member of the class) on the basis of other contextual inferences (as Hippocrates knew quite well).

In verbal language a similar process takes place, since I can name an entity by synecdoche from genus to species. Instead of saying 'human beings', I can say 'mortals'.

The prognostic sign from cause to effect involves a number of problems as well. Thomas Aquinas says (*Summa Theologiae* 1.70.2 – 2; 3.62) that the instrumental cause can be a sign of its possible effect: if the hammer, then the operations that it can be expected to perform. This is how the police operate. If weapons are found in an apartment, their possible criminal usage is deduced. This type of sign is obviously open to contextual inferences. The nature of the clue changes, depending upon whether the weapons are found in the house of a presumed terrorist, of a police officer, or of a gunsmith. And why does Aquinas not mention, for instance, the efficient cause? Cannot the presence of a well-known murderer in town be a sign of criminal intent on his or her part? As for the final cause, is it not the basis for the *cui prodest* type of argumentation?

It appears, then, that all prognostic signs are weak because of the epistemological nature of inference (the link is not a necessary one), whereas all diagnostic signs can be weak because of the generality of the implicatum (the class of the consequents is too wide). Today epistemology, inductive logic, and probability theory know how to measure the various degrees of epistemological force. One might ask why Aristotle and, above all, Quintilian did not hesitate to list as possible evidence every type of sign, even though they were aware of their different epistemological force. But, at the rhetorical level, links are mostly based on conventions and common opinions. Quintilian cites as verisimilar the following argument: if Atalanta goes walking in the woods with boys, then she is probably not a virgin any more. In certain communities this verisimilitude can be as convincing as a necessary sign. It depends on the codes and on the scripts (cf. Eco 1979) which the community registers as 'good'.

The hiatus between 'scientific' certitude and 'social' certitude constitutes the difference between scientific hypotheses and laws, on the one hand, and semiotic codes, on the other. The necessity of scientific evidence has little in common with the necessity of semiotic evidence. Scientifically, the whale is a mammal, but in many people's competence it is a fish. Scientifically, a lemon is necessarily a citrus fruit, and it is not necessarily yellow. But for a reader of poetry (Montale: "The golden trumpets of solarity"), the lemon is a yellow fruit, and its being a citrus is irrelevant.

Therefore, at the semiotic level, *the conditions of necessity of a sign are socially determined*, either according to weak codes or according to strong codes. In this way, an event can be a sure sign, even though scientifically it is not so. This hierarchy of semiotic necessity supports the correlational links between antecedents and consequents, and renders them as strong as the correlations between expression and content.

A typology of the various coding levels can be found in Eco (1976, ch. 3), with a theory of the modes of sign production. This review of the possibilities of sign production shows that there is a semiosic continuum which goes from the strongest kind of coding to the most open and indeterminate. The task of a *general semiotics* is that of tracing a single formal structure which underlies all these phenomena, this structure being that of the inference which generates interpretation.

The task of specific semiotics, on the other hand, will be that of establishing — according to the sign system in question — the rules of greater or lesser semiotic necessity for inferences (institutionalization rules).

When — still in semiotic terms — the class of the consequents is very imprecise, we have a sign which is either not yet coded, vaguely coded (the 'symbol'), or in the process of being coded (see Eco 1979, ch. 3 for the process of code invention; and Chapter 4 of this book). Usually, code invention takes the form of the most daring of inferences, that of *abduction or hypothesis*.

## 1.11. Abduction and inferential nature of signs

Compared to deduction and induction, abduction gives rise to three different inferential schemes (Figure 1.3), where the solid-line boxes indicate propositions which are already verified and where the broken-line boxes indicate tentative propositions produced in the process of reasoning.

If signs were rooted in mere equivalence, their understanding would represent a simple case of *modus ponens:* every time one utters /man/ one means «rational mortal animal». But one uttered /man/; therefore, one meant «rational mortal animal». This is in fact the absolutely deductive process we implement when dealing with substitutional tables, as it happens with the dots and dashes of the Morse alphabet. But it does not seem that we do the same with all the other signs, that is, when we are not invited to recognize the conventional equivalence between two expressions belonging to two different semiotic systems, but when we have to decide what content should be correlated to a given expression.

If we did not know the meaning of a sign and had to reconstruct it through repeated experiences, the correct process to develop would appear to be of an inductive type. Apparently, this is how ostensive definitions work. Each time a native speaking a language unknown to us utters the expression /x/, he or she either points to the object 'y' or there is a recurrence of experience 'y'. Therefore, that word can reasonably be interpreted as meaning that class of objects or of actions. The induction by ostensive interpretation is shown to be very precarious by Augustine in *De Magistro*. When Augustine asks Adeodatus how he would explain the meaning of the verb /to walk/, Adeodatus answers that he would start walking. And when Augustine asks him what he would do if the question were posed to him while walking, Adeodatus answers that he would start walking faster. Augustine then replies that the answer could be understood to mean that the sense of /to walk/ is «to hurry up». Obviously, the accumulation of ostensive signs does not clarify the meaning of a term by simple induction. A frame of reference is necessary, a

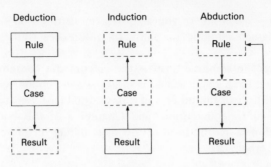

FIGURE 1.3

metalinguistic (or, rather, metasemiotic) rule expressed in some way, prescribing what rule should be used in order to understand ostension. But at this point we have already arrived at the mechanism of abduction. Only if I hypothesize that Adeodatus' behavior (in which his hurry acts as a metasemiotic mechanism which should make evident the act of walking) constitutes the interpretation of the linguistic term am I able to suppose that what he calls to my attention (Result) is a case of the hypothesized Rule. This procedure occurs in the decoding of known linguistic terms as well, when one is uncertain about what language they belong to. When someone tells me /cane!/ in an excited voice, in order to understand whether it is a Latin imperative («sing!») or an Italian holophrastic indexical proposition («dog!»), I must hypothesize *a* language as a frame of reference. The fact that there are circumstantial and contextual clues to direct me toward the determination of the rule does not change in principle the structure of the interpretive process.

Abduction is, therefore, the tentative and hazardous tracing of a system of signification rules which will allow the sign to acquire its meaning.

Abduction occurs with those natural signs which the Stoics called indicative and which are thought to be signs, yet without knowing what they signify. Kepler noticed that the orbit of Mars passes through points $x$ and $y$ (this example is given by Peirce, *C. P.* 2.96): this was the Result, but the Rule of which this was a Case was not yet known (the consequents of this antecedent being, therefore, equally unknown). Points $x$ and $y$ could have been points of, among other possible geometrical figures, an ellipse. Kepler hypothesized the Rule (and this was an act of imaginative courage): they are the points of an ellipse. Therefore, if the orbit of Mars were in point of fact elliptical, then its passing through $x$ and $y$ (Result) would have been a case of that Rule. The abduction, of course, had to be verified. In the light of the hypothesized rule, $x$ and $y$ were 'signs' of the further passage of Mars through the points $z$ and $k$. It was obviously necessary to wait for Mars at the spot where the first 'sign' had led one to expect its appearance. Once the hypothesis was verified, the abduction had to be widened (and verified): the behavior of Mars was hypothetically thought to be shared by all the other planets. The behavior of a planet thus became a sign for the general behavior of planets.

Abduction is a very complex mode of inference, and there are probably many types of abduction, ranking from the simplest and easiest to the more complex and tentative. Thagard (1978) has distinguished between hypothesis and abduction in connection with the distinction between overcoding and undercoding (Eco 1976, 2.14); Bonfantini and Proni (1983) have outlined three types of abduction, and I have elaborated on this proposal (Eco 1983). The three types of abduction I shall outline here represent a typological abstraction, a sort of rough segmentation of a more finely segmentable continuum. In other words, one could find concrete examples of abduction which cover intermediate positions between the first and the second or between the second and the third types, as well as complex processes that combine these different types.

(a) There is a *hypothesis* or an *overcoded abduction* when the law is given automatically or quasi-automatically. This 'quasi' is to be taken very seriously. Let us suppose that a verbal language represents a system of absolute equivalences and that in this language /man/ stands for «rational mortal animal». When someone utters /man/, I must first assume that this utterance is the token of a type of English word. It seems that usually we do this kind of interpretive labor automatically, but it is enough that we are living in an international milieu in which people are supposed to speak different languages, and we realize that our choice is not completely an automatic one. To recognize a given phenomenon as the token of a given type presupposes some hypothesis about the circumstances of utterance, the nature of the speaker, and the discursive co-text. Thagard suggests that this kind of hypothesis corresponds to my notion of *overcoding* and says that, since the rule is already given, the inference concerns only the decision to recognize the Result as the Case of that Rule. I agree, but I insist on the fact that, since one has *to decide* to connect that Rule with that Result through the mediation of the Case, then the process is never fully automatic.

Abductions of this type are also implemented in co-textual interpretation. The example provided by Augustine apropos of *ex* (see 1.9) represents an interesting instance of such an inferential process. Augustine knew that /ex/ meant the separation of something from something else; he still had to decide how to identify the two terms of this relationship within the co-text he was interpreting. His decision was quasi-automatic; however, he had to figure out a hypothesis — even though a hardly challengeable one.

(b) There is an *undercoded abduction* when the rule must be selected among a series of equiprobable alternatives. In Chapter 2 of this book it is maintained that our semantic representations do not follow the model of a dictionary but of an encyclopedia. Therefore, we have no guarantees that the meaning of /man/ is necessarily, and in every context, «rational mortal animal». According to different contextual and circumstantial selections (see Eco 1976, 2.11), a man also can be a very virile person, a brave male, a two-footed creature, and so on. Therefore, when one utters /this is a man/, we have to decide whether one says that this is a rational animal, a mortal creature, or a good example of virility, and so on. Likewise, /this is not a man/ can mean either «this is not rational» or «this is not mortal», depending on whether the sentence is about a monster produced by Doctor Frankenstein or about an angel. The decision as to whether certain properties (belonging to the meaning of a term) must be blown up or narcotized (see Eco 1979 and Chapter 2 of this book) represents a good case of undercoded abduction. Thagard calls this kind of reasoning an abduction *stricto sensu:* the rule selected can be, in a given co-text, the most plausible one, but it is not certain whether it is the most correct or the only correct one. Thus the explanation is *entertained,* waiting for further tests.

A case of undercoded abduction, working for nonlinguistic signs, is the one of Kepler's discovery, quoted above. Kepler met a surprising fact, and then he had to select among alternative explanations: there were many geometrical curves that could account for the movement of Mars. Their number was not infinite, and some previous assumptions about the regularity of the universe suggested to Kepler that he had to look only for closed, nontranscendental curves; therefore, ellipsis seemed more plausible than spyrals or sinewaves. Notwithstanding this hierarchy of plausibilities, Kepler had *to try*.

(c) There are, finally, cases of *creative abduction*, in which the rule acting as an explanation has to be invented *ex novo*. This could be the case of Copernicus when he had the intuition of heliocentrism in *De revolutionibus orbium coelestium*. Copernicus felt that the Ptolemaic system was inelegant, without harmony, like a painting in which the painter reproduced all the members without composing them into a unique body. Then he decided that the sun *ought to be* at the center of the universe because only in this way the created world would have displayed an admirable symmetry. He figured out a possible world whose guarantee was its being well structured, 'gestaltically' elegant. As in every case of creative abduction, this way of reasoning required a sort of meta-abduction, which consisted in deciding whether the possible universe (or state of things) outlined by the creative abduction was the same as the 'real' universe. In over- and undercoded abduction this metalevel of inference is not compulsory, because there are preexisting explanations of the same kind that have already proved to be plausible in other cases. In other words, in over- and undercoded abductions one uses explanations that already held for different results. In creative abductions one is not sure that the explanation one has selected is a 'reasonable' one.

We implement creative abduction when dealing with poetic texts, as well as when solving criminal cases. Many interpretive decisions concerning symbols (see Chapter 4 of this book) involve creative abductions. Many cases in which language is used not to confirm but to challenge a given world view or a scientific paradigm, and to decide that certain properties cannot belong any longer to the meaning of a given term (see Chapter 2 of this book) require an interpretive cooperation that displays many characteristics of a creative abduction.

So far, inferences are at work at every level of semiosis, in verbal language as well as in the understanding of so-called natural signs. In this sense, there is a link between theory of meaning and theory of evidence that, according to Harman (see 1.4 above), is to be carefully distinguished. If there is a difference, it is not between linguistic and natural signs or between words and symptoms, but rather between *semiotic* and *scientific* inference, or between two kinds of certitude.

The semiotic plausibility is based on social habits, whereas the scientific plausibility is based on other criteria of verifiability. This difference is of the greatest relevance under many respects, indeed. But it should not blur that other evidence: that we deal both with language and with every other kind of sign by implementing inferential processes. These processes can be defined as interpretive processes. The understanding of signs is not a mere matter of recognition (of a stable equivalence); it is a matter of *interpretation*.

## 1.12. The criterion of interpretability

Thus substitution (*aliquid stat pro aliquo*) is not the only necessary condition for a sign: the possibility of *interpretation* is necessary as well. By interpretation (or criterion of interpretability) we mean the concept elaborated by Peirce, according to which every *interpretant* (either a sign or an expression or a sequence of expressions which translate a previous expression), besides translating the Immediate Object or the content of the sign, also increases our understanding of it. The criterion of interpretability allows us to start from a sign in order to cover, step by step, the entire circle of semiosis. Peirce maintained that a term is a rudimentary proposition and that a proposition is a rudimentary argumentation (*C. P.* 2.342 – 44). By saying *father* I have already produced a two-argument predicate: if father, then someone who is a child of this father.

The interpreted content allows me to go beyond the original sign and makes me see the need for future contextual occurrence of another sign. From the proposition 'every father has or has had a child', one can go on to analyze whole argumentative topics, while the intensional mechanism leads us in the direction of propositions to be analyzed extensionally.

At this point it is clear that the death sentence pronounced on the sign on the basis of the charges of equality, similitude, and reduction of differences was quite unfounded. It based itself on the blackmail of a 'flat' linguistic sign, seen as a type of correlation based on dead-end equivalence, on the substitution of the same. In truth, the sign always *opens up* something new. No interpretant, in adjusting the sign interpreted, fails to change its borders to some degree.

To interpret a sign means to define the portion of continuum which serves as its vehicle in its relationship with the other portions of the continuum derived from its global segmentation by the content. It means to define a portion through the use of other portions, conveyed by other expressions. If the interpretation is pushed to its extreme, it is possible to cast doubt on the content determined at the beginning, and even the global criterion of segmentation. This implies that we must cast doubt on the way in which the form of the content has segmented the continuum.

Hjelmslev leads us to believe in the existence of two separate continua, one for the expression and one for the content. But the sign-function model should, in the light of Peirce's semiotics, be reformulated (Figure 1.4). The *matter*, the *continuum* about which and through which signs speak, is always the same. It is the Dynamic Object that Peirce talked about that motivates the sign, though the sign does not render it immediately, since its expression only conveys an Immediate Object (the *content*). A specific civilization organizes the content in the shape of fields, axes, subsystems, and partial systems which are often not coherent with each other. They are articulated according to a specific contextual perspective (and the context can be the culture of a millennium as well as a poem or a diagram). These content-segments can correspond to physical entities (woman, dog, house), abstract concepts (good, evil), actions (to run, to eat), genera and species (animal, plane figure), as well as directions and relations (above, before, toward, if and then, or). These portions are articulated in larger sequences according to the inferential links we described above. In order to express them, one must choose formalized or formalizable portions of the continuum, which *are the same* as what is talked about, that is, the same continuum segmented by the content. Sometimes the material elements, chosen in order to express them, utilize portions of the continuum different from the expressed continuum (sounds can be used in order to express spatial relations). At other times the same portion of the continuum is used as material both for the expression and for the content (spatial relationships in a diagram used to express spatial relationships on a tridimensional surface).

FIGURE 1.4

The matter segmented in order to express something expresses other segmentations of that matter. Through this interplay from sign to sign, the world (the continuum, the pulp itself of the matter which is manipulated by semiosis) is called into question. The form that we attribute to the Dynamic Object is continuously changed through the formulation of Immediate Objects and their constant redefinition by successive interpretants.

## 1.13. Sign and subject

The notion of sign as expression of equality and identity could be legitimately claimed to support a sclerotic (and ideological) notion of the subject. The sign as the locus (constantly interrogated) for the semiosic process constitutes, on the other hand, the instrument through which the subject is continuously made and unmade. The subject enters a beneficial crisis because it shares in the historical (and constitutive) crisis of the sign. The subject is constantly reshaped by the endless resegmentation of the content. In this way (even though the process of resegmentation must be activated by *someone*, who is probably the collectivity of subjects), the subject is spoken by language (verbal and nonverbal), by the dynamic of sign-functions rather than by the chain of signifiers. As subjects, we are what the shape of the world produced by signs makes us become.

Perhaps we are, somewhere, the deep impulse which generates semiosis. And yet we recognize ourselves only as semiosis in progress, signifying systems and communicational processes. The map of semiosis, as defined at a given stage of historical development (with the debris carried over from previous semiosis), tells us who we are and what (or how) we think.

# DICTIONARY VS. ENCYCLOPEDIA

## 2.1. Porphyry strikes back

### 2.1.1. Is a definition an interpretation?

The aim of this chapter is to demonstrate the untenability of that model for definition, structured by genera, species, and differentiae, known as the Porphyrian tree and elaborated from Boethius through the whole Middle Ages, as an interpretation of the *Isagoge* written by the Phoenician Porphyry in the third century A.D. It would seem preposterous to criticize such a venerable and outdated theory. But every revisitation of the history of signs is fruitful, because it helps to discover the remote origins of some contemporary theoretical 'cramps'. Porphyry is still alive in many semantic theories.

A sign is not only something which stands for something else; it is also something that can and must be interpreted. The criterion of interpretability allows us to start from a given sign to cover, step by step, the whole universe of semiosis.

This criterion (as we have shown in the first chapter of this book) held for the classical notion of natural signs, based on an inferential model ($p \supset q$), but it should hold also for linguistic signs, even though they were based, by a long historical tradition, on the model of equivalence ($p \equiv q$). This latter idea of sign as identity was due to the persuasion that the meaning or the content of a given linguistic expression was either a synonymous expression or its definition. Irrespective of whether the definition is provided by genus and differentia (/man/ $\equiv$ « rational mortal animal») or by a series of semantic components or markers (/man/ $\equiv$ «human + male + adult»), there should be a biconditional link between *definiens* and *definiendum*. One can say that not even this model excludes an interpretive process: undoubtedly «rational mortal animal» says something more than the verbal utterance /man/, especially if 'mortal', 'rational', and 'animal' are interpreted in their turn. However, every decision about this matter concerns the choice between a *dictionary* and an *encyclopedia*, a crucial question widely discussed in the course of the last decades (see, for instance, Wilson 1967; Katz 1972; Putnam 1975; Rey-Debove 1971; and, for the most complete and convincing overview of the problem, Haiman 1980). Naturally, one must distinguish between the opposition dictionary/encyclopedia as it is intended in the publishing world and the same opposition as conceived in semiotic or philosophical terms. It suffices to read some of the analyses of the current dictionaries and encyclopedias (see, for instance, Weinreich 1980; Rey-Debove 1971) to realize that, if so-called encyclopedias are in some way encyclopedic, so-called dictionaries are rather impoverished encyclopedias.

If one consults the 1974 edition of the Merriam-Webster dictionary, one finds that /bull/ is defined as an «adult male bovine animal» (a definition that would titillate every fan of a semiotic dictionary); but /tiger/ is defined as «a large tawny black striped Asiatic flesh-eating mammal related to cat», and this definition is as if it were conceived to support Putnam's idea of 'stereotypes'.

## 2.1.2. The idea of a dictionary

The first semiotician to outline the idea of a dictionary was probably Hjelmslev. After having analyzed expressions into minor elements or *figurae* so that "unrestricted inventories are resolved into restricted" (1943:71), he tried to do the same for the content-plane. If the analysis of the expression-plane consists "in the resolution of entities that enter unrestricted inventories (*e.g.*, word-expressions) into entities that enter restricted inventories, and this resolution is carried on until only the most restricted inventories remain" (ibid.), the same procedure must be followed for the content plane:

> While the inventory of word-contents is unrestricted, in a language of familiar structures even the minimal signs will be distributed (on the basis of relational differences) into some (selected) inventories, which are unrestricted (*e.g.*, inventories of root-contents), and other (selecting) inventories, which are restricted (*e.g.*, inventories embracing contents of derivational and inflexional elements, *i.e.*, derivatives and morphemes). Thus in practice the procedure consists in trying to analyze the entities that enter the unrestricted inventories purely into entities that enter the restricted inventories. (Ibid.)

The example given by Hjelmslev concerns a series of word-contents corresponding to the common nouns *ram, ewe, man, woman, boy, girl, stallion, mare, sheep, human being, child,* and *horse* and to the pronouns *he* and *she.* Hjelmslev reduces the inventory in a way that can be represented by the diagram in Figure 2.1. He thought that the word-contents of the expressions *horse, sheep, human being,* and *child* belonged to unrestricted inventories, while *she* and *he* belonged to a category "with a restricted number of members."

|     | SHEEP | HUMAN | CHILD | HORSE |
|-----|-------|-------|-------|-------|
| SHE | ewe | woman | girl | mare |
| HE | ram | man | boy | stallion |

FIGURE 2.1

Hjelmslev's proposal seems to account for some linguistic phenomena that, according to the further semantic literature, should be explained by a dictionary. If a dictionary concerns purely our linguistic knowledge without giving instructions as to how to use linguistic terms in order to mention things or states of the world, Hjelmslev's dictionary undoubtedly explains why such sentences as *a ewe is a female sheep* and *if x is a ewe then x is not a stallion* are semantically well formed, even though the user of that language never had a direct acquaintance with a sheep or with a stallion. In fact, other dictionary theories, in order to provide instructions for reference, provide another kind of information; see, for instance, the idea of 'distinguishers' in Katz and Fodor (1963) and the reformulation of this principle in Katz's 'neoclassical theory of reference' (1979).

Hjelmslev's dictionary seems to explain (as usually requested to a dictionary) at least the following phenomena: (a) synonymy and paraphrase (a *ewe* is a *female sheep*); (b) similarity and difference (*ram/stallion, ewe/mare,* and *stallion/mare* have a common semantic component, but in a different respect a stallion is different from a mare, and a mare is different from a ewe); (c) antonymy (*girl/boy*); (d) hyperonymy and hyponymy (*horse/stallion*); (e) meaningfulness and semantic anomaly (*stallions are male* makes sense, whereas *a female stallion* is anomalous); (f) semantic ambiguity (a more complete dictionary should explain the possible ambiguity between *ram* as male sheep and *ram* as a warship); (g) redundancy (unfortunately in such a limited dictionary redundancy coincides with meaningfulness; *a male ram* is both meaningful and redundant); (h) analytic truth (for the same reason as above *rams are male* is at the same time meaningful, redundant, and analytically true, since the meaning of the subject contains the meaning of the predicate); (i) contradictoriness (*rams are female*); (j) syntheticity (the dictionary recognizes expressions such as *sheep provide wool* as depending on one's world knowledge); (k) inconsistency (*this is a ram* and *this is a ewe* cannot be true at the same time if referred to the same individual); (l) containment and semantic entailment: these two phenomena are strictly dependent on each other since, by virtue of the dictionary, every term is supposed to 'contain' certain properties; on the basis of these semantic rules (and independently of any other logical law) the sentence *this is a ram* entails *this is a sheep,* the sentence *this is not a sheep* entails *this is not a ram,* and the sentence *this is not a ram* leaves unprejudiced whether this is a sheep or not.

I have severely limited my list of requirements for a dictionary (other authors introduce more controversial requirements; see, for instance, Katz 1972, 5–6). In any case, Hjelmslev's proposal for a dictionary leaves unsolved two important questions: how to define the meaning of the components or *figurae* (in other words, if *ram* means male sheep, what does *sheep* mean?) and how to obtain a finite or unrestricted inventory.

Let us first consider the second problem. The most rigorous supporters of a theoretical dictionary maintain that the meaning of linguistic expressions should be represented through a *finite* number of semantic *primitives* (components, markers, properties, universal concepts).

It is not strictly necessary to assume that the set of *definienda* be a finite one. Naturally, the ideal condition for a dictionary is that this dictionary, being "the reconstruction of an aspect of the speaker's semantic competence," storing "only finitely many bits of information about a particular lexical item," be "a finite list of entries" so that "each entry consists of a finite number of lexical readings, and that each lexical reading contains a finite number of semantic markers" (Katz 1972:59–60). However, it is theoretically possible to conceive of a consistent number of primitives whose combination permits the description of an open number of *definienda*.

At this point the problems are (a) how to determine the primitives and (b) how to guarantee that their number be a finite one. As far as the determination of the primitives is concerned, the discussion is still open. Haiman (1980) remarks that (according to the current philosophical and semiotic literature) these primitives can be identified only in three ways:

(a) Primitives are 'simple' (or the 'simplest') concepts. It is, however, very hard to decide what a 'simple' concept is. In terms of the speaker's intuition, 'human' is simpler than 'mammal' (since every speaker is able to tell whether something or somebody is a human being or not, whereas we have problems in telling whether a dolphin is more a 'mammal' than a platypus). It must be clear that in this case 'simpler' or 'simplest' does not mean more general; therefore, 'simplest' concepts risk being more numerous than the 'complicated' ones. It is true that it is not necessary that the primitives be less than the *definienda:* "a phonological features analysis would not be invalidated by the discovery that there are more features than phonemes in some language" (Dean Fodor 1977:147). However, this remark can hold in phonemics, since a language has a finite number of phonemes. But if a language has a potentially open number of expressions to be defined, can one accept that this open series be defined by a series of primitives that is indefinitely open as well? Moreover, the quest for 'simple' concepts leads one to the second way, and the strictures holding for the latter also hold for the former.

(b) The primitives are rooted in our world experience, that is, they are 'object words' (in the sense of Russell 1940). The meaning of an object word is given by direct *ostension* of a state of the world, that is, of things that we meet in the course of our experience. A child learns by ostension what *red* means. On the contrary, there are 'dictionary words' that must be defined in terms of other dictionary words. It is, however, difficult to ascertain whether a word is an 'object' or a 'dictionary' one; as Russell remarks, *pentagram* is to most people a dictionary word, but to a child brought up in a house decorated with pentagrams it might be an object word (1940:70). Wierzbicka (1972:21) lists among object words *sea, river, field, wood, cloud, mountain, wind, table, house, book, paper, bird, fish, insect, plant, animal, cat, apple, rose, birch, gold, salt,* and so on — a very 'open' series, indeed, which reminds one of the open list of 'natural kinds' conjured up by the theories of 'rigid designation' (Kripke 1972; Putnam 1975). But, once one has decided to go on in this direction, the list of primitives cannot be a finite one. Moreover, the idea of a list of semantic primitives is devised in order to conceive of a dictionary-like competence free of any commitment to world knowledge, but, if one takes the option (b), then the dictionary competence is entirely dependent on the world knowledge.

(c) The primitives are Platonic ideas. This position is philosophically impeccable, but there is a historical (and therefore empirical) inconvenience: not even Plato succeeded in limiting in a satisfactory way the system of these universal and innate ideas. Either there is an idea for every 'natural kind', and the dictionary is not finite, or there are few very general ideas (One, Good, Multiplicity, and so on), and they do not succeed in distinguishing the meaning of any single expression.

One can, however, conceive of a fourth and more theoretical way. Suppose there is the possibility of establishing a system of primitives such that, by virtue of their systematic relationship, they must be finite in number. If one's mind succeeds in doing this, this can be taken as proof that such a systematic arrangement in some way 'mirrors' the structure of the human mind (and probably also the structure of the world).

Fortunately, we have a good example of such a system: it is represented by a purely lexical system of hyponyms and hyperonyms organized in the format of a tree such that every $n$-tuple of hyponyms postulates a single hyperonym, and every $n$-tuple of hyperonyms becomes an $n$-tuple of hyponyms of a higher single hyperonym, and so on, until the point where, irrespective of the number of hyponyms to be classified at the lower row of the tree, the tree necessarily *tapers* at a single uppermost node. Figure 2.2 represents a tree of this kind by simply reorganizing the terms provided by Hjelmslev. One can say that *ewe* contains or comprises 'sheep' and (by a transitive property of this classification) contains or comprises 'animal'. One can also say that this tree represents a system of *meaning postulates* in the sense of Carnap (1974). In fact, if the form of a meaning postulate is

$$(x)\ (Sx \supset Ax),$$

the fact that *x is a sheep* postulates the fact that *x is an animal* and *this is a sheep* entails *this is an animal*.

FIGURE 2.2

A set of meaning postulates is, however, different from the system of Figure 2.2. Carnap's formula holds even though $S$ stands for *raven* and $A$ stands for *black*. According to this meaning postulate, *if this is a raven, this is black* is an instance of analytic truth, and, if there was not a meaning postulate establishing that sheep are animals, *this sheep is an animal* would be an example of synthetic or factual truth. A set of meaning postulates is established on 'pragmatic' grounds (cf. Lyons 1977:204) and does not distinguish between encyclopedia and dictionary (see Carnap 1966).

The system of Figure 2.2 represents, on the contrary, an *ordered* set of meaning postulates, because it is *hierarchically structured;* for this reason it *must* be finite. One can think that it can be so because the way in which a lexicon of a natural language establishes relationships of hypo/hyperonomy reproduces some (as yet mysterious) structure of the human mind. Fortunately, one can disregard such a tremendous question. In any case, the system of Figure 2.2 (even were it 'true' or 'natural' or 'universal') is *not* an instance of a 'powerful' dictionary. Its inconveniences are the following: (a) it does not say what *sheep* or *animal* means (once again it does not explain the meaning of *figurae*); (b) it does not help one to distinguish a ram from a ewe, since both are sheep and animals; (c) it does account for such phenomena as hyperonomy, hyponymy, meaningfulness and anomaly, redundancy, analytic truth, contradictoriness, inconsistency, containment, and entailment, but it *does not account* for such phenomena as synonymy, paraphrase, and semantic difference.

To conclude, the tree of Figure 2.2 cannot provide the means for giving definitions. As Aristotle knew very well, there is a good definition when, in order to identify the essence of something, one selects attributes such that, although each of them has wider extension than the subject, *all together* they have not (*Post. An.* 2.96a.35). There must be full reciprocability between *definiendum* and *definiens*.

Supposing that /ram/ can be defined as the only «horned male sheep», then not only does *this is a ram* entail *this is a horned male sheep* but also *this is a horned male sheep* entails *this is a ram* as well as *this is not a ram* entails *this is not a horned male sheep*, and vice versa. *Definiens* and *definiendum* can be substituted for each other in *every* context.

This cannot happen with the tree of Figure 2.2. Not only does *this is an animal sheep* not entail *this is a ram*, but also *x is my preferite ram* does not entail *this is my preferite animal, all rams are horned* does not entail *all animals are horned*, and, if one deletes the hyponym, one does not necessarily delete the hyperonym.

Thus we must now think of a different system that, while displaying the same 'good' characteristics of the tree of Figure 2.2, is also able to account for the phenomena that the latter leaves unsolved. Let us try, then, a second tree (Figure 2.3), which in some way reproduces the procedure used by naturalists in order to classify animal species.

It is certainly imprudent to equate linguistic inventories with taxonomies in natural sciences: Dupré (1981) has demonstrated not only that, where a layman identifies a species (for example, beetle), the entomologist identifies something like 290,000 species, but also that the lexical system of a natural language and scientific taxonomies overlap in a very 'fuzzy' way. We call *tree* both an elm and a pine tree, while a naturalist would say that the former is an 'angiosperm' and that the latter is not. There is no taxonomic equivalent of *tree* and no ordinary language equivalent of *angiosperm*.

However, Hjelmslev's proposal can allow one to conceive of a sort of taxonomic tree as in Figure 2.3, designed to define without ambiguity and with the maximum economy a series of words, namely, *dog, wolf, fox, cat, tiger, lynx, bachelor* (as a seal), *horse, ox, buffalo, sheep, mouflon, elephant* and *echidna*. In such a linguistic (and natural) universe, one is not supposed to distinguish a horse from an ass or an elephant from a rhinoceros, and this explains why only certain lower disjunctions are called for. In this sense, the tree of Figure 2.3 overlaps only partially a current scientific taxonomy.

The tree of Figure 2.3 provides the picture of a very restricted universe made up of natural kinds (of which the words in italic in the lower row provide *names*). We are obliged to consider this universe as a restricted one for the sake of our experiment: this universe is scarcely similar to the one of our actual experience, but when speaking of dictionaries one must conceive not only of very artificial languages but also of very artificial worlds. For instance, this universe takes into account neither 'artificial' kinds (such as a house or a chair) nor predicates, nor actions, nor social roles (such as 'king', 'bachelor', 'pilot'). It has been remarked how it is difficult to account for all these problems at the same time (see Schwartz 1977:37–41). Aristotle (and Porphyry) dealt with natural kinds in the tree of substances, admitting that all the other phenomena should have been dealt with in one of the possible trees for the other nine categories (see 2.2.1). As for artificial kinds, Aristotle was convinced that one can deal with them *as if* they were substances, but according to some analogical procedures (see *Metaphysics*, 1043b21, 1070a– b).

It is not necessary to decide whether the linguistic terms in each node of the tree names *classes* included within larger classes or *properties* in some way contained or postulated by the terms naming the natural kinds listed in italic in the lowest row. One can say that any name of a subclass postulates its class or that every name of natural kinds postulates a hierarchical series of properties. In lexicographical representations of a system of hypo/hyperonyms, it is usual to assume that, if the meaning of a word is included within the meaning of another, then "each 'included' meaning has all the features of the 'including' meaning . . . plus at least one more feature which serves to distinguish the more restricted area" (Nida 1975:16).

In any case, the whole system of Figure 2.3 is a *finite* one, which accounts also for *synonymy, paraphrase,* and *semantic difference* and which permits the production of *definitions*. Only a cat is a «felis catus, felis, felid, fissiped, carnivorous placental animal», and, if something does not have *all* these properties *in conjunction*, then it cannot be a cat.

This tree accounts for all the phenomena that a good dictionary is supposed to explain. It is a very flexible tool. Suppose one has to explain also the meaning of /halibut/; it will be sufficient to insert the disjunction 'fish/mammal' under the node 'animal', and the tree would equally taper toward an ultimate node. With further complications one could also distinguish /bachelor/ as a seal from /bachelor/ as a human being. The tree would always result in being finite.

The tree does not offer the possibility of distinguishing between male

and female, adult and young. It is a pity; we shall see apropos of the
Porphyrian Tree (in 2.1.3) how embarrassing these kinds of 'accidents'
are. But before coming to grips with these formidable questions, we
have to raise a more urgent criticism.

### 2.1.3. The interpretation of the markers

The tree explains without ambiguity that a cat is nothing else but a 'felis
catus'. But in Latin (even though at two different historical stages of this
language) both /felis/ and /catus/ (or *cattus*) are synonymous with the
English word /cat/. Thus the *definiens* and the *definiendum* are certainly
interchangeable, but only because they are absolutely and redundantly
synonymous: a cat is a cat is a cat is a cat. If one asks what a *felis catus* is,
one knows that it is a felis, which is not enough to distinguish a cat from
a tiger.

However, when a zoologist says that what we call cat is a *'Felis catus'*
he is not merely playing on words. He uses *Felis* as the name of a genus
and *catus* as the name of a differentia, but by these short-hand expressions he intends to signify other biological properties. To be a *catus*
means to have the properties $p_1, p_2 \ldots p_n$, and to be a *Felis* means to
have the properties $p_1, p_2, \ldots p_n$ (and so on for the upper nodes).

The taxonomy of the zoologist does not intend to be a way to analyze
the meaning of the word /cat/; it represents a mere *classification* of natural kinds, accidentally labeled with certain names (changing from natural
language to natural language). The zoologist as such is strongly interested in defining the actual properties of the species he classifies, yet
these properties are simply *contained* or *meant* by the terms he uses as
taxonomic labels.

If a zoologist is told that *gorillas grow in Ireland*, he can react in two
ways. Either he understands the sentence in the sense that *some* gorillas
are born in Ireland, and in this case he is eager to concede that similar
events happen in zoological gardens, or he takes the sentence as conveying an 'eternal' proposition (all the animals belonging to this species
grow in Ireland), and then he would say that the proposition is
*analytically* false because it challenges some information that belongs to
his definition of gorillas. Likewise he would not discuss the statement
*this sheep has three feet*, since he knows that there can be handicapped
sheep, but he would challenge the statement *sheep are not four-footed* because in his definition of a sheep there is a marker (probably 'ungulata')
that must be *interpreted* in terms of four-footedness. Perhaps the zoologist
would not say that sheep are four-footed *necessarily* or *analytically*, but he
would say that the property of being four-footed belongs to sheep in
some strong sense of /belonging/.

Zoologists know that their classificatory markers are *interpretable* and

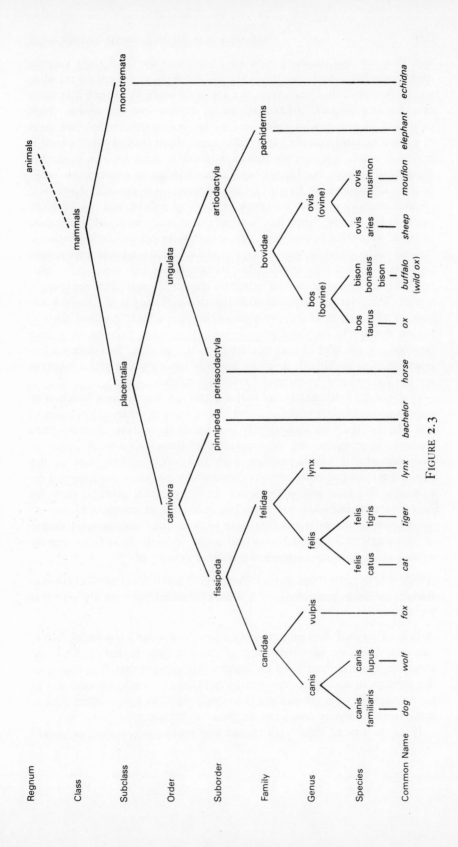

FIGURE 2.3

that they are not metalinguistic constructs but *words* of their specific object-language. Zoologically speaking, 'mammal' is not only a metalinguistic construct that guarantees the semantic anomaly of such assertions as *a stone is a mammal:* /mammal/ means more or less «an animal which nourishes its young with milk secreted by mammary glands». Speakers of natural language do the same, obviously: when they say that a land is rich in minerals, they do not intend only that that land is rich in nonliving natural objects, but intend many other interesting properties as well. In natural language we frequently use expressions as animal, object, and vegetal as many times as we speak of cats and wolves, and maybe more often. This means either that we are using many terms of a metalanguage as items of a natural language or that there is a difference between 'animal' as a semantic marker and /animal/ as a linguistic expression. But this is indeed a mere wordplay; in fact, when lexicographers or philosophers of language use the semantic marker 'animal' they are using a word of their natural language to build up a metalanguage. One can say that, as soon as a natural expression has become a metalinguistic term, it should not be further interpreted; such a rigorous decision is indeed possible and the tree of Figure 2.1 proves it, but, once this decision has been made, it is difficult to know not only what a sheep and a mouflon are but also what /sheep/ and /mouflon/ mean.

It would be sufficient to say that a dictionary has the sole function of providing a computer with the capability of parsing sentences in order to test whether they are semantically consistent, redundant, or analytically true, without explaining the meaning of their component words to someone who is not acquainted with any corresponding state of the world. Yet even the most rigorous theories of a dictionary competence try to escape this fate, and in two ways: from a practical point of view, by matching a representation of meaning with some instructions for the individuation of the referents (see Katz 1979 for the "neoclassical" theory of meaning), and from a theoretical point of view, *by defining even the analytic markers.* Katz analyzes the lexeme /chair/ as

(Object) (Physical) (Non living) (Artifact) (Furniture) (Portable) (Something with legs) (Something with a back) (Something with a seat) (Seat for one)

so mixing up analytical properties and pieces of world knowledge; but at the same time he says that each of the concepts represented by the semantic markers "can itself be broken into components. For example, the concept of an object represented by '(object)' might be analyzed as *an organization of parts that are spatio-temporally contiguous which form a stable whole having an orientation in space*" (1972:40).

If so, the tree of Figure 2.3 should host other markers such as 'organ-

ization', 'part', 'orientation', 'space', 'contiguous', and so on. Even admitting that all these markers can be inserted into a bidimensional tree
(and without asking what will happen when one decides to analyze,
along with 'object', also 'living' or 'furniture', not to mention all the
rest), we are not sure that markers such as 'contiguous' are of the same
nature as 'space' or 'animal'.

Moreover, to make the markers interpretable, usually a theory has to
give up on their hierarchy and consider them as an unordered set, that
is, it has to adopt a cross-classificatory criterion (cf. the remarks of Dean
Fodor 1977:153). We have demonstrated that, if the tree is not hierarchically organized, one has no more guarantees of dealing with a finite
number of markers.

Thus either the primitives cannot be interpreted, and one cannot explain the meaning of a term, or they can and must be interpreted, and
one cannot limit their number. The latter is the case of the Porphyrian
tree, in which the notion of *differentia specifica* is posited exactly in order
to provide a minimal, but sufficient, interpretation for *every* marker. Unfortunately, as we shall see, as soon as the differentiae are introduced, a
Porphyrian tree loses the properties of a dictionary and becomes an encyclopedia.

## 2.2.  Critique of the Porphyrian tree

### 2.2.1.  Aristotle on definition

Aristotle says that "definition is of the essence or essential nature" (*Post.
An.* 2.90b30). To define a substance means to establish, among various
accidental attributes, the essential ones, particularly that one which
causes the substance to be as it is — its substantial form. The problem is
then to "hunt" for the right attributes that must be predicated as elements in the definition (96a15). Aristotle gives the example of the attributes that can apply to the number 3: an attribute such as 'being' undoubtedly applies to 3, but also to other things that are not numbers. On
the contrary, 'oddness' applies to every 3 and, even though it has a wider
application (it also applies to 5), it nevertheless does not extend beyond
the genus 'number'. "We must select attributes of this kind, up to the
point where, although each of them has a wider extension that the subject, all together they have not; this will be the essence of the thing"
(96a35). Aristotle means that, if one defines man as a rational, mortal
animal, each of these attributes, singly, also applies to other entities (for
instance, also horses are animals, dogs are mortals, angels are rational),
but, taken as a whole, as a definitional cluster, these attributes apply
only to man (thus *definiens* and *definiendum* are convertible or biconditionally linked: $p \equiv q$).

However, a definition is not a demonstration: to show the essence of a thing is not the same as to prove a proposition about it; a definition reveals what an object is while a demonstration proves *that* something can be said of a given subject (91a1). In a definition we are assuming what we are required to prove in a demonstration (91a35), and those who define do not prove that something exists (92b20). A definition explains the meaning of the name (93b30).

In his attempt to find out a right method for inferring satisfactory definitions, Aristotle develops the theory of *predicables*, that is, the modes in which the categories can be applied to a subject. In *Topics* (1.101b17–24) Aristotle lists only four predicables, namely, genus, property (*proprium*), definition, and accident. Since Porphyry will definitely list five predicables (genus, species, differentia, property, and accident), this discrepancy has aroused many discussions. There was a serious reason why Aristotle did not insert the differentia among predicables: the differentia "being generic in character, it should be ranged with the genus" (*Topics* 1.101b20), and to define consists in putting the subject into its genus and then adding the differentiae (*Topics* 6.139a30). Thus one can say that, in a way, the differentia is automatically (via genus and definition) inserted into the list. As far as the species is concerned, Aristotle does not mention it because the species cannot be predicated of anything, being the ultimate subject of any predication. Since, however, the species is expressed by the definition, this probably explains why Porphyry in his lists replaces species with definition.

### 2.2.2. The Porphyrian tree

In a long discussion in *Posterior Analytics* (2. 12.96b25–97b15), Aristotle outlines a series of rules for developing a right division from the most universal genera to the *infimae species*, by isolating at every step the right differentiae.

This is the method carried out by Porphyry in his *Isagoge*. The fact that Porphyry develops a theory of division in commenting upon Aristotle's *Categories* (where the problem of differentia and genus is just mentioned) is a matter that requires serious discussion (see Moody 1935) but is not relevant for the purposes of the present analysis. We can also disregard the discussion on the nature of universals, opened by the *Isagoge* though the commentary of Boethius. Porphyry says that he intends to "put aside the investigation of certain profound questions," namely, whether genera or species exist in themselves or reside in mere concepts alone. As a matter of fact, he is the first to translate Aristotle's suggestion on definition under the form of a tree, and it is difficult to avoid the suspicion that he is portraying (rather iconically) a Neoplatonic chain of beings. But we can disregard the metaphysics underlying the Porphyrian tree, since we are interested in the fact that this tree, inde-

pendent of its alleged metaphysical grounds and conceived as a representation of mere *logical* relationships, has influenced all subsequent discussions on the method of definition. We are not interested in the
metaphysical perspective according to which Porphyry outlines a *unique*
tree of substances, and it is doubtful whether Aristotle thought in this
way or was more flexibly eager to imagine different and differently structured trees according to the definitory problem he had to solve. Aristotle
deals cautiously with this method of division and, if he seems to ap-
preciate it in the *Posterior Analytics,* he seems to be more skeptical in
*Parts of Animals (*6426*bff).* Nevertheless, Porphyry designed a *unique* tree
for substances, and it is from this model that every subsequent idea of a
dictionary-like representation stems.

Porphyry lists five predicables: genus, species, differentia, property,
and accident. The five predicables establish the modes of definition for
all the ten categories (substance plus nine accidents). It is therefore possible to think of ten Porphyrian trees: one for substances, which allows,
for instance, the definition of man as a rational mortal animal, and one
for each of the other nine categories; for instance, a tree of qualities will
allow the definition of purple as a species of the genus 'red'. Aristotle
said that even accidents are susceptible to definition, even though an
accident can be said to have an essence only in reference to substances
(*Metaphysics* 8.1028a10– 1031a10). There are, thus, ten possible trees,
but there is not a tree of the ten trees, because the Being is not a
*summum genus.*

Undoubtedly, the substance-tree proposed by Porphyry aims at being
considered a *finite* set of genera and species (we will see in which sense
this assumption is untenable); it is not said whether the other nine possible trees are to be finite or not, and Porphyry is rather elusive on this
subject.

The definition Porphyry gives of genus is a purely *formal* one: a genus
is that to which the species is subordinate. Likewise the species is what
is subordinate to a genus. Thus genus and species are relative to each
other, that is, mutually definable. Any genus posited on a given node of
the tree encompasses its dependent species, but each species becomes
at its turn the genus of another underlying species, and so on, until the
last row of the tree, where the *species specialissimae* or second substances
are located. At the upper node of the tree there is the *genus generalissimus*
(represented by the name of the category), and this genus cannot be the
species of something else.

Thus every species postulates its upper genus, while the opposite
does not hold. A genus can be 'predicated of' its species, while species
'belong to' their genus. However, a Porphyrian tree cannot be composed
only of genera and species; otherwise, it would assume the format represented in Figure 2.4. (Incidentally, in the Neoplatonic tradition, gods

are listed among bodies and animals because they are intermediate natural forces, not to be identified with the inaccessible and immaterial One. The Christian medieval tradition adopts this example as a conventional assumption, more or less as modern logicians assume that the Morning Star is identical with the Evening Star).

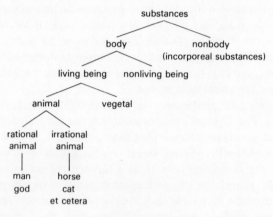

FIGURE 2.4

In a tree of this sort, man and god, as well as horse and cat, could not be distinguished from each other. Man is different from god because the former is mortal and the latter is not. The mortality of man represents his *differentia*. Now, the tree of Figure 2.4 does not account for *differentiae*.

In order to understand better the nature of *differentia*, one must carefully distinguish between accident, *differentia*, and *proprium*. This is a crucial point, since accidents are not required to produce a definition, and the 'property' (*proprium*) has a curious status: it belongs to the species, but it is not required to build up the definition. There are different types of propria: (a) occurring in one species, although not in every member of it (as the capability of healing in men); (b) occurring in the whole species, but not in a single species only (as being two-footed); (c) occurring in the whole species, and only in a single one, but only at some time (as being grey in old age); (d) occurring in a whole species, only in a single one, and at every time (as the capacity of laughing in man). This last case is the one most frequently quoted in classical literature and has an interesting feature: it is biconditionally equivalent with its subject (only men are laughing beings, and vice versa). The nature of proprium remains mysterious, both in Aristotle and in Porphyry, since it looks like something midway between an essential and analytic property and an encyclopedic and synthetic one.

Let us come back to the differentia. Differentiae can be *separable* from the subject (as to be hot, moving, ill), and in this sense they are mere accidents. But they can also be *inseparable:* some of them are inseparable but still accidental, as to be hook-nosed, but there are differentiae that belong to the subject *per se,* or *essentially*, as being rational, mortal, and capable of knowledge. These are the *specific differentiae* which are added to the genus in order to form the definition of the species.

Differentiae can be both *divisive* and *constitutive*. For instance, the genus 'Living Beings' is potentially divisible into the differentiae 'sensitive/insensitive' (endowed or not with sensitivity), but the differentia 'sensitive' can be composed with the genus 'living being' to constitute the genus 'animal'. The genus 'animal' is divisible into 'rational/ irrational', but the difference 'rational' is constitutive (along with the genus it divides) of the species 'animal rational animal'. Thus the differentiae divide a genus (the genus *potentially* contains these opposites) and are selected to constitute in fact a lower genus.

The *Isagoge* only suggests verbally the idea of the tree, but the medieval tradition has definitely built it up, as in Figure 2.5. In the tree of Figure 2.5, the dotted lines marks the *divisive* differentiae, while the continuous lines mark the same differentiae insofar as they are considered *constitutive*.

## 2.2.3. A tree which is not a tree

It seems that the tree of Figure 2.5 does show the difference between man and God, but not the one between man and horse. As a matter of fact, all the instances of a Porphyrian tree, following a common standard, aim at showing how man can be defined and are therefore incomplete. In order to isolate the essence of horses, the diagram should display a different series of disjunctions on its right side so as to isolate (along with a rational animal) an irrational (and mortal) one. Even in this case, however, a horse could not be distinguished from a dog; one should therefore postulate some complication of the right side of the tree so as to insert into the diagram many more disjunctions. Aristotle would have had serious problems in doing so: in *Parts of Animals* he criticizes the method of division and, so to speak, provides many possible small trees according to the specific problem he has to solve.

However, the tree of Figure 2.5 encourages a stronger objection. What distinguishes God from man is the difference mortal/immortal; but horse and man are both mortal and are distinguished by the difference 'rational/irrational'. Therefore one has to choose either of the following alternatives: (a) the differentia 'mortal/immortal' is not divisive of the genus 'rational animal' but, rather, of the genus 'animal' (but in this first case it would be impossible to tell the difference between man and God); (b) the differentia 'mortal/immortal' occurs twice, one time under 'rational animal' and one time under 'irrational animal'.

GENERA AND SPECIES

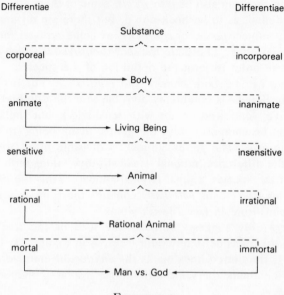

FIGURE 2.5

Porphyry would not have discouraged this second decision, since he says that the differentia "is often observed in many species, as four-footed in many animals which differ in species" (18.20). This is a very important remark. Also, Aristotle says that, when two or more genera are *subordinate* to an upper genus (as it happens to man and horse insofar as they are both animals), nothing prevents them from having the same differentiae (*Cat.*, 1b.15*ff*; *Topics*, 4.164b.10).

In *Posterior Analytics* (2.90b*ff*) Aristotle shows how it is possible to arrive at an unambiguous definition of the number 3. Keeping in mind that for Greeks 1 was not a number (but rather the source and the measure of any successive number), the number 3 can be defined as that odd number which is prime in both senses of being neither measurable by number nor composed of numbers. This definition is (biconditionally) equivalent with the expression *three*. But it is interesting to represent (Figure 2.6) how Aristotle reaches this conclusion by a careful work of division.

This sort of division displays two interesting consequences: (a) the properties registered in italic are not exclusive of a given node but can occur under more nodes; and (b) a given species (2, 3, 9) can be defined by the conjunction of more of the above properties. In fact, these properties are differentiae. Thus Aristotle shows by a clear example, not only

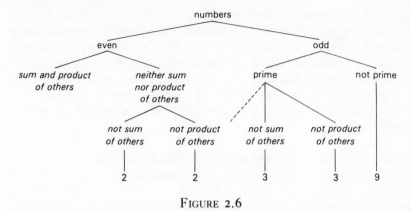

FIGURE 2.6

that many differentiae can be attributed to the same species, but also that *the same couple of differentiae can occur under diverse genera*. Moreover, he shows that, once a given difference has served to define unambiguously a given species, one is not obliged to take into account all the other subjects or which it is predicable: in other words, once one or more differentiae have served to define without ambiguities the number 3, it is irrelevant that they can also serve to define the number 2. (For a clear statement in this sense, see *Post. An.* 2.13.97a15– 25.)

But at this point we can try a further step. Once it has been said that, given subordinate genera, nothing prevents them from having the same differentiae, and since the tree of substances is wholly made of genera that are all subordinate to the uppermost one, it is hard to tell how many times the same couple of differentiae can occur. In *Topics* (1.15.106*aff*) Aristotle says that we can call both a sound and a material substance 'sharp'. It is true that 'sharp' does not mean the same differentia in both cases, since in the former case it is opposed to 'flat' and in the latter case to 'dull' (thus the same name is used equivocally for two diverse differentiae). However, the same opposition 'white/black' occurs when one speaks either of colors or of sounds. Aristotle is convinced that this equivocality is a merely lexical one, since the same couple of contraries is referred to two different cases of sense-perception (sight and hearing). However, this equivocality is similar to the nonunivocal use of *to be* for the propositions *men are animals* (which is a matter of substantial being) and *these men are white* (which is a matter of accident): a case in which Aristotle speaks of "being used in various senses but with reference to one central idea" (ηρòς έν: *Metaphysics* 4.1003a30). This reference to a central idea will be translated (by medieval philosophers) in terms of analogy, of proportion, not in terms of mere equivocality.

In *Topics* 1.15.107b30) Aristotle will also say that the couple 'white/

black' when referred to a body is a *species* of color, whereas when referred to a sound it is a *differentia* (for one note differs from the other in being more or less clear or white). The whole matter is very complex, but how to avoid the suspicion that the entire universe of differentiae is polluted by metaphorical ambiguities (be they due to mere equivocality or to analogy)? Is 'two-footed' as referred to man the same as 'two-footed' as referred to a bird? Is 'rational' as applied to man the same as 'rational' as applied to God?

### 2.2.4.  The tree is entirely made up with differentiae

Many medieval commentators on the *Isagoge* seem to encourage our suspicions. Boethius (*In Isagogen, C. S. E. L.* 256.10– 12, 266.13– 15) writes that 'mortal' can be a differentia for 'irrational animal' and that the species 'horse' is constituted by the differentia 'irrational and mortal'. He also suggests that 'immortal' can be a differentia for celestial bodies which are inanimate and immortal: "In this case the differentia *immortal* is shared between species that differ not only in their proximate genus but also in all their genera up to the subaltern genus second from the top of the tree" (Stump 1978:257).

According to Stump, the suspicion aroused by Boethius is "surprising" and "disconcerting"; in fact, it is only reasonable. Aristotle and Porphyry say that a differentia is greater (encompasses more) than its subject, and this could not be if *only* men were mortal and *only* gods were immortals. In order to have such a result 'mortal/immortal' must occur under more than a genus, and so on for the other differentiae. Otherwise it would be incomprehensible why (according to *Topics* 4.144a25) the species entails the difference, but the difference *does not* entail the species: 'mortal' has a wider extension than 'animal rational and mortal'.

Abelard, in his *Editio super Porphyrium* (157v.15), suggests that a given differentia is predicated of more and different species: "falsum est quod omnis differentia sequens ponit superiores, quia ubi sunt permixtae differentiae, fallit." Thus, given that (a) the same differentia can encompass more species, (b) the same couple of differentiae can occur under more than one genus, (c) different couples of differentiae can be represented under many genera by using the same names (equivocally or analogically), and (d) it is an open question how high in the tree the common genus can be in respect to which many *subordinate* genera can host the same differentiae, then one is entitled to reformulate the Porphyrian tree as in Figure 2.7.

The tree of Figure 2.7 displays many interesting characteristics: (a) it provides the representation of a possible world in which many new and still unknown natural kinds can be discovered and defined (for instance, incorporeal, animate, and irrational substances); (b) it shows that so-

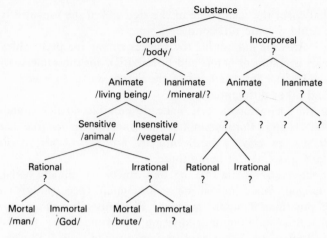

FIGURE 2.7

called genera and species are *names* by which one labels only clusters of differentiae; (c) according to this tree, one cannot predict that if mortal then rational, or if irrational then corporeal, and so on; (d) as a consequence of (c) it can be freely reorganized according to alternative hierarchies.

As for the characteristic (a), we have seen what Boethius said apropos of celestial bodies. As for the characteristic (b), it must be clear that *this tree is composed only of differentiae*. Genera and species are only the names that we assign to the nodes represented by disjunctions of differentiae. Boethius, Abelard, and other medieval scholars knew this so well that they continually complain about the *penuria nominum*, that is, about the fact that we do not have enough lexical items to name the nodes of the tree represented by differentiae added to differentiae of upper differentiae.

Consider the case of the constitutive node obtained by adding the differentia 'rational' to the genus 'animal': the traditional tree labels this node with the expression *rational animal*, which is blatantly redundant and only repeats the name of the upper genus and of the differentia constitutive of the unnamed species. This laziness in providing names for species is rather inconceivable. The medieval imagination could have coined some new term. But it is a merely empirical circumstance that somebody found the name /animal/ for labeling the node composed by adding the difference 'sensitive' to /living being/, which is in turn the mere name of the composition 'animate + corporeal'. The names of genera are insufficient because they are mere shorthand: a genus is no more than a cluster of differentiae. Genera and species are linguistic ghosts that cover the real nature of the tree and of the universe it represents: a world of pure differentiae.

Thus, if Aristotle did not list the species among the predicables (since the species is a sum of genus and differentia), for the same reason also genera could be eliminated, since they, too, are mere sums of upper genera and other differentiae.

As for the characteristic (c), since differentiae do not contain each other, the classical Porphyrian tree (as unveiled in its true nature in Figure 2.7) *is no longer a hierarchical and ordered structure*. It does not provide any guarantee of being finite.

As for the characteristic (d), the tree can be continually reelaborated and rearranged. Since 'mortal' does not contain (necessarily) 'rational', why not put 'mortal' upon 'rational'? Boethius (*De divisione* 6,7) says clear'y that this kind of optional division is possible for accidents. We can say tl at all white are either hard (pearl) or liquid (milk). But we can at the same time say that, given the genus of hard things, some of them are white (pearl) and some of them are black (let us say, ebony); or that, given the genus of liquid things, some are white (milk) and some are black (let us say, ink). Therefore Boethius suggests that (at least for accidents) many trees can be arranged playing upon the same entities, as shown in Figure 2.8.

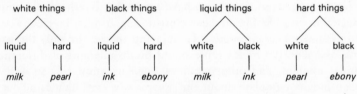

FIGURE 2.8

Boethius, however, says something more (*De divisione* 37), namely, that the same freedom of choice holds as far as every genus is concerned. We can divide numbers between prime and not prime as well as between even and odd. We can divide triangles either according to their sides or according to their angles. "Fit autem generis eiusdem divisio multipliciter . . . generis unius fit multiplex divisio . . . genus una quodammodo multarum specierum similitudo, est . . . atque ideo collectivum plurimarum specierum genus est."

The same is said by Abelard (*Editio super Porphyrium* 160v.12): "pluraliter ideo dicit genera, quia animal dividitur per rationale animal et irrationale; et rationale per mortale et immortale dividitur; et mortale per rationale et irrationale dividitur" (that is to say, as in Figure 2.9). In a tree composed with pure differences, these differences can be rearranged *according to the description under which a given subject is considered*.

FIGURE 2.9

### 2.2.5. Differentiae as accidents and signs

Differentiae enjoy such a singular status because they are accidents, and accidents are infinite, or at least indefinite, in number.

Differentiae are qualities, and it is not by chance that, whereas genera and species are expressed by common nouns, differentiae are expressed by adjectives. They belong to a tree different from the one of substances. According to Aristotle, their number cannot be known a priori (*Metaphysics* 8.2.6.1042b2 – 1043a). It is true that he says this of nonessential differentiae, but who really knows which differentiae are strictly essential or specific? Aristotle plays upon a few examples (such as rational and mortal, followed by the whole medieval tradition), but when he speaks of other natural kinds, such as animals, and of artificial objects, he is more vague, so as to make his readers suspect that he could have never thought of a *finite* Porphyrian tree.

However, the notion of specific differentia conceals an oxymoron: a specific differentia is an *essential accident*. Is it possible to solve such a philosophical puzzle? The most striking answer to this question is given by Aquinas. In *De Ente et Essentia* Aquinas asserts that the differentia specifica corresponds to the substantial form (the difference corresponds to the form, and the genus to the matter, and together they make up the essence of the substance of which they provide the definition). At this point it would appear rather whimsical to identify an accident (a quality) with a substantial form, but Aquinas excogitates a brilliant solution: "in rebus sensibilibus etsi ipsae differentiae essentiales nobis ignotae sunt: unde significantur per differentiae accidentales quae ex essentialibus oriuntur, sicut causa significatur per suum effectum, sicut bipes ponit differentia hominis" (*De Ente* 6). Essential differences cannot be known directly by us; we know (we infer!) them *by semiotic means*, through the effects (accidents) they produce, and these accidents are the sign of their unknowable cause.

This idea is repeated, for instance, in the *Summa Theologiae* (1.29.2 – 3; or 1.77.1 – 7). Thus we discover that differentiae such as rational are not the actual substantial form that constitutes the species as such: Aquinas makes clear that the *ratio* as *potentia animae* appears outside *verbo et facto*, through external actions (and actions are not substances, but accidents); men are told to be rational because they manifest their rational potency through their activity of knowing, an activity that they perform by internal thought and external discourse (1.79.8*ff*). In a decisive text (*Contra Gentiles* 3.46), Aquinas says that human beings do not know what they are (*quid est*); they know *quod est* (that they are so), insofar as they perceive themselves as performing a rational activity. *What* in reality our spiritual potencies are, we know "ex ipsorum actuum qualitate," through the quality of the acts of which they are the potencies.

Thus, 'rational' is an accident, and so we are all the differentiae in which the traditional Porphyrian tree dissolves itself.

The tree of genera and species, the tree of substances, blows up in a dust of differentiae, in a turmoil of infinite accidents, in a nonhierarchical network of *qualia*. The dictionary is dissolved into a potentially unordered and unrestricted galaxy of pieces of world knowledge. The dictionary thus becomes an encyclopedia, because it was in fact *a disguised encyclopedia*.

## 2.3. Encyclopedias

### 2.3.1. Some attempts: registering contexts and topics

If a dictionary is a disguised encyclopedia, then the only possible representation of the content of a given lexical item cannot be provided except in terms of an encyclopedia. If the so-called universals, or metatheoretical constructs, that work as markers within a dictionary-like representation are mere linguistic labels that cover more synthetic properties, an encyclopedia-like representation assumes that the representation of the content takes place only by means of *interpretants,* in a process of unlimited semiosis. These interpretants being in their turn interpretable, there is no bidimensional tree able to represent the global semantic competence of a given culture. Such a global representation is only a semiotic postulate, a regulative idea, and takes the format of a multidimensional network that has been described as the Model Q (Eco 1976, 2.12).

Local representations of the Model Q are implemented every time a given text requires a background encyclopedic knowledge in order to be interpreted. These local representations of the encyclopedic knowledge assume the form of a set of instructions for the proper textual insertion of the terms of a language into a series of contexts (as classes of co-texts) and for the correct disambiguation of the same terms when met within a given co-text. An encyclopedic version of componential semantics should then appear as an *Instruktionssemantik* which is text-theoretically oriented (see, for instance, Schmidt 1976).

In *A Theory of Semiotics* I have outlined a model of componential analysis in an encyclopedic format, where the spectrum of the sememe (corresponding to the content of a given expression) was analyzed in terms of *contextual* and *circumstantial selections*. I have also maintained that this kind of representation should hold not only for so-called categorematic terms but also for the syncategorematic ones, and I have provided examples of an instruction-like or a text-oriented analysis of not only verbal expressions but also indexical signs, as a pointing finger.

In *The Role of the Reader* I have insisted on the fact that a sememe is a virtual or potential text and that a text is the expansion of one or more sememes. The encyclopedic representation of the sememe has been reinforced with the reference to frames, scripts, and other instructions concerning coded circumstantial and contextual occurrences. As a consequence, it is clear that an encyclopedic representation, insofar as it is text-oriented, must take into account this kind of so-called pragmatic factor as well. In an encyclopedic representation, semantics must translate into its own terms most of the phenomena studied by pragmatics. There are many contextual operators which work exclusively in relation with a given co-text, but their co-textual fate must be established, foreseen, and predicted by coded contextual selections.

Take a co-textual operator such as the Italian syncategorematic expression /*invece*/, basically translatable as /instead/. When syntagmatically linked with /di/ (*invece di* = instead of) it is basically a sentence operator. Without preposition, /*invece*/ is an adverb and works as a textual operator, and can be translated as /on the contrary/ or /on the other hand/. As such it seems to express some opposition, but it is doubtful what it is opposed to. Take the following expressions:

(1) Mary ama le mele. John invece le odia. (Mary loves apples. John on the other hand hates them.)

(2) Mary ama le mele. Invece odia le banane. (Mary loves apples. On the other hand she hates bananas.)

(3) Mary ama le mele. Invece John adora le banane. (Mary loves apples. John on the other hand is fond of bananas.)

(4) Mary sta suonando il violoncello. John invece sta mangiando banane. (Mary is playing her 'cello. John on the other hand is eating bananas.)

We realize that in (1) /*invece*/ (on the other hand) marks an alternative to the subject and her action; in (2) it marks an alternative to the action and to the object; in (3) it marks an alternative to the subject and the object; in (4) everything seems to be challenged.

Now let us try to insert these expressions into a more comprehensive co-text; let us look at them as the appropriate answers to the following questions:

(1a) Do Mary and John love apples?
(2a) What kind of fruit does Mary love?
(3a) What kind of fruit does John love?
(4a) What the hell are those kids doing? They were supposed to have
their music lesson!

It has repeatedly been asserted (see, for instance, van Dijk 1977) that
a textual topic can be detected by formulating the implicit question
dominating a given text or portion of a text. That is the case. The four
questions listed above are establishing four different textual topics,
namely:

(1b) People who love apples.
(2b) Fruit Mary loves.
(3b) Fruit John loves.
(4b) Music lesson.

At this point it is intuitively clear that /invece/ (on the other hand) in
(1) is opposed to (1b), in (2) is opposed to (2b), and so on. This means
that our encyclopedic competence has stored a semantic analysis of
/invece/ where, after a general semantic marker of alternative, a contextual selection is recorded, such as "in the cases in which the textual
topic is $x$, the expression under consideration marks an opposition to $X$"
(Figure 2.10).

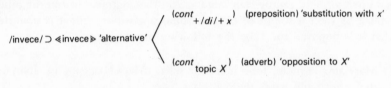

FIGURE 2.10

### 2.3.2.  Some attempts: registering frames and scripts

Nevertheless, there are cases in which such notions as contextual selections are not enough to establish the possible textual insertion of given
lexemes. Take an expression such as the following:

(5) John was sleeping when he was suddenly awakened. Somebody was
tearing up the pillow.

I imagine that a computer fed with dictionary-like information would be
able to understand what /to sleep/ and /pillow/ mean, but would be
unable to establish what the relation is between John and the pillow (and
which pillow?). Current research in Artificial Intelligence has elaborated
the notion of *frame* (Minsky 1974; Winston 1977; Schank 1975, 1981;

van Dijk 1977): the addressee (be it a computer or a human being) is endowed with an enlarged encyclopedic competence which encompasses also a set of frames, or scripts, among which — for instance — are the frames 'sleeping' and 'bedroom'. By resorting to this storage of competence, the addressee knows that human beings usually sleep in bedrooms and that bedrooms are furnished with beds, beds with pillows, and so on. By amalgamation of two or more frames, the addressee realizes that the pillow just mentioned can only be the one John was resting his head on.

To what extent can one assume that the frames, too, are elements of an encyclopedia-like componential analysis (an extremely rich one indeed)? Do they belong to a sort of additional competence (that which is called *overcoding* in Eco 1976)? Probably the very notion of the encyclopedia has to be revised and reorganized according to different rates of social accessibility or of textual necessity. For instance, when reading *John was sleeping and was dreaming of . . .* , one does not need to have recourse to the frame 'bedroom' (even though one shares this piece of knowledge), and only the co-text leads one to *blow up* and to *narcotize* given sememes or frames (see Eco 1979).

The notion of frame (before being postulated by the empirical engineering of Artificial Intelligence scientists) was already indirectly advocated by Peirce. Take, for instance, his example of a possible definition of lithium. According to a general dictionary (*Webster's New Collegiate*), lithium is "a soft silver-white element of the alkali metal group that is the lightest metal known and that *is used esp. in nuclear reactions and metallurgy*" (I have stressed the most evident elements of encyclopedic information).

According to a scientific handbook, lithium is definable as that element which has an atomic number 3, atomic weight 6.393, fusion point 108.5 degrees centigrade, boiling point 1330 degrees centigrade, density 0.53. This second definition, even though expressed in technical jargon, looks more similar to the following definition given by Peirce than it does to the one given by Webster:

If you look into a textbook of chemistry for a definition of *lithium* you may be told that it is that element whose atomic weight is 7 very nearly. But if the author has a more logical mind he will tell you that if you search among minerals that are vitreous, translucent, gray or white, very hard, brittle, and insoluble for one which imparts a crimson tinge to an unluminous flame, this mineral being triturated with lime or witherite rats-bane, and then fused, can be partly dissolved in muriatic acid; and if this solution be evaporated, and the residue be extracted with sulphuric acid, and duly purified, it can be converted by ordinary methods into a chloride, which being obtained in the solid state, fused and electrolyzed with half a dozen powerful cells, will yield a globule of a pinkish silvery metal that will float on gasolene; and the material of *that* is a specimen of lithium. The peculiarity of this definition — or rather this precept that is more serviceable than a definition — is that it tells you what the word *lithium* denotes by prescribing what you are to *do* in order to gain a perceptual acquaintance with the object of the world. (*C. P.* 2.330)

This 'operational' definition looks more like an informal frame than an encyclopedic description (for descriptions of this kind, see Charniak 1975, 1980). It satisfies the needs of an *Instruktionssemantik*. Gathering together the definition of Webster and that of Peirce, one is able to understand why, let us suppose, in a text a certain Professor Smith should need lithium for an atomic experiment and look for lime or witherite rats-bane. A textual assertion of this type undoubtedly elicits a lot of presuppositions, but these presuppositions are governed by preexisting frames.

Therefore, when a text theory aims to establish a "frame for frames" (Petőfi 1976), it is attempting both to discover textual rules and to set up a more organized and comprehensive notion of code as encyclopedic knowledge.

Schank and Abelson (1977) attempt to represent not only the lexical meaning of a given expression but also all the connected forms of world knowledge that allow the interpreter to draw (from the utterance of a term or of a sentence made up with the analyzed terms) co-textual inferences. Thus (through the use of certain primitives representing fundamental human operations, such as ATRANS, EJECT, INGEST, MOVE, and so on) Schank represents the verb *to eat* as an item susceptible of being inserted into contexts such as *John ate a frog* (Figure 2.11).

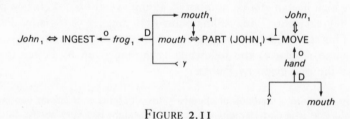

FIGURE 2.11

An interesting semiotic problem (which has escaped the notice of Artificial Intelligence theorists up to now) is the question of how to interpret in their turn not only the primitives expressed verbally but also the visual expressions of the diagram in Figure 2.10. In a general semiotic framework, a linguistic term can be interpreted by nonlinguistic interpretants, but even these interpretants are semiotic devices which must be in turn interpreted. In Eco (1976, 3.6.5) they have been studied as topo-sensitive *vectors*.

The project for an encyclopedic semantics is still in progress. Up to now we have been witnessing a series of alternative or complementary proposals. The structural semantics of Greimas (1966, 1979), with its notion of actant and of classemes or contextual semes, as well as with the idea of 'narrative programs', is encyclopedia-oriented; the early case grammar of Fillmore (1968), along with the more recent researches of Fillmore (1975, 1976a, 1976b, 1977, 1981), as well as the proposals by Bierwisch (1970, 1971), are encyclopedia-oriented. A new semantics in terms of encyclopedia and world knowledge (and phenomenological experience) is evident in the last researches of Lakoff (1980) and Lakoff and Johnson (1980).

Since all of these representations concern coded sequences of actions, relationships between agents (actors or abstract actants), they can be retraced together to the idea of frame.

### 2.3.3. Some attempts: stereotypes and commonsense knowledge

Undoubtedly, any encyclopedia-like semantics must blur the distinctions between analytic and synthetic properties, and in this sense nothing better has been said after and beyond Quine's "Two Dogmas of Empiricism" (1951). Naturally, nothing prevents one from using analytical markers, provided one knows that they are shorthand devices used in order to include other analytic properties they entail and to summarize all the synthetic markers they name (in the same way as the names of genera, in a Porphyrian tree, name clusters of accidental properties or differentiae). In this sense, the proposal of Putnam (1975) is more than acceptable:

> The normal form of description of the meaning of a word should be a finite sequence, or 'vector', whose components should certainly include the following (it might be desirable to have other types of components as well): (1) the syntactic markers that apply to the word, e.g., 'noun'; (2) the semantic markers that apply to the word, e.g., 'animal', 'period of time'; (3) a description of the additional feature of the stereotype, if any; (4) a description of the extension. The following convention is a part of this proposal: the components of the vector all represent a hypothesis about the individual speaker's competence, *except the extension*. Thus the normal form description for 'water' might be, in part:

| Syntactic markers | Semantic markers | Stereotype | Extension |
|---|---|---|---|
| mass noun, concrete | natural kind liquid | colorless transparent tasteless thirst-quenching etc. | H₂O (give or take impurities) |

The idea of the stereotype represents probably the most fruitful suggestion coming from Putnam's theory of language: according to our normal competence it is doubtful whether tigers are 'felidae' or 'felis tigris' or 'metazoa', but they are undoubtedly 'yellow', 'like a big cat', and 'black striped'.

Semantic markers are pseudoanalytic shorthand labels, since there should be a stereotype also for 'liquid' and perhaps for 'natural'.

As for the extension, Putnam's proposal is dependent on his sharing of Kripke's theory of rigid designation (Kripke 1972). It is hard to say whether Putnam's idea of rigid designation really corresponds to that of Kripke; Putnam thinks of the something rigidly designated by a linguistic term as an essence that can be defined in scientific terms. However, such an expression as '$H_2O$' is composed by chemical symbols, which, in turn correspond to linguistic terms such as /hydrogen/ and /oxygen/, and these should in turn be interpreted in terms of other formulas or chemical symbols (or expressions of natural language) expressing the properties of these elements (atomic number, atomic structure, plus many of their functional properties — for instance, that oxygen is the element that permits combustion, and so on).

As a matter of fact, the ultimate referent of a rigid designation (intended as the possible extension of a given term) can be defined in two ways. If rigid designation is (as Kripke seems to suggest) a process of mentions leading backward to an initial and aboriginal baptismal ceremony (and therefore to a primeval act of ostension accompanied by the utterance of the name), then the chain of mediatory information that guarantees the link with the original christening is made up of an uninterrupted series of discourses, descriptions, stories told about other stories up to the initial event; and in this case there is no difference between rigid designation and the encylcopedia, the sum of all these links representing the encylcopedic competence of a society in its very progress through time.

But the process of rigid designation can also be described in the terms used by Putnam (1975:200). Suppose, suggests Putnam, that I were standing next to Benjamin Franklin when he made his experiment on electricity and that Franklin told me that 'electricity' is phenomenon so and so. He would have given me an approximately correct definite description of the phenomenon. Now when I use the term /electricity/, I refer to the *introducing event,* the moment I learned that term, and everyone of my uses of the name will be causally connected to that event, even though I forgot when I first learned what I know about that name. Now suppose that I teach someone the word by telling him that the term /electricity/ names a physical magnitude so and so (listing some properties of the magnitude) without mentioning the causal link occurring between my present use of the word and the introducing event. The being of this word in someone's vocabulary will still be *causally connected* to the introducing event. End of Putnam's example.

Even in this case, what makes my (and someone's) language work is not the introducing event but the encyclopedic set of more or less definite descriptions I was able to provide (and that Franklin was able to give me). The introducing event was something similar to Peirce's Dynamic Object (intending the Dynamic Object both as electricity as physical magnitude and as my original experience of it). But what permits communication between me, Putnam, and someone else is the outline, via definite descriptions, of an Immediate Object, which is the encyclopedic representation of /electricity/. It would be possible that among the interpretants of the word /electricity/ there be also a photograph of Putnam speaking with Franklin; as a matter of fact, among my own (Eco's) interpretants of /electricity/, there are some images of Franklin performing his experiment. But, since even introducing events can be spoken of through interpretants (disregarding the fact that even Putnam's memories of his own introducing event, if any, could be viewed as mental interpretants or mental icons), what remains is only an encyclopedic chain.

Finally, if the introducing event described by Putnam really took place (in the way he describes it in Putnam 1975:200), the only things one can semiotically test are just the printed expressions at page 200 of Putnam 1975, along with their interpretable content.

There is a further objection to the theory of rigid designation (at least such as it is proposed by Kripke and by many of his interpreters). Maybe we call a halibut *halibut* because of a first baptismal ceremony, and a halibut will still be a halibut (with an essence of its own, as Putnam suggests) even though we change by counterfactual conditionals every possible definite description of it. Let us accept this view. Now let us suppose that, in order to avoid future world wars, the United Nations decided to establish a Peace Corps of ISC (Inter-Species Clones). This corps will be composed by half-human beings, to be produced by cloning, through a genetic hybridation of human punk rockers and speaking chimps trained in ASL. Such clones would guarantee a fair and unbiased international control, because they are independent of any national or ethnic heritage. The UN Assembly has to speak a lot about this new 'natural kind' because the members must reach a final agreement — that is, they have to speak about ISCs before ISCs exist, and just in order to make them exist. It is clear that, if there were any baptismal ceremony, what the UN christened as ISC was not an original 'thing', but the encyclopedic description of such a thing. There was neither original ostension, nor causal link; there will be only an established correspondence between an expression and the operational description of its content (with the understanding that, in the future, such an expression, along with its content, will be used in order to mention some state of affairs, as yet merely possible).

It is evident that we use linguistic expressions or other semiotic means to name 'things' first met by our ancestors; but it is also evident that we frequently use linguistic expressions to describe and to call into life 'things' that will exist only after and because of the utterance of our expressions. In these cases, at least, we are making recourse more to stereotypes and encyclopedic representations than to rigid designators.

Many of Putnam's suggestions (for instance, the distinction between stereotyped knowledge and expert knowledge) are accepted by Petőfi's theory of encyclopedical representation. Let us consider, for instance, the tentative representation (Figure 2.12) of *chlorine* proposed by Neubauer and Petőfi (1980:367). Chlorine is more interesting than electricity because we have good reasons to believe that not even Putnam was witnessing its baptismal ceremony when Scheele christened it in 1774. (Incidentally, I suspect that he baptized it in German as *Chlor,* and this fact shuffles the causal chain.)

One can say that the fact that chlorine is a gas is a piece of common knowledge as well as the fact that it is a disinfectant. But Petőfi's proposal is tentative: the difference between commonsense knowledge and expert knowledge should be traced each time according to the specific co-text. What is important is to assume that all the items of information listed (Figure 2.11) are part of a possible linguistic competence, irrespective of the difference between dictionary and encyclopedia. There are novels in which many of the 'industrial' properties of chlorine are more important than the one of being a chemical element. (Incidentally, Petőfi records as commonsense knowledge what Putnam would record as semantic information, since to be an element is an 'analytical' property.)

The advantage of Petőfi's model over Putnam's is that the former definitely gives up the distinction between intension and extension. Any item of expert knowledge can be intended as a meaning component that serves to establish the extension of the term under certain circumstantial conditions: since we are not living on the Twin Earth (see Putnam 1975), when someone is invited to look in some closet for some chlorine, it is enough that he looks for a greenish liquid, disagreeable to smell, and his subsequent indexical assertion *there is some chlorine* can be evaluated in terms of truth values even according to Tarskian criteria.

There are many other models for an encyclopedic representation, and, at the present state of the art, it would be embarrassing to decide which one is the more suitable. Rey-Debove (1971) speaks, apropos of the work of lexicographers and of their 'natural' definitions, of *bricolage;* she also remarks that, looking at the existing dictionaries, it seems that it is easier to define infrequent expressions such as /infarct/ than frequent ones such as /to do/. A semiotic encyclopedia, even though only de-

A. *Sector of commonsense knowledge*

- generic term     · element
- color            · greenish
- smell            · disagreeable, bad

B. *Sector of expert knowledge*

1. *Chemical knowledge*
- element category          nonmetallic

- family                    *halogen*
- valence                   *univalent*
                            *polyvalent*

- chemical symbol           *Cl*
- natural occurrence        *In chlorides*
- chlorine compounds,       *NaCl, HCl*
  etc.

2. *Physical knowledge*
- natural state or matter   *gas*
- other states              *liquid chlorine*
- weight                    *2½ times as*
                            *heavy as air*

- atomic weight             *17*
- atomic number             *33.453*

3. *Biological knowledge*
- effect on living          *poison*
  organisms

4. *Geological knowledge*
- amount in earth's crust   *0.15%*

5. *Historical information*
- discovery                 *Scheele 1774;*
                            *Davy 1810*
- further research          *production of liquid*
                            *chlorine in 1823*

6. *Etymological information*
- origin                    *Greek chloros*

7. *Industrial knowledge*
- production                *electrolysis from*
                            *common salt*

- uses                      *bleaching in paper*
                            *and textile industry*
                            *disinfectant (germicide*
                            *and pesticide)*
                            *chemical warfare*
- storage                   *cool, dry conditions,*
                            *in iron, etc. containe*

FIGURE 2.12

signed under the form of local examples, is subjected to the same restrictions. However, the choice of the encyclopedia over the dictionary is
not a free one: we have shown that dictionaries cannot exist if not as
theoretical figments. The universe of natural languages (and not only of
verbal ones) is the universe of *semiosis*. The regulative idea of encyclo-

pedia is the only way to outline a possible format of such a universe and to try tentative devices for describing part of it.

### 2.3.4. Clusters

According to the last representation we have examined, it is clear that, when the content of an expression is represented in the format of encyclopedia, there is no way to establish — out of any context — a hierarchy among properties. In Figure 2.3 we have refrained from inserting sexual differences into the tree. After the critique of the Porphyrian tree, we are now in the position of understanding the reason for this act of prudence. When differences like the sexual ones are taken as specific differentiae (a decision that Porphyry would not have encouraged), they can occur in many nodes of the tree, so compromising once again its structure. Following the suggestion of Boethius (2.4), one can play upon the opposition 'male/female' in many ways (for example, as shown in Figure 2.13), so creating (according to different contexts) different oppositions, antonymies, and semantic similarities.

At this point, which kind of information is deleted by a negative statement such as *this is not a man?*

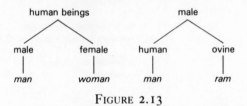

FIGURE 2.13

Katz designs, for an ideal dictionary competence, a criterion: "an ideal speaker of a language receives an anonymous letter containing just one sentence in that language, with no clue about the motive, circumstances of transmission, or any other factor relevant to understanding the sentence on the basis of its context of utterance . . ." (1977:14). This criterion draws a sharp line that divides semantic (dictionary) competence and pragmatic and encyclopedic competence. The semantic component represents only those aspects of meaning that an ideal speaker/hearer would know in such an anonymous letter situation.

Now, we can certainly admit that an anonymous letter reading *when you will enter that log cabin you will find a man* is absolutely unambiguous. According to the dictionary he or she refers to, the addressee will be sure to meet, in that log cabin, either an adult male human being or a mortal rational animal. The situation turns out badly if the anonymous letter reads *whatever you will find entering that log cabin it will not be a man.* What should one expect to see in that place? A woman, a crocodile, a ghost, a bronze statue?

Since the speakers of natural languages have few opportunities of receiving anonymous letters, let us consider a more 'normal' situation. During the night, looking out of the window of her home in the countryside, a wife tells her husband: *Honey, there is a man on the lawn near the fence!* Now, suppose that her husband controls the situation and answers: *No, honey, it's not a man. . . .* It would be absolutely unclear what the husband means, what he is negating and what survives his negation. The 'thing' in the lawn can be a boy, a boa constrictor escaped from the nearby zoological garden, a tree, an alien invader, a dog, the giant teddy bear left there by their children, the shadow of a tree.

Naturally, the husband can have the intention of scaring his wife by producing a feeling of uneasiness and suspense; but, in this case, we are no longer concerned with semantic questions, but with a more complex pragmatic strategy based on *reticence*. The husband, in this case, exploits the nature of the encyclopedia in order to achieve a rhetorical effect.

However, we are now considering the case in which the husband really wants to say something 'clear' in order to communicate to his wife that he actually thinks about the thing in the lawn. He should then say that that thing is not a man but (alternatively) a boy, a dog, a spatial creature, a tree, and so on. In doing so, he has not to go on without a dictionary; he must simply build up and presuppose the same 'local' portion of dictionary he assumed as implicitly outlined by his wife in uttering her sentence. The husband must make some conjecture or abduction about the *ad hoc* dictionary that both speakers, in that situation, take for granted. Once having evaluated the situation of the utterence, the husband has reasonably conjectured that, by uttering *man*, his wife was magnifying or *blowing up* certain semantic properties and *narcotizing* some others (see Eco 1979, 0.6.2).

Probably the wife was not interested in the fact that men are mortal or hot-blooded animals; she was interested in their being rational only insofar as to be rational means to be able to conceive evil intentions. In other words, a man was to her something potentially aggressive, able to move inside. If the thing were a child, it would be felt as nonpotentially aggressive; if it were a dog, it would be felt as unable to intrude; if it were a tree or a giant teddy bear, it would be felt as unable to move. On the contrary, a spatial alien would be viewed as a moving and potentially aggressive being. We can also suppose that each alternative elicits the retrieval of a given frame such as 'burglars in the night', 'lost child', 'space invaders', 'the thing from the outer world', and so on.

Thus the husband is committed to utter, along with the negation of *man*, the assertion of some other being that does not contain one or more of the frightening properties. Consequently, he should figure out an *ad hoc* Porphyrian tree, more or less in the format of the one in Figure 2.14.

The encyclopedia is the regulative hypothesis that allows both speakers to figure out the 'local' dictionary they need in order to ensure the good standing of their communicative interaction. The success of the interaction will eventually prove that their hypothesis was the good one. Moreover, even if the husband wanted to implement a strategy of reticence, he equally needed this hypothesis, in order to know how to create the due suspense. He had to know that by deleting *man* he was excluding that the thing in the lawn was a human, dangerous, walking thing, but he was not excluding that it was a nonhuman, dangerous, walking thing.

A natural language is a flexible system of signification conceived for producing texts, and texts are devices for blowing up or narcotizing pieces of encyclopedic information.

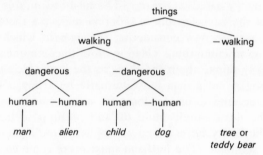

FIGURE 2.14

### 2.3.5. The encyclopedia as labyrinth

The project of an encyclopedia competence is governed by an underlying metaphysics or by a metaphor (or an allegory): the idea of labyrinth. The utopia of a Porphyrian tree represented the most influencial attempt to reduce the labyrinth to a bidimensional tree. But the tree again generated the labyrinth.

There are three types of labyrinth. The first, the classical one, was linear. Theseus entering the labyrinth of Crete had no choices to make: he could not but reach the center, and from the center the way out. That is the reason by which at the center there was the Minotaur, to make the whole thing a little more exciting. Such a labyrinth is ruled by a blind necessity. Structurally speaking, it is simpler than a tree: it is a skein, and, as one unwinds a skein, one obtains a continuous line. In this kind of labyrinth the Ariadne thread is useless, since one *cannot* get lost: the labyrinth itself itself is an Ariadne thread. This kind of labyrinth has nothing to do with an encyclopedia, irrespective of its important and venerable symbolic meanings.

The second type is called in German *Irrgärten* or *Irrweg;* a good En-

glish term for it is *maze*. The maze is a Manneristic invention; iconologi-
cally speaking, it does not appear before the late Renaissance. A maze
displays choices between alternative paths, and some of the paths are
dead ends. In a maze one can make mistakes. If one unwinds a maze,
one gets a particular kind of tree in which certain choices are privileged
in respect to others. Some alternatives end at a point where one is obliged to return backwards, whereas others generate new branches, and
only one among them leads to the way out. In this kind of labyrinth, one
does need an Ariadne thread; otherwise, one might spend one's life in
turning around by repeating the same moves. A Porphyrian tree can become a maze of this type, especially if reformulated as in 2.4. A maze
does not need a Minotaur: it is its own Minotaur: in other words, *the
Minotaur is the visitor's trial-and-error process.*

In a labyrinth of the third type is a net (maybe the word *meander*
characterizes it as different from a maze and from a *plain labyrinth*). The
main feature of a net is that every point can be connected with every
other point, and, where the connections are not yet designed, they are,
however, conceivable and designable. A net is an unlimited territory. A
net is not a tree. The territory of the United States does not oblige
anybody to reach Dallas from New York by passing through St. Louis,
Missouri; one can also pass through New Orleans. A net — as Pierre
Rosenstiehl (1980) suggests — is a tree *plus* corridors connecting its nodes
so as to transform the tree into a polygon, or into a system of embedded
polygons. But this comparison is still misleading: a polygon has some
borderlines. On the contrary, the abstract model of a net has neither a
center nor an outside.

The best image of a net is provided by the vegetable metaphor of the
rhizome suggested by Deleuze and Guattari (1976). A rhizome is a
tangle of bulbs and tubers appearing like "rats squirming one on top of
the other." The characteristics of a rhizomatic structure are the following: (a) Every point of the rhizome can and must be connected with
every other point. (b) There are no points or positions in a rhizome;
there are only lines (this feature is doubtful: intersecting lines make
points). (c) A rhizome can be broken off at any point and reconnected
following one of its own lines. (d) The rhizome is antigenealogical. (e)
The rhizome has its own outside with which it makes another rhizome;
therefore, a rhizomatic whole has neither outside nor inside. (f) A
rhizome is not a calque but an open chart which can be connected with
something else in all of its dimensions; it is dismountable, reversible,
and susceptible to continual modifications. (g) A network of trees which
open in every direction can create a rhizome (which seems to us equivalent to saying that a network of partial trees can be cut out artificially in
every rhizome). (h) No one can provide a global description of the whole

rhizome; not only because the rhizome is multidimensionally complicated, but also because its structure changes through the time;
moreover, in a structure in which every node can be connected with
every other node, there is also the possibility of contradictory inferences:
if $p$, then any possible consequence of $p$ is possible, including the one
that, instead of leading to new consequences, leads again to $p$, so that it
is true at the same time both that *if p, then q* and that *if p, then non-q*. (i)
A structure that cannot be described *globally* can only be described as a
potential sum of *local* descriptions. (j) In a structure without outside, the
describers can look at it only by the inside; as Rosenstiehl (1971, 1980)
suggests, a labyrinth of this kind is a *myopic algorythm;* at every node of it
no one can have the global vision of all its possibilities but only the local
vision of the closest ones: every local description of the net is a
*hypothesis,* subject to falsification, about its further course; in a rhizome
blindness is the only way of seeing (locally), and thinking means to *grope
one's way.* This is the type of labyrinth we are interested in. This represents a model (a Model Q) for an encyclopedia as a regulative semiotic
hypothesis.

A midway solution between the tree and the rhizome was the one
proposed by the Encyclopedists of the Enlightenment. Trying to transform the tree into a map, the eighteenth-century encyclopedia, the
*Encyclopédie* of Diderot and of d'Alembert, made in fact the rhizome
thinkable.

In respect to its hierarchical structure, the eighteenth-century encyclopedia was not necessarily different from a tree. What does make it
distinct is, in the first place, the hypothetical nature of the tree: it does
not reproduce a presumed structure of the world, but presents itself as
the most economic solution with which to confront and resolve a particular problem of the reunification of knowledge. In the second place, the
encyclopedist knows that the tree organizes, yet impoverishes, its content, and he hopes to determine as precisely as he can the intermediary
paths between the various nodes of the tree so that little by little it is
transformed into a geographical chart or a map.

D'Alembert, in his preliminary discourse on the *Encyclopedie*, furnished information about the criteria for the organization of the work. In
one respect, he develops the metaphor of the tree; in another, he puts it
into question, speaking instead of a word map and a labyrinth:

> The general system of the sciences and arts is a kind of labyrinth, a tortu-
> ous road which the spirit faces without knowing too much about the path to
> be followed.
> But this disorder (however philosophical it be for the mind) would disfig-
> ure, or at least would entirely degrade an encyclopedic tree in which it

would be represented. Our system of knowledge is ultimately made up of different branches, many of which have a simple meeting place and since in departing from this point it is not possible to simultaneously embark on all the roads, the determination of the choice is up to the nature of the individual spirit. . . . However, the same thing does not occur in the encyclopedic order of our knowledge which consists in reuniting this knowledge in the smallest possible space and in placing the philosopher above this vast labyrinth in a very elevated point of perspective which would enable him to view with a single glance his object of speculation and those operations which he can perform on those objects to distinguish the general branches of human knowledge and the points dividing it and uniting it and even to detect at times the secret paths which unite it. It is a kind of world map which must show the principal countries, their position and their reciprocal dependencies. It must show the road in a straight line which goes from one point to another; a road often interrupted by a thousand obstacles which might only be noticed in each country by travelers and its inhabitants and which could only be shown in very detailed maps. These partial maps will be the different articles of the encyclopedia and the tree or the figurative system will be its world map. Yet like overall maps of the world on which we live, the objects are more or less adjacent to one another and they present different perspectives according to the point of view of the geographer composing the map. In a similar way, the form of the encyclopedic tree will depend on the perspective we impose on it to examine the cultural universe. One can therefore imagine as many different systems of human knowledge as there are cartographical projections.

D'Alembert says with great clarity that what an encyclopedia represents has no center. The encyclopedia is a pseudotree, which assumes the aspect of a local map, in order to represent, always transitorily and locally, what in fact is not representable because it is a rhizome — an inconceivable globality.

The universe of semiosis, that is, the universe of human culture, must be conceived as structured like a labyrinth of the third type: (a) It is structured according to *a network of interpretants*. (b) It is virtually *infinite* because it takes into account multiple interpretations realized by different cultures: a given expression can be interpreted as many times, and in as many ways, as it has been actually interpreted in a given cultural framework; it is infinite because every discourse about the encyclopedia casts in doubts the previous structure of the encyclopedia itself. (c) It does not register only 'truths' but, rather, what has been said about the truth or what has been believed to be true as well as what has been believed to be false or imaginary or legendary, provided that a given culture had elaborated some discourse about some subject matter; the encyclopedia does not register only the 'historical' truth that Napoleon died on Saint Helena but also the 'literary' truth that Juliet died in Verona. (d) Such a semantic encyclopedia is never accomplished and exists only as a *regulative idea;* it is only on the basis of such a regulative idea that one is able actually to isolate a given portion of the social encyclopedia so far as it appears useful in order to interpret certain portions of actual discourses (and texts). (e) Such a notion of encyclopedia does not deny the existence of structured knowledge; it only suggests that such a knowledge cannot be recognized and organized as a global system; it provides only 'local' and transitory systems of knowledge, which can be contradicted by alternative and equally 'local' cultural organizations; every attempt to recognize these local organizations as unique and 'global' — ignoring their partiality — produces an *ideological* bias.

The Porphyrian tree tried to tame the labyrinth. It did not succeed because it could not, but many contemporary theories of language are still trying to revive this impossible dream.

### 2.3.6.   The dictionary as a tool

After having demonstrated that the theoretical idea of a semantic representation in the format of a dictionary is untenable, we should, however, remind ourselves that dictionary-like representations can be used as suitable tools.

The system of hyperonyms provided by a dictionary represents a way to save 'definitional energies'. When one says that a rose is a flower, one does not suggest that 'flower' is a primitive that cannot be interpreted; one simply assumes that, for the sake of economy, in that specific context, all the properties that are commonly assigned to flowers should not be challenged. Otherwise, one would say *a rose is a flower, but.* . . .

In the example of husband and wife provided above (2.3.4), the husband knows that there is no absolute and unique representation of *man*, but — exactly because of this — he is obliged to figure out an *ad hoc* dictionary-like local representation in order to ensure the good standing of that conversational interaction. In Chapter 3 of this book we shall see that, in order to generate and to interpret metaphors, according to the model proposed, one must rely also on dictionary-like representations. D'Alembert has suggested that, in order to make up a flesh-and-body encyclopedia, one certainly knows that each of its items can be included in different classes according to the description under which it is considered, but at the end (and even though transitorily) an item must be included in *a* given class, thus 'freezing' its representation in the format of a provisional dictionary.

When Putnam lists 'liquid' among the semantic markers of *water*, he uses that hyperonym because he assumes that, in order to provide a definition of *water*, he is not interested in challenging all the properties that are usually assigned to liquids. It is by virtue of this shorthand decision that he can exclude from the stereotypical properties of water those of being physically perceptible, wet, and subject to evaporation; he assumes that these are all properties that we assign to liquids without challenging them — until the moment that a sudden change in the scientific paradigm will oblige our culture to cast in doubt the very notion of liquid. The function of hyperonyms in a lexical system depends exactly on the epistemological decisions that govern the life of a culture. We can make up dictionary-like representation in order to save definitional energies in any context in which certain 'central' assumptions of a cultural system are *taken for granted*. We presuppose a local dictionary every time we want to recognize and to circumscribe an area of consensus within which a given discourse should stay, because no single discourse is designed to change globally our world view.

Thus, if the encyclopedia is an unordered set of markers (and of frames, scripts, text-oriented instructions), the dictionary-like arrangements we continuously provide are transitory and pragmatically useful hierarchical reassessments of it. In this sense, one should turn upside down a current distinction between dictionary (strictly 'semantic') and encyclopedia (polluted with 'pragmatic' elements); on the contrary, *the encyclopedia is a semantic concept and the dictionary is a pragmatic device*.

One could wonder about a more profound reason for all this. One can legitimately ask whether there is a 'universal' or 'biological' reason by which certain properties seem to be more 'dictionarial' than others. Undoubtedly, we frequently challenge the opinion that men are cruel or reasonable and that dogs are men's best friends, but less frequently we challenge the common and strong belief that both are animals. Quine (1951) has already answered this question: every culture has a strongly organized 'center' and a more and more fuzzy 'periphery', and, in order to change its central concepts, one must expect a radical scientific revolution. Certain dictionary properties are such — and more resistantly remain as such — by virtue of this *cultural inertia*. These properties are not 'dictionarial' on logical or biological grounds, but on *historical* grounds. Our representations usually respect this heritage, for many intuitive reasons. Many properties that inhabit the higher nodes of so many dictionary-like trees (such as 'living being' or 'body' or 'physical') have been profoundly rooted in the world view of our culture for millennia. It is not impossible, however, to think of a new discourse in which these concepts become the target of a critical deconstruction of our cultural paradigm. Chapter 3, on metaphor, will show that sometimes a poetic text aims at destroying exactly our most unchallengable assumptions; in these cases it can happen that colorless green ideas can (and maybe *must*) sleep furiously, and we are obliged to suspect that perhaps ideas are more 'physical' than we usually believe. Thus the interpretation of a metaphorical text requires the greatest flexibility, on the part of the interpreter, in rearranging the most venerable and higher nodes of current dictionaries.

In more common contexts, one can decide that certain properties are more 'focal', more 'central', more 'diagnostic', more resistant than others. Once having recognized that the dictionary is not a stable and univocal image of a semantic universe, one is free to use it when one needs it.

# [3]

# METAPHOR

## 3.1.  The metaphoric nexus

The "most luminous and therefore the most necessary and frequent" (Vico) of all tropes, the metaphor, defies every encyclopedic entry. It has been the object of philosophical, linguistic, aesthetic, and psychological reflection since the beginning of time. Shibles' (1971) bibliography on the metaphor records around 3,000 titles; and yet it overlooks authors such as Fontanier, and almost all of Heidegger and Greimas — and of course it cannot mention, after the research in componential semantics, the successive studies on the logic of natural languages, the work of Henry, Groupe $\mu$ of Lièges, Ricoeur, Samuel Levin, and the latest text-linguistics and pragmatics.

The term *metaphor* for many authors — and this is true for Aristotle and Emanuele Tesauro — has served to indicate every rhetorical figure in general; the metaphor, as the Venerable Bede put it, is "a genus of which all the other tropes are species." To speak of metaphor, therefore, means to speak of rhetorical activity in all its complexity. And it means, above all, to ask oneself whether it is out of blindness, laziness, or some other reason that this peculiar synecdochic view of metaphor has arisen, whereby the part is taken as representative of the whole. It is very difficult indeed to consider the metaphor without seeing it in a framework that necessarily includes both synecdoche and metonymy — so difficult, in fact, that a trope that seems to be the most primary will appear instead as the most derivative, as the result of a semantic calculus that presupposes other, preliminary semiotic operations. A curious situation for a figure of speech that has been recognized by many to be the basis of every other.

Not the least of the contradictions encountered in a *metaphorology* is that, of the thousands and thousands of pages written about the metaphor, few add anything of substance to the first two or three fundamental concepts stated by Aristotle. In effect, very little has been said about a phenomenon concerning which, it seems, there is everything to say. The chronicle of the discussion on metaphors is the chronicle of a series of variations on a few tautologies, perhaps on a single one: "A metaphor is that artifice which permits one to speak metaphorically." Some of these variations, however, constitute an 'epistemic break', allowing the concepts to drift toward new territories — ever so slightly, but just enough. It is with these variations that we shall be concerned.

Every discourse on metaphor originates in a radical choice: either (a) language is by nature, and originally, metaphorical, and the mechanism of metaphor establishes linguistic activity, every rule or convention arising thereafter in order to discipline, to reduce (and impoverish) the metaphorizing potential that defines man as a symbolic animal; or (b) language (and every other semiotic system) is a rule-governed mechanism, a predictive machine that says which phrases can be generated and which not, and which from those able to be generated are 'good' or 'correct', or endowed with sense; a machine with regard to which the metaphor constitutes a breakdown, a malfunction, an unaccountable outcome, but at the same time the drive toward linguistic renewal. As can be seen, this opposition retraces the classical one between *phusis* and *nomos*, between analogy and anomaly, motivation and arbitrariness. But the problem is to see what ensues when we accept one or the other of the two horns of this dilemma. If it is metaphor that founds language, it is impossible to speak of metaphor unless metaphorically. Every definition of metaphor, then, cannot but be circular. If instead there exists first a theory of language that prescribes 'literal' linguistic outputs, and if within this theory the metaphor constitutes a scandal (that is, if the metaphor is a deviation from such a system of norms), then the theoretical metalanguage must speak of something to define which has not even been devised. A merely denotative theory of language can indicate those cases where language is incorrectly used but *appears to say something* — but such a theory is embarrassed to explain what and why. Consequently, it reaches for tautological definitions of the following type: "There is a metaphor every time something unexplainable happens which the users of a language perceive as a metaphor."

But the problem does not end there. When closely studied in connection with verbal language, the metaphor becomes a source of scandal in a merely linguistic framework, because it is in fact a semiotic phenomenon permitted by almost all semiotic systems. The inner nature of metaphors produces a shifting of the linguistic explanation onto semiotic mechanisms that are not peculiar to spoken languages; one need only think of the frequently metaphorical nature of oneiric images. However, it is not a matter of saying that visual metaphors *also* exist, or that there perhaps *also* exist olfactory or musical metaphors. The problem is that the verbal metaphor itself often elicits references to visual, aural, tactile, and olfactory experiences.

And, finally, we must ask whether the metaphor is an expressive mode with *cognitive value*. As an ornament, the metaphor is of no interest to us, because, if it says more pleasantly that which can be said otherwise, then it could be explained wholly within the scope of a semantics of denotation. We are interested in the metaphor as an additive, not substitutive, instrument of knowledge.

Nevertheless, seeing the metaphor as a cognitive tool does not mean studying it in terms of truth values. For this reason, discussions on the aletic logic of metaphor (that is, whether a metaphor is truthful and whether it is possible to draw true inferences from a metaphorical utterance) are not sufficient. It is obvious that when someone creates metaphors, he is, literally speaking, *lying* — as everybody knows. But someone who utters metaphors does not speak 'literally': he *pretends* to make assertions, and yet wants to assert *seriously* something that is beyond literal truth. How may one 'signal' such an ambiguous intention?

While it may be possible, then, to bypass an extensional semantics of metaphor, it is impossible to avoid a *pragmatics*. From the point of view of *conversational maxims* (Grice 1967), the making of metaphors is a way of flouting the maxim of Quality ("Make your contribution one that is true"), that of Quantity ("Make your contribution to the conversation as informative as possible"), that of Manner ("Avoid obscurity and ambiguity"), and that of Relation ("Be relevant"). Someone uttering metaphors apparently lies, speaks obscurely, above all speaks of something other, all the while furnishing only vague information. And thus, if somebody who is speaking violates all these maxims, and does so in such a way as to not be suspected of stupidity or awkwardness, an *implicature* must click in the listener's mind. Evidently, that speaker meant something else. The question that we want to discuss here is, if we want to avoid any appeal to ineffable intuition, on what encyclopedic rules must the solution of the metaphorical implicature base itself?

## 3.2.  Traditional definitions

Current dictionaries are usually uneasy about defining the metaphor: "the transfer of the name of one object to another object through a relation of analogy" (but what is a relation of analogy in itself if not a metaphorical relation?); "the substitution of an appropriate term with one that is figurative" (*qua* species of the genus of figures, the metaphor is defined by a synecdoche); "an abbreviated simile. . . ." These all fall into the classical definitions (cf. Lausberg 1960); and even in the best of cases, there are typologies of the various kinds of substitution, from animate to inanimate, from inanimate to animate, from animate to animate, and from inanimate to inanimate, either in a physical or moral sense; or otherwise there are substitutions of names, adjectives, verbs, adverbs (cf. Brooke-Rose 1958).

As far as synecdoche is concerned, it is spoken of as a "substitution of two terms for each other according to a relation of greater or lesser extension" (part for the whole, whole for the part, species for genus, singular for plural, or vice versa), whereas metonymy is spoken of as a "substitution of two terms for each other according to a relation of contiguity" (where contiguity is a rather fuzzy concept insofar as it covers the relations of cause/effect, container/content, instrument for operation, place of origin for original object, emblem for object emblematized, and so on). And when it is specified that the synecdoche carries out a substitution within the *conceptual content* of a term, while metonymy acts outside of that content, it is hard to see why the part for the whole is a synecdoche and the material for the object a metonymy—as though it were 'conceptually' essential for an object to have constituent parts and not to be made of some material.

As will be seen in 3.11.2, this confusion is due to an 'archaeological' and extrarhetorical reason. It will also be shown that the synecdoche could be limited to semantic representations in the form of a dictionary, reserving metonymy for representations in the form of an encyclopedia. But in effect the dictionaries' embarrassment is the same as that of the classical manuals, which constructed a typology of rhetorical figures (still useful today for various aspects) that is quite admirable but riddled with ambiguities: (a) it considers tropes as operations on single words (*in verbis singulis*), precluding thus their contextual analysis; (b) it introduces, as we said above, the distinction synecdoche/metonymy on the basis of the unexamined category of *conceptual content;* (c) it does not distinguish between syntactic and semantic operations (asyndeton and zeugma, for example, are two cases of figures of words by detraction, where the first concerns pure syntactic distribution but where the second implies semantic decisions); (d) above all, it defines metaphor as a trope characterized by a dislocation or leap, where /dislocation/ and /leap/ are themselves metaphors for «metaphor», and where /metaphor/ is in its turn a metaphor, insofar as it means (etymologically) «transfer» or «displacement».

Because the tradition has left several disconnected notions, we shall have to look for a theory of metaphor in the moment when it is proposed for the first time, that is, when it is proposed by Aristotle.

### 3.3. Aristotle: synecdoche and Porphyrian tree

Aristotle first confronts the issue of metaphor in the *Poetics* (1457-b1 – 1458a17). In order to enliven language, it is possible to use, beside common words, also foreign words, artificial coinages, lengthened, shortened, or altered expressions (in the *Rhetoric* many of these verbal games, actual puns, will be analyzed), and, finally, metaphors. The metaphor is defined as the recourse to a name of another type, or as the transferring to one object of a name belonging to another, an operation that can take place through displacements from genus to species, from species to genus, from species to species, or by analogy.

Clearly, in laying the basis for a metaphorology, Aristotle uses *metaphor* as a generic term: his first two types of metaphors are in fact synecdoches. But it is necessary to look carefully at his entire classification and at the examples woven into the commentary if we are to find the origins of all that in the following centuries has been said on the metaphor.

First type: from genus to species. Following the definition of Groupe $\mu$ (1970), this type will now be called a 'generalizing synecdoche in $\Sigma$'. The example used by Aristotle is *This ship of mine stands there*, since standing is the genus that contains among its species lying at anchor. An example that is more obvious and more canonical would be the use of /animal/ for «men», man being a species of the genus animal.

According to *Categories* (1a1 – 12), two things are named 'synonymous' when they are both named according to their common genus (so both a man and an ox can be called animal). Therefore a metaphor of the first type is a form of synonymy whose generation and interpretation depend on a preexisting Porphyrian tree (see chapter two in this book). In both cases (synonymy and metaphor of the first type), we are witnessing a sort of 'poor' definition. A genus is not sufficient to define a species, and it does not entail its underlying species. In other words, to accept /animal/ for «man», one should rely on an invalid inference: $((p \supset q) \cdot q) \supset p$. From a logical point of view, Aristotle's second type of metaphor seems more acceptable, since it represents a correct case of *modus ponens:* $((p \supset q) \cdot p) \supset q$. Unfortunately, a material implication can sound very unconvincing from the point of view of natural language. Thus the metaphor of the second type (which is another synecdoche, the one that Groupe $\mu$ calls 'particularizing synecdoche in $\Sigma$') is a really unsatisfactory one. The example provided by Aristotle is *Indeed ten thousand noble things Odysseus did*, where /ten thousand/ stand for «many», a genus of which it is allegedly a species. The clumsiness of Aristotle's example is self-evident. In fact, /ten thousand/ is *necessarily* «many» only in a Porphyrian tree that is based on a certain scale of quantity. One can well imagine another scale oriented toward astronomic sizes, in which ten thousand, even a hundred thousand, is a rather scarce quantity.

In other words, though it may seem more or less necessary for a man to be mortal, it is not so necessary that ten thousand be a lot. This notwithstanding, /ten thousand/ suggests «many» intuitively and with an undeniably hyperbolic tone, whereas /men/ for «animal» is not intuitively perceived as an interesting figure of speech — both examples depend, however, on the same logical scheme. Probably, according to the code of the Greek language in the fourth century B.C., the expression /ten thousand/ was already *overcoded* (as a ready-made syntagm) and was used to designate a great quantity. In other words, Aristotle explains the modes of interpretation of this synecdoche taking as already disambiguated the synecdoche itself — a new example of confusion between the structure of language, or of the lexicon, and the structure of the world. The surprising conclusion is that metaphors of the second type (particularizing synecdoches in Σ) are logically correct but rhetorically insipid, whereas metaphors of the first type (generalizing synecdoches in Σ) are rhetorically acceptable but logically unjustifiable.

### 3.4.   Aristotle: metaphors of three terms

As for the third type, the Aristotelian example is two-fold: *Then he drew off his life with the bronze* and *Then with the bronze cup he cut the water*. Another translation would have a bronze sword, in the second case, cutting the flow of blood, or life. These are, in any case, two examples of a passage from species to species: /drawing off/ and /cutting/ are two cases of the more general «taking away». This third type genuinely seems to be a metaphor: it could be said right away that there is something 'similar' between drawing off and cutting, for which reason logical structure and interpretive movement could be represented as in Figure 3.1, where the passage from a species to its genus and then from that genus to a second species can take place from right to left or from left to right, according to which of Aristotle's two examples one should want to discuss.

FIGURE 3.1

This third type so truly seems to be a metaphor that many of the later theories work out of preference on examples of this type. Different authors have represented this third kind of metaphor using the following diagram, where *x* and *y* are respectively the metaphorizing and metaphorized terms (Richards' *vehicle* and *tenor*) and where Z is the intermediary term (the genus of reference) that permits the disambiguation as shown in Figure 3.2.

FIGURE 3.2

The diagram accounts for such expressions as *the tooth of the mountain* (peak and tooth partake of the genus 'sharpened form') and *she was a birch* (girl and birch partake of the genus 'flexible body'). Contemporary theories say that birch acquires a 'human' property or that girl takes on a 'vegetal' property, and that, at any rate, the units in question lose some of their own properties (see, for example, the theory of *transfer features* in Weinreich 1972). But at this point, two problems arise.

First, to define which properties survive and which must drop away, we must by rights construct an *ad hoc* Porphyrian tree, and this operation must be oriented by a universe of discourse or frame of reference (for one of the first assertions of this principle, see Black 1955). Second, in this operation of sememic intersection, a phenomenon arises that is new with respect to synecdoches or metaphors of the first two types. Consider the twofold movement that is at the basis of both the production and the interpretation of *tooth of the mountain* as shown in Figure 3.3.

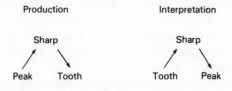

FIGURE 3.3

In a synecdoche, in which a peak were named as something sharp, peak would lose some of its characteristic properties (that of being mineral, for example) and share instead with the genus to which it is reduced some morphologic properties (in particular, that of being sharp). In a metaphor of the third type, peak loses some properties in becoming a sharp thing and regains others in becoming a tooth. While peak and tooth, however, have *in common* the property of sharpness, their mutual comparison also focuses on those very properties that stand *in opposition*. This is so much the case that the phenomenon is referred to as a transfer of properties, as mentioned above (peak becomes more human and organic, tooth acquires the property of being mineral). What makes theories of 'transfer features' questionable is always the fact that we cannot tell who gains what and who loses instead something else. More than of a transfer, we could speak of a 'back-and-forth' of properties. This phenomenon is what in 3.6 will be called 'condensation', as it was called by Freud, and it is the phenomenon that characterizes the fourth type of metaphor. At any rate, what likens the metaphor of the third type with the fourth type is that mere identifications or absorptions (from species to genus) are no longer the rules of the game: now it is both 'similarity' and 'opposition', or identity and difference, that are in question.

### 3.5.   Aristotle: the proportional scheme

The metaphor by analogy or by proportion is a metaphor with four terms, which are no longer $A/B = C/B$ (for example, peak is to the genus of sharp things in the same way as tooth), but $A/B = C/D$. The cup is to Dionysus as the shield is to Ares, suggests Aristotle. In this way, the shield can be defined as *the cup of Ares* or the cup as *the shield of Dionysus*. And again: old age is to life as sunset is to day, and thus old age can be defined as *the sunset of life* and the evening as *day's old age*.

Aristotle's definition has always seemed superb for its concision and clarity. In fact, it is; and undoubtedly the idea of finding a sort of propositional function, in which infinite concrete instances can be inserted, represented a stroke of genius. Even more so given that this proportional formula permits the representation of even those cases of strict catachresis where the vehicle stands for a tenor that, lexically speaking, does not exist: $A/B = x/D$. Aristotle provides his own, linguistically complex example, but we can also turn to two familiar catachreses, *the leg of the table* and *the neck of the bottle*. A leg is to a body as an unnamed object is to the body of a table.

It becomes clear right away that the way leg is related to body is not the same way in which neck is related to body. The leg of a table resembles a human leg provided we have a frame of reference that puts into relief the property of 'support', whereas the neck of a bottle is not exactly the support of a cork nor, on the other hand, of the entire container. It seems that the analogy of leg plays on *functional* properties at the expense of *morphologic* similarities (themselves reduced to very abstract equivalences, and quantity having been put aside as nonpertinent), while the analogy of neck drops the functionally pertinent features and insists on those that are morphological. Which is to say that, yet again, different criteria for constructing a Porphyrian tree are in question — if it were even still possible, though, to speak of Porphyrian tree *tout court*. Consider the typical situation of a metaphor of the fourth type, such as cup/Dionysus = shield/Ares. How can we accommodate it into any Porphyrian tree?

To begin with, the relation cup/Dionysus, according to the criteria of the later theories of rhetoric, is of a metonymic type. Cup and Dionysus are commonly associated *by contiguity*, through the relation subject/ instrument, through a cultural habit (without which cup could *stand for* many other objects). This relation is not at all amenable to being expressed by a Porphyrian tree, unless we want to draw broadly inclusive equivalencies (of the following type: cup belongs to the class of things characterizing Dionysus, or, alternatively, Dionysus belongs to the class of all beings that use cups). And the same goes for the relation shield/Ares. In other words, it is very difficult to recognize in this relation a case of embedding of genus within species.

The case of man/animal presents us with analytic properties, whereas that of cup/Dionysus presents us with synthetic properties. Man is animal in virtue of its definition, whereas cup does not necessarily refer to Dionysus, except in a very restricted co-textual situation in which the various pagan gods are listed iconographically along with their characteristic attributes. Panofsky and Caravaggio would both hold that *if Dionysus then cup;* but they themselves would agree that whereas it is not possible to think of a man who is not an animal, it is always possible to think of Dionysus without thinking of cup. Even if one should grant that it is possible to group together the relations cup/Dionysus and man/animal, a new problem surfaces: why should Dionysus be placed in a relation with Ares and not, for example, with Ceres, Athena, or Vulcan?

While it is prudent to exclude the speaker's intuition from this type of consideration (since the speaker's intuition is determined by cultural contexts), it is to an extent intuitive that Aristotle himself would find it difficult to name the spear of Athena as the cup of Athena and the wheaten sheaves of Ceres as the shield of Ceres (even if baroque contexts where that is possible are not excluded). Intuition says that shield and cup can entertain a relation because both are round and concave (round and concave in different ways, yes, but therein is the metaphor's cleverness, in making us see a certain resemblance between different things). But what matches Dionysus and Ares? In the pantheon of pagan gods, it is their diversity that unites them (strange oxymoron). Dionysus the god of joy and of the peaceful rites, Ares the god of death and war: a play of *similarities*, then, mingling with *dissimilarities*. Cup and shield become similar because of their roundness, dissimilar because of their functions; Ares and Dionysus are similar because both are gods, dissimilar because of their respective domains of action.

Before this nexus of problems, a few observations immediately arise. What was not clear and evident to Aristotle was thereafter developed at different stages of later metaphorology.

### 3.6. Proportion and condensation

The metaphor with four terms does not set into play verbal substances alone. No sooner has the proportion been established than it is possible to see, as something incongruous, Dionysus actually drinking out of a shield or Ares defending himself with a cup. In the first two types of metaphor, the metaphorizing term absorbes (or confuses itself with) the metaphorized term, much as a figure enters a multitude — or leaves it — without our cognitive habits coming into question. At best, the result is something impoverished, both conceptually and perceptually. In the third type of metaphor, instead, a superimposition of plant and girl is created that is almost visual, as in the fourth type.

Albeit confusedly, Aristotle realizes that, by naming one thing with something else's name, one denies the first thing those qualities proper to it. Ares' shield could also be called *cup without wine* (*Poetics* 1457b32). Henry (1971) notes that this is no longer a metaphor, but instead a "secondary phenomenon," as a consequence of the preliminary metaphor. That is true, but it means that, as the metaphor starts to be understood, the shield becomes a cup, even as this cup, while remaining round and concave (though in a different way from the shield), loses the property of being full of wine. Or, in reverse, one forms an image wherein Ares possesses a shield that acquires the property of brimming with wine. In other words, two images are conflated, two things become different from themselves, and yet remain recognizable, and there is born a visual (as well conceptual) hybrid.

Could it not be said that we have before us a kind of oneiric image? The effect of such a proportion having been established is quite like what Freud (1889) called "condensation": where noncoincident traits can be dropped while those in common are reinforced. The process is typical not only of dreams but also of jokes (*Witzen*), that is, of those puns or compound words (ψυχρὰ) (*Rhetoric* 1406b1) or, even better, of those witticisms ('αστεῖα) (ibid., 1410b6) which seem so similar to some of the categories of *Witze, Kalauer*, and *Klangwitze* analyzed by Freud (1905). If the Freudian typology can be compared to a typology of rhetoric, there can be no doubt that, at least, the final result of the Aristotelian proportion is a process very much like Freudian condensation, and that this condensation, as will be better demonstrated later, can be described as far its semiotic mechanism is concerned in terms of the acquiring and losing of *properties* or *semes*, however we should wish to call them.

### 3.7.  Dictionary and encyclopedia

According to what has been said in chapter two of this book, clearly the properties set into motion by the third and fourth types of metaphor do not have the same logical status as those set in motion by the first two types. To obtain the condensation cup/shield, it is necessary to activate properties or semes such as 'round' and 'concave', 'war' and 'peace', 'life' and 'death'. It is clear here that a difference is being outlined between a semantic description in the form of a dictionary and a description in the form of an encyclopedia, or even, with inconsistent variations, between Σ properties and Π properties (Groupe μ 1970), between semantic properties and semiological properties (Greimas 1966), or between dictionary markers and world knowledge.

Groupe μ distinguishes between an 'endocentric' series of semes or 'conceptual' properties (mode Σ) and an 'exocentric' series of parts or 'empirical' properties (mode Π). An example of an endocentric series would be the entailment oak – tree – plant (curiously, the authors consider only one direction – "If *x* is a tree, then it is *either* a poplar *or* an oak *or* a birch" – without considering that, if *x* is a poplar, then it is necessarily a plant; but the two directions are obviously complementary). An example of an exocentric series would be the relation between a tree and its parts: trunk *and* branches *and* leaves. The distinction between the two modes could be represented as in Figure 3.4.

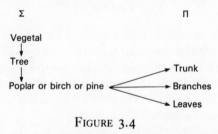

FIGURE 3.4

Groupe μ knows very well that "these endoseries [that is, endocentric series] exist *in posse* in the vocabulary; but it is we who trace their existence there, for each word or concept can, in principle, be the crossing point of as many series as it contains semes" (1970; Eng. tr., p. 100). But after having shown this critical awareness of a dictionary's metalinguistic mechanisms, Groupe μ does not draw from that the consequences it should, and falls into a sort of Aristotelian identification of categories with things. Consider the way in which the various metaphorical constructions are explained by means of a double synecdochic exchange, from a generalizing synecdoche (Sg) to a particularizing synecdoche (Sp), and vice versa, whether in the Σ mode or the Π mode.

The rule proposed is that the term $I$, which remains absent from the metaphorical interpretation, must be a synecdoche of the term of origin $D$, while the term of arrival $A$ must be a synecdoche of $I$. The condition is that $A$ and $D$ must be on the same level of generality. According to mode $\Sigma$, the resulting metaphor will be based on semes common to $D$ and $A$, while in mode $\Pi$ it will base itself on their common parts. The material part must be smaller than the whole, while the semic part must be more general. (See Figure 3.5.)

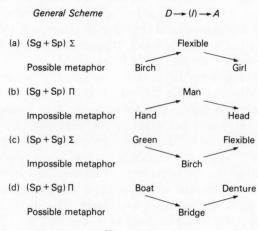

FIGURE 3.5

Example (a) is incorrect. That a birch is flexible is a $\Pi$ property, unless one should change the dictionary tree and consider the genus of all flexible things (of which obviously birches are one among the species). If we look again carefully at the preceding scheme, a (more) acceptable example would be /poplar of the desert/ for «palm tree» (from palm to tree and from tree to poplar).

Example (b) is correct, because one cannot say /he shook my head/ in place of «he shook my hand». But the mechanism it exemplifies is not at all impossible. The oneiric situation (or an instance of *Witz*) in which a nose represents the penis (both being parts of a human body) is not at all unthinkable. Why should nose be able to metaphorize penis, and hand not be able to metaphorize head? The answer is suggested at various moments by Greimas (1966): two semes can be opposed or joined according to their 'classeme' (which is nothing other than a 'contextual selection'; cf. Eco 1976, 1979). Nose and penis have in common the characteristics of being 'appendages' and of being 'long' (besides the fact that both are canals, both are pointed, and so on). A head instead has semes of 'roundness', 'apicality', and 'oneness', which a hand does not have. The substitution, then, is not based only on a play of synecdoches — it puts into question a semic relation that is far more complex, where the common reference of both nose and penis to human body is contextually irrelevant. Only in this way does the effect of superimposition that is typical of the processes of condensation take place.

As regards example (c), again it seems that Groupe $\mu$ has chosen as dictionary (or $\Sigma$) properties those that seem more appropriately $\Pi$ properties — without making clear the contextual reasons that make it necessary to assume them as dictionary properties in the first place. It is true, though, that the metaphor in (c) appears impossible inasmuch as it passes from a genus to a species, proceeding then from that species to another genus that has nothing in common, however, with the first. According to Group $\mu$ such would be the case where there were a passage from the genus 'iron' to the species 'blade' and then from the species 'blade' to the genus 'flat object'. The coexistence in one same object of ferrous and flat qualities would not produce an intersection of properties.

Finally, we come to case (d). Groupe $\mu$'s example is acceptable. One can also think of the passage from *crude oil* to 'precious' (a $\Pi$ property of crude oil): from the property 'precious' one ascends to another lexeme to which the same marker could be ascribed, for example, *gold*, and there would follow the substitution gold/oil in a metaphor such as /the gold of the sheikhs/ or /black gold/ for «oil». But, even in this case, other properties would come into question, such as 'black' or 'of the sheikhs', which Groupe $\mu$'s scheme does not take into consideration. These are all problems that we will try to resolve further on.

At the close of this discussion of the Aristotelian proposal, we can say that two clusters of problems have been brought into relief: (1) the existence of processes of condensation, which the proportional relation is hard put to explain; and (2) the need for a more flexible consideration of the relations between dictionary properties and encyclopedic properties, which can only be distinguished according to contextual exigencies. Why then has Aristotle's proposal held myriad interpreters in fascination through the centuries? Two facts have played a role in the matter, that is, responsibility lies with a misunderstanding, on the one hand, and an extremely lucid insight, on the other.

### 3.8.   The cognitive function

That misunderstanding or ambiquity arises when Aristotle, in passing from his consideration of the first three types of metaphor to the fourth type, *changes his game* without even being aware of it: in speaking of the first three types, he explains *how* a metaphor is produced and understood, whereas in speaking of the fourth type he explains *what* a metaphor enables us to know. In the first three cases, he says *how* the metaphorical production and interpretation *function* (and that he can do because the mechanism, which is synecdochic, is rather simple and is based on the inflexible logic of a Porphyrian tree, however that tree is selected). In the fourth case, Aristotle tells *what the metaphor says*, or in what way it increases our knowledge of the relations between things — though he explains it only partly. The metaphor *cup of Ares* certainly raises the suspicion that some indeterminate relation exists between cup and shield, and between Ares and Dionysus. But the theory of condensation explains that what we learn is not just that. The Aristotelian proportion is an empty schema where infinite pieces of encyclopedic information can be inserted; but what a metaphor allows us to know has more to do with those inserted items of knowledge than with the schematic relation that is filled up. The later periods of the metaphorological tradition hold up the theory of the proportion or analogy as an explanation of the metaphor's mechanisms — at the cost of a self-debasing chain of tautologies (for example, "a metaphor is that thing that permits us to have knowledge that is analogical, in other words, metaphorical") — and frequently ignore the most ingenious and vigorous of Aristotle's conclusions, that the metaphor is not only a means of delight but also, and above all, a tool of cognition (as Freud, moreover, was able to show with regard to *Witze*).

When reading the Aristotelian texts (the *Poetics* and the *Rhetoric*), one is struck by the fact that examples of metaphor that are not convincing often appear, where the translator-philologist himself admits to not being able to grasp the obviousness of a proportion assumed as self-evident. One often has the same response, moreover, when confronting texts from distant cultures. Consider, for example, the Song of Songs: "I have compared thee, O my love, to a company of horses . . ." (Song 1:9); "Thy teeth are as a flock of sheep which go up from the washing" (ibid., 4:2); "Her legs are as pillars of marble . . ." (ibid., 5:15); "Thy nose is as the tower of Lebanon . . ." (ibid., 7:4). Notice that these are similes and therefore give the proportion in advance rather than suggest it in the form of an enigma. If a metaphor were only the contraction of an already posited proportion — so that, from the perspective of production, one starts from the simile and, interpretively speaking, one arrives at it — a simile would always be convincing. And yet it cannot be denied that one is led to see sheep coming out of the water as *shaggy, dripping* creatures (bleating and smelly, as well): a terrible premise on which to build an analogy on the "black but comely" maiden whose "two breasts are like two young does that are twins" (ibid., 7:3).

Nevertheless, we can imagine how the biblical poet drops all those properties of sheep negatively identified above, so as to preserve only the characteristic of their *aequalitas numerosa,* their splendid unity in variety — as well as their whiteness. It is understood that the poet is able to do so because within his culture these most probably were the properties associated with sheep, *at least within the poetic tradition.* And it is also clear that the qualities chosen to define the beauty of a healthy and sturdy country girl, destined to tend the flocks among the rocky Palestinian hills, single out her upright solidity (like that of columns), her unbroken state of perfection, in the same way that it is not so much the cylindrical shape of columns that is preeminently chosen as is their whiteness, instead, and their grace of line.

But, to reach these conclusions, one must undertake an impassioned 'hermeneutic circle'; one assumes a code, which is verified against the simile, whose metaphorical transformations are appraised in advance; or one starts from the simile in order to infer a code that makes it acceptable; one starts to become familiar, at one and the same time, with both the biblical poet's aesthetic ideology and the maiden's properties; in other words, one learns something extra about the maiden *and* about the intertextual universe of the biblical poet, simultaneously. Analyzing further this process of trial and error, we would realize that we are dealing with multiple inferential movements: hypothesis (or abduction), induction, and deduction. The same process takes place when we understand a catachresis — not the institutionalized catachresis, transformed into a codified lexeme (for example, the leg of a table), but the institutive catachresis, which later will be identified by many as the 'auroral' moment of language. *Inflationary spiral* is an institutive catachresis (language creates metaphors even outside of poetry, simply out of a need to find names for things). And if institutive catachreses require interpretive labor, it is because the latent proportion (which could be expressed in a simile) does not exist before the metaphor; it must be found, whether by the person who invents the catachresis or by the person interpreting it (at least, for a brief stretch of the trope's circulation), after which discovery language absorbs the trope, lexicalizes it, and registers it as an *overcoded* expression.

This is precisely what Aristotle meant to say when he assigned a *cognitive* function to the metaphor — not only when he associates metaphor with enigma, an extended sequence of metaphors, but also when he says that creating metaphors "is a sign of a natural disposition of the mind," because knowing how to find good metaphors means perceiving or grasping the similarity of things between each other (τὸ ὅμοιον ϑεωρεῖν) (*Poetics* 1459ᵃ6 – 8). But if the proportion between cup and shield and between Ares and Dionysus were already overcoded, that metaphor would not say anything other than *what is already known.* If it says something new, it means that either (a) the proportion was not so commonly accepted, or (b) if it was accepted it was then soon forgotten. And thus the metaphor *posits* ('posits' in a philosophical sense, but also in a physical sense, as 'in *putting before the eyes*', το ηρὸ ὀμμάτωνηοιεῖν a proportion that, wherever it may have been deposited, was not before the eyes; or it was before the eyes and the eyes did not see it, as with Poe's purloined letter.

To point out, or teach how to see, then. To see what? The likeness between *things*, or the subtle network of proportions between *cultural units* (that is, the fact that sheep are indeed unique and equal in their variety or the fact that a certain culture sees a flock of sheep as an example of unity within variety)? To this question Aristotle gives no answer, as was only appropriate for one who had identified the modes of being of Being (the categories) with the modes of being of language.

What Aristotle understood was that the metaphor is not an ornament (κόσμος), but rather a cognitive instrument, at once a source of clarity and enigma:

> Accordingly, it is metaphor that is in the highest degree instructive [. . .]. It follows, then, for style and reasoning [enthymenes] alike, that in order to be lively [lively expressions are the ἀστεῖα, which in the Baroque period will be the metaphorical witticisms] they must give us rapid information. Consequently, we are not highly gratified by enthymemes that are obvious — and "obvious" means absolutely plain to everyone, not demanding a bit of mental inquiry — nor by those which, when stated, we do not understand. What we like are those that convey information as fast as they are stated — so long as we did not have the knowledge in advance — or that our minds lag only a little behind. With the latter two kinds there is some process of learning. (*Rhetoric* 1401b14– 25; Eng. tr., p. 207)

Aristotle provides the most luminous confirmation of the metaphor's cognitive function when he associates it with *mimesis*. Ricoeur (1975) warns that if metaphor is *mimesis* it cannot be an empty, gratuitous game. In the *Rhetoric* (1411b25*ff*) there is no room for doubt: the best metaphors are those that "show things in a state of activity." Thus metaphorical knowledge is knowledge of the dynamics of the real. That definition seems rather restrictive, but it can be reformulated as follows: the best metaphors are those in which the cultural process, the dynamics itself of semiosis, shows through. Aristotle defeats right from the start the theorists of the easy metaphor, whether they are the classical moralists, who feared the metaphor's cosmetic and deceitful nature, or the Baroque immoralists, who privileged its 'spicy' nature, or, finally, the current semanticists who see rhetorical *ornatus*, at the most, as a structure even more superficial than surface structure, incapable of tapping deep structures, whether these are syntactic, semantic, or logical. To all of these theorists Aristotle had already said, "Metaphors . . . should be drawn from objects that are related to the object in question, but not obviously related; in rhetoric as in philosophy the adept will perceive resemblances even in things that are far apart" (ibid., 1412a11 – 12; Eng. tr., p.212).

And that these likenesses were not only in things but also (perhaps above all) in the ways in which language defines things, the philosopher knew well when he lamented (ibid., 1405a25 – 27) how pirates in his time had the gall to call themselves purveyors, and how wily the orator is in a calling crime an error or an error a crime. All that pirates had to do, it seems, was find a genus that fitted their species and adapt to the purpose a creditable Porphyrian tree; it is true that they transport merchandise by sea, as do commercial purveyors. What is manipulatory of reality, or *ideological,* is to select only that *one* out of *all* the other properties that were characteristic of pirates, and through that choice *make themselves known,* put themselves before others' eyes in this perspective and *under that particular description.*

### 3.9.   The semiosic background: the system of content

#### 3.9.1.   The medieval encyclopedia and *analogia entis*

We have seen how Aristotle's limitation consists in his identifying the categories of language with the categories of being. This identification is not questioned by post-Aristotelian rhetoric — from the *Rhetorica ad Herennium,* through Cicero and Quintilian, all the way to the medieval grammarians and rhetoricians. In the meantime, the traditional classification of figures has been worked out in this period. However, a *panmetaphorical* attitude, established in the Middle Ages, deserves a brief discussion, since it helps resolve (even if in a negative manner) the question with which we are concerned.

Saint Paul had already affirmed that "we see through a glass, darkly" (1 Corinthians 13:12). Medieval Neoplatonism gives a metaphysical frame to this hermeneutic tendency. In a universe that is nothing other than an emanative outpouring from the unknowable and unnameable One down to the furthest ramifications of matter, every being functions as a synecdoche or metonymy of the One. When Hugh of Saint Victor affirms that the "entire sensible world is, so to speak, a book written by the hand of God," and that "all visible things, visibly presented to us by a symbolic instruction, that is, figured, are proposed for the declaring and signifying of things invisible" (*Didascalicon,* PL, CLXXVI, col. 814), he gives us to understand that there exists a sort of code that, assigning to things emergent properties, allows them to become metaphors for supernatural things, in accordance with the traditional theory of the four levels of exegesis (the literal, allegorical, moral, and analogical). This is the project taken up in bestiaries, the *lapidaria*, the *imagines mundi*, all formed on the Hellenistic model of the *Physiologus:* certain properties are predicated of every animal, plant, part of the world, or event in nature, and, on the basis of an identity between one of these properties and one of the properties of the supernatural being that is to be metaphorized, a correlation is established. There exists a network of cultural information, which functions as a cosmological code.

The code is ambiguous, nevertheless, since of all the properties there are to choose from it chooses only a few, and those are contradictory. The lion erases his tracks with his tail to throw the hunters off his track and is thus a figure of Christ canceling the traces of sin; but in Psalm 21 the terrible maw of the beast — *"Salva me de ore leonis"* — becomes a metaphor of Hell, and *"per leonem antichristum intelligitur"* definitively.

Even though medieval Neoplatonism was not aware of it (but the medieval rationalists, from Abelard to Ockham, would not fail to realize this), the universe, which seems to be a *rhizomatic* or mazelike network of real properties, is in effect a mazelike network of *cultural* properties, and those properties are attributed both to the earthly beings and to the heavenly beings in order that metaphorical substitutions may be possible.

What medieval Neoplatonists knew was that, in order to decide whether the lion must be seen as a *figura Christi* or as a figure of the Antichrist, a *co-text* is necessary. The tradition provides a typology of possible co-texts, so that the best interpretation is always the one recorded by some (intertextual) *auctoritas*. That the question is merely one of cultural networks, and not of ontological realities, Thomas Aquinas was well aware, and he disposes of the problem in two ways. On the one hand, he admits that there is only one portion of reality in which things and events themselves acquire metaphorical and allegorical value, inasmuch as they have been created and disposed thus by God himself: sacred history, and for this reason the Bible in itself is literal (it is the things of which it speaks literally that are *figures*). There remains as well the figure of the parable, as it is used in poetry (but in this sense one need not leave the bounds of classical rhetoric). But, on the other hand, insofar as it is necessary to speak of God in accordance with the dictates of reason, and given that God is at an immense distance from the created world, with which He is not in a Neoplatonic identity, but which He keeps alive through an act of *participation*, Aquinas turns to the principle of the *analogia entis*. Inasmuch as God's perfection transcends that of His creations, it is impossible to speak of Him univocally, nor can one limit oneself to speaking of Him equivocally; He must be spoken of, then, *through analogy* or, in other words, by means of a proportion between cause and effect. Through a kind of metonymy, therefore, which is held up, however, by a proportion of metaphorical type.

What is the foundation of the analogy? Is this a case of a logical-linguistic artifice, or of an actual ontological network? The interpreters are discordant. Among the modern exegetes, Gilson admits that "what Saint Thomas calls our knowledge of God consists in our aptitude for forming affirmative propositions about Him" (1947:157). We only have to push a bit further to affirm, with no threat to Thomist orthodoxy, that the analogy speaks only of the knowledge men have of reality, of their way of naming concepts, and not of reality itself. The metaphor derived from that knowledge is a *suppositio impropria* based on a proportion between *intentiones secundae*, where, in other words, the expression /dog/ (whether verbal or visual) does not mean the real dog, but rather the word *dog* or the concept of «dog» (McInerny 1961). In a universe comprehensible by means of the proportion between God and things, the fundamental mechanism is actually found in an identity between names, even if for Thomas (unlike the nominalists) those names reflect the properties of things.

### 3.9.2. Tesauro's categorical index

An interesting return to the Stagyrite's model is found in the *Cannocchiale aristotelico (The Aristotelian Binocular)* of Emanuele Tesauro (1655), written at the very height of the Baroque period. From Aristotle, Tesauro inherits the tendency to call every trope and figure a metaphor. I shall not speak here of the detail and enthusiasm with which the author of the treatise studies puns both in single words and in actual microtexts, and of how he extends the metaphorical mechanism to visual puns, painting, sculpture, actions, inscriptions, proverbs, truncated phrases, laconic messages, mysterious characters, hierograms, logographs, cryptograms, gestures, medallions, columns, ships, garters, chimeric bodies. I shall not speak of those sections in which Tesauro borders on modern speech-acts theory, showing how language states, narrates, affirms, denies, swears, corrects, holds back, exclaims, doubts, approves, admonishes, orders, praises, derides, invokes, questions, thanks, vows, and so on. (With regard to all these aspects and to the others of which I will speak, I direct the reader to Speciale's reconstruction, 1978.) Tesauro knows that metaphors are not created out of a pure joy of invention, but that they impose on one a *labor*, to master which takes practice.

The first exercise is the reading of catalogues, anthologies, hieroglyphic collections, medallions (and their reverse sides), emblems — in a way, a pure invitation to intertextuality, to the imitation of the 'already said'. But the second stage of the exercise presupposes learning a *combinatory* mechanism.

Tesauro invites his reader to draft a *categorical index,* that is, *a model of an organized semantic universe.* Such a model begins with Aristotle's categories (Substance, Quantity, Quality, Relation, Place, Time, Position, Possession, Activity, Passivity; see *Categories* 1b25 – 2a8) and then organizes under each of these categories the various members that are inclusive of everything susceptible to such categorization. Suppose we have to make a metaphor on a dwarf. We leaf through the categorical index until we find the entry Quantity; we then identify the concept 'little things', and all such microscopic things as may be found under that rubric may be divided still further according to contextual selections (as we would say now): astronomy, human organism, animal, plant, and so on. But an index organized by substances would have to be integrated with a *second index* in which each substance were analyzed according to the particles that define how the object in question manifests itself. (For example, under the category of Quantity we would then have to find what measurements it has, what weight it has, how many parts it has; and under Quality there would be the specificiations whether it is visible, whether it is hot, and so on.) As can be seen, this is essentially a system of content organized as an encyclopedia. At this point, we will find that the smallest measure is the Geometric Thumb, and we will say that in order to measure a dwarf's body, a geometric thumb would be too gross a measure.

While he is a careless structuralist, Tesauro knows nevertheless that it is no longer ontological relations but the structure itself of language that guarantees the metaphorical transfers. Look, for example, at the Aristotelian metaphor of old age as the sunset of life (or of youth as spring). Tesauro still proceeds by analogy, but the relation is one of *contiguity in the index.* The transfer is structured as in Figure 3.6.

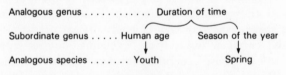

FIGURE 3.6

The higher nodes become classemes or contextual selections of the lower nodes. One can see that the analogy Aristotle perceived between *draw off* and *cut* functions when the act of drawing off is considered under the category of Passivity; but, if it is considered under the category of Possession, drawing off becomes analogous to other processes of acquisition and not to processes of deprivation (take away). Henceforth, there is the possibility of searching through the categorical index ad infinitum, and of uncovering a reserve of untapped metaphors, and of metaphorical propositions and arguments.

Tesauro's model still represents the framework of medieval Neoplatonism — which it has deliberately resolved, though, into a network of units of purely cultural content. It is, however, announcing the model of an unlimited semiosis. While being a still too hierarchical system of semes, it produces a web of interpretants.

### 3.9.3. Vico and the cultural conditions of invention

An overview of the history of metaphorology and of its epistemic breaks, however brief, must not leave out Vico, not least because of the fact that *La Scienza Nuova* (and its chapter "Della logica poetica") seems to put into question the existence of a cultural network, of semantic fields and universes, and of a preestablished process of semiosis, which should precede (on the basis of the foregoing observations) the production and interpretation of metaphors.

Certainly, Vico discusses the "first tropes," and the phenomenon of speaking by means of animate substances, whereby natural objects and phenomena are named by reference to parts of the body (1744; Eng. tr., p. 129), for example, the eyes of needles, the lips of a vase, and so on. Now, much too much has been said about this 'auroral' moment of language; in the view of some interpreters, Vico argues that the creating of metaphors is an inborn ability in beings who are at the dawn or awakening of their own intelligence; metaphorical speech, furthermore, would be iconic, insofar as it instituted a kind of native onomatopoeic relation between words and things. But the fact is, Vico knows and says that, outside the utopia of an Adamic language (an idea already in Dante and later elaborated in seventeenth-century England, as well as in Vico's own time), what is indisputable is the diversity of languages. In fact,

> as the people have certainly by diversity of climates acquired different natures, from which have sprung as many different customs, so from their different natures and customs as many different languages have arisen. For by virtue of the aforesaid diversity of their natures they have regarded the same utilities or necessities of human life from different points of view, and there have thus arisen so many national customs, for the most part differing from one another and at times contrary to one another; so and not otherwise there have arisen as many different languages as there are nations. (Ibid., p. 148)

Given which, evidently, Vico makes the following fundamental observations: languages, like customs, are born as the response of groups of human beings to the material environment in which they live; even if the disposition toward language functions and develops in all human societies according to the same logic, and even if the utilities and necessities of life are the same for everybody, nevertheless, human societies have looked at these material universals *from different viewpoints,* which is to say, they have *made pertinent different aspects of their universe.*

Catachreses are created out of transpositions of natural objects "according to their natural properties or sensible effects" (ibid., p. 147); in this sense the labor of metaphor is always motivated. What must be asked here is if those effects and properties — given that metaphors are the result of a selection of pertinent aspects — are not already cultural constructions. If metaphors require an underlying cultural framework, then the *hieroglyphic* language of the gods cannot be a merely primitive stage of human consciousness: it needs the presence of both the *symbolic* language of heroes and the *epistolary* language of men as its starting point. Thus Vico is not speaking of a linear development from a metaphorical language to a more conventional language, but of a continual, cyclical activity.

The language of the gods is a heap of unrelated synecdoches and metonymies: thirty thousand gods as identified by Varro, as many as the Greeks counted, including stones, fountains, reefs, brooks, minute objects, signifiers of forces, causes, connections. The language of heroes already creates metaphors (which thus are not so primeval), but the metaphor or catachresis invents a new term using at least two terms that are already *known* (and expressed) and presupposing at least another one that is unexpressed. Could that symbolic language establish itself without the support of an epistolary language, the only language recognizedly conventional? On this point Vico is very explicit:

> To enter now upon the extremely difficult [question of the] way in which these three kinds of languages and letters were formed, we must establish this principle: that as gods, heroes, and men began at the same time (for they were, after all, men who imagined the gods and believed their own heroic nature to be a mixture of the divine and human natures), so these three languages began at the same time, each having its letters, which developed along with it. (Ibid., p. 149)

In light of these considerations, Vico's semiotic resembles, more than an aesthetics of ineffable creativity, a cultural anthropology that recognizes the categorical indices on which metaphors are based, indices whose historical conditions, birth, and variety it researches even as it explores the variety of brave deeds, of medallions, and of fables.

### 3.10.   The limits of formalization

At this point we cannot ignore the fact that formal semantics, in the effort to transform itself into a logic of natural languages, has recently made several important strides toward reducing the scandal of the metaphor; that is, formal semantics has sought to expand a logic of truth conditions so as to recognize the legitimacy of metaphorical expressions — expressions that speak about the world *by lying*. What we want to suggest here is that, at most, a formal semantics can define the place that a metaphorical calculus might occupy within its framework — yet again, it does not explain what it means to understand a metaphor.

Take one conjecture, among the many, which is perhaps the most recent of the efforts to formalize the phenomenon. The model put forth is intended "to reflect the context-sensitivity of the metaphor, and to give a metaphorical interpretation to statements which may be literally true and nondeviant" (Bergmann 1979:225). A vocabulary is proposed that is outfitted with monadic predicates $P_1$, $P_2$, with a dyadic predicate =, with individual constants $a_1$, $a_2$, with individual variables $v_1$, $v_2$, and with normal logical connectives. Grammatical rules are provided (of the type if $t_1$, $t_2$ are terms, then $t_1 = t_2$ is a formula), and a class of "ideal contexts" $C$ is added to the semantics of this language $L$.

> Let $D$ be a non-empty class; it is the domain of discourse and is assumed to be comprised of possible (actual and non-actual) individuals. An interpretation function assigns to every monadic predicate of $L$ a subset of $D$, and to every constant an element of $D$. Let $F$ be the class of all interpretation functions on $D$. Choose some element of $F$ as the *literal* interpretation function — it assigns to the monadic predicates and constants of the language their literal interpretations. Call this function '$f^0$'. Let $F^0$ be the class of all interpretation functions $f$ in $F$ which agree with $f^0$ in the values assigned to the constants. Let g be the metaphorical disambiguating function: it assigns to every $c \in C$ a member of $F^0 - (f^0)$. The idea here is that g tells us, for each ideal context, what the metaphorical interpretations of predicates in that context are. Finally, let a model for $L$ be the 5-tuple M = $\langle D, C, f^0, F^0, g \rangle$. (Ibid., p. 226)

Obviously, this defintion does not say anything about metaphors. In effect, it does not at all pretend to say anything: the author is not interested in understanding how metaphors function, but, rather (once it has been *intuitively* accepted that in natural languages metaphors are easily produced and understood), she is interested in introducing this phenomenon into the formal representation of a natural language. True, the author herself warns that, at least, the model she proposes permits her better to consider certain questions and to formulate such in a manner that is formally acceptable. For example, what must be understood by literal paraphrasability; whether metaphorical interpretations depend on those that are literal, and whether every linguistic expression is interpretable metaphorically in some context, or in every context, and so on. But these are questions the answers to which are not given (at least for the time being) by formal semantics: "without an ideal context there are no strict rules for interpretation of metaphors" (ibid., p. 228) — which is what metaphorology already knew; it is important, however, that the several formal semantics become aware of this.

There are formal approaches, of course, that by virtue of their taking into consideration the contributions of linguistics, of lexicology, and of semiotics in general allow their (tendential) preoccupations with concreteness to show through to a greater degree. In the meantime, though, it is to studies of this sort that the distinction is owed between what could be called an 'intensional' metaphor and one that is 'extensional'. An example of the first type is *The girl is a birch,* which, given certain meaning postulates (for example, *if young girl then human; if reed then nonhuman*), clearly mainfests its metaphoricity (otherwise it would be a semantically incorrect expression, or an outright lie). An example of the second type is *the emperor entered,* an expression which in itself is literal and, semantically speaking, unambiguous, unless it should refer in a particular circumstance to the entrance of an office manager. This example would occur only in an absurd universe in which metaphors appeared only in expressions isolated from their context, and where only one semantic system were engaged, that of verbal language; that is, such a situation verifies itself only in books of linguistics and in books of formal semantics. In fact, a sentence of that sort is usually uttered (a) in a context in which it has already been said or will immediately be said that the office manager is entering, (b) while one is showing an image of the office manager as he is entering, (c) while indicating a person whom anyone recognizes as the office manager and, in any case, as someone who is not an emperor. All of which means that, the isolated expression having been put into contact with the linguistic context and the elements of extralinguistic systems, it would immediately be retranslated as *the office manager (who is) the emperor is entering* (given that there is not a question here of information *de dicto:* the office manager, whom *we call* the emperor, is entering). At this point, the second example falls into the category of the first: the girl is not a birch, just as the office manager is not the emperor. (In any event, for all these cases of mentioning and referring, see Eco 1976, 3.3).

Van Dijk admits that "only a fragment of a serious theory of metaphor can be covered by the formal semantics approach. A formal semantics specifies the conditions under which metaphoric sentences may be said to have a truth-value" (1975:173). And he makes clear that a formal semantics with such ambitions cannot but be 'sortal', that is to say, it must be a semantics that accounts for "selection restrictions" (for example, if *automobile* includes the seme 'mechanical' or 'inorganic' and if *to eat* includes semes such as 'human' and 'the object is inorganic', then it is semantically deviant to say *John ate the automobile;* if *to eat* includes a seme 'human' one will not be able to say *The automobile ate up the road,* that is, it will be necessary to admit that this sortal deviation has metaphorical intentions). Hence the difference between expressions that are sortally incorrect (such as *The square root of Susy is happiness,* whose very negation is false) and which do not seem to have any possible metaphorical interpretation (naturally that is not true; it depends on the context), expressions that are sortally incorrect but with a possible metaphorical interpretation (*The sun smiled high up in the sky*), and expressions that are sortally correct and that can, in particular situations of referring, be metaphorical (*The emperor is entering*). A sortal specification would then be a function that assigns to each predicate of the language a "region of logical space."

It seems that such a region, which a formal semantics identifies as an abstract and 'empty' entity, once filled up cannot be anything other than a portion of Tesauro's categorical index. Given that this region would be populated by 'points', 'possible individuals', or 'possible objects', the problem of the metaphor would entail the question of the similarities and differences between these objects. Right, but not enough. Naturally the theory is not as dumb as it seems: within its framework it is possible to give a formal definition, once differences and similarities have been granted, of the greater or lesser distance between the metaphorizing and metaphorized terms. *The horse growls* is less daring a metaphor than *The theory of relativity growls,* because in the play of related properties there is undoubtedly more of a relation between a growl and the 'animal' property of a horse than there is between a growl and the 'abstract object' property of the Einsteinian theory. But this useful definition of distance is not capable of deciding which of the two metaphors is better. All the more so, in view of the fact that at the end the author (who knows more about metaphors than the method he chooses in his article allows him) finishes by admitting that "the choice of typical criteria for the similarity function is pragmatically determined on the basis of cultural knowledge and beliefs" (ibid., p. 191).

No greater satisfaction is given by another attempt at formalization, by a logician who takes off right from Aristotle, Guenthner: "If metaphors are to be analyzed within the framework of formal semantics, the first thing will obviously be to provide for a way of implementing information about the meaning structure of predicates which is relevant for their metaphorical behavior" (1975:205). But immediately he says that it will not be necessary, however, to construct this semantic information in the form of an encylopedia, and a few sortal specifications will be enough. Which is exactly the way to preclude an understanding of a trope. Such is the case that, when he analyzes some examples borrowed from Groupe $\mu$, Guenthner rediscovers the same old relation of girl-birch. And as we shall see, the fact that a girl and a birch tree are both flexible is properly an item of encyclopedic information. At any rate, Guenthner's model (useless for understanding how a metaphor functions) seems more useful than the others for expanding a formal semantics of natural languages. Its author starts, in fact, from a distinction between natural kinds (fish, lion, and so on), opposing these against nonnatural kinds (such as president), and plays on the fact that the properties of a natural kind must be contextually selected (obviously on the basis of the context) in order to make the metaphor acceptable and comprehensible. A sortal model is a 4-tuple $M = \langle D, f, k, s \rangle$, such that $D$ is a nonempty domain of objects, or a universe of discourse, $f$ a function of interpretation, $k$ a function that assigns to every object in $D$ the kinds to which the object belongs in the model, and $s$ is a function drawn from the group of those predicates not assigned as natural kinds by $k$. A sortal model determines which statements are true, false, or meaningless (that is, literally nonsignificant).

> If we now add a function p which assigns to each predicate P in L a set of 'prominent' properties, a sortal model accounts for the metaphorical meaning of an expression in roughly the following way. If a sentence $\phi$ is neither true nor false in M and if $\phi$ translates for example the English sentence: *John is a mule* ($\phi$ = E x(x = j & Mx) or Mj) then $\phi$ can be interpreted metaphorically if there is a 'prominent' property assigned to M such that that property holds true of John. (Note that in our culture such properties are usually rather well delimited, but never related to the basic meaning of the expression — this can be easily tested in translating metaphorical sentences from one natural language into another.) (Ibid., p. 217)

Because entities such as the prominent properties, and every other possible insertion into the sortal apparatus, cannot be accounted for by a formal semantics, the present inspection of this universe of discourse must stop here. And we have to go back, as I said above, to a componential semantics.

## 3.11. Componential representation and pragmatics of the text

### 3.11.1. A model by 'cases'

We can venture at this point an explanation of the metaphorical mechanism that (a) is founded on a componential semantics in the format of an

encyclopedia and that (b) takes into account, at the same time, rules for
contextual insertion. An encyclopedic semantics is undoubtedly more interesting than a dictionary. The format of a dictionary, we have seen,
permits us to understand the mechanism of the synecdoche, but not that
of the metaphor. We only have to look at the efforts made by transformational grammar and interpretive semantics approaches. (For a synthetic account, see Levin 1977.) Establishing that a 'transference' or
transfer of properties occurs in the sentence *She is a birch*, whereby a girl
would acquire the seme 'vegetal' or birch the seme 'human', tells us
very little about what happens in the interpretation and production of
that trope. In fact, if we try to paraphrase the result ("This girl is human
but also has a vegetal property") we see that it is not very far from being
a parody of itself. The issue here is obviously one of flexibility (but,
again: a birch tree is not flexible in the same way that a young girl is
. . .), and it cannot be considered within a semantics in the format of a
dictionary.

A componential representation in the format of an encyclopedia, however, is potentially infinite and assumes the form of Model Q (Eco
1976), that is to say, of a polydimensional network of properties, in
which some properties are the *interpretants* of others. In the absence of
such a network, none of these properties can attain the rank of being a
metalinguistic construction or a unit belonging to a privileged set of
semantic universals. In a model dominated by the concept of unlimited
semiosis, every sign (linguistic and non-) is defined by other signs (linguistic and non-), which in turn become terms to be defined by other
terms assumed as interpretants. With the advantage that an encyclopedic
representation (even if ideal), based on the principle of unlimited interpretation, is capable of explaining in purely semiotic terms the concept of 'similarity' between properties.

By similarity between two semes or semantic properties we mean the
fact that in a given system of content those properties are named by the
same interpretant, whether it be verbal or not, and independently of the
fact that the objects or things for the designation of which that interpretant is customarily used may manifest perceptual 'similarities'. In other
words, the teeth of the maiden in the Song of Solomon are *like* the sheep
if, and only if, in that given culture the interpretant *white* is used to
designate both the color of teeth and that of sheep's fleece.

But metaphors set up not only similarities but also oppositions. A cup
and a shield are alike in their *form* (round and concave), but opposite in
their *function* (peace vs. war), just as Ares and Dionysus are alike insofar
as they are gods, but opposite with regard to the *ends* they pursue and to
the *instruments* they use. To account for these phenomena, an
encyclopedic representation has to assume the form of a *case grammar*,
which should recognize therefore the Subject Agent, the Object on

whom the agent executes his action, the Counter Agent who may possibly opposed himself to that action, the Instrument used by the agent, the Goal of the action, and so on. A semantics of this type has been elaborated by various authors (cf. Greimas' and Tesnières' *actants*, Fillmore's grammatical cases, Bierwisch's semantics, irrespective of their substantial differences; see also Nef 1979).

As a first approach, let us say that the properties that a case-like representation associates with a given action display a metonymic character: goal, instrument or agent seem to be metonymically linked to the represented action. We shall see later in which sense this kind of metonymic relationship also accounts for synecdochic relationships and ought to be considered as the basis for every metaphoric substitution.

### 3.11.2. Metonymy

From this perspective *a metonymy becomes the substitution of a sememe with one of its semes* (for example, /Drink a bottle/ for «drink wine», because a bottle will be registered among the final destinations of wine) or of *a seme with the sememe to which it belongs* (for example, /Weep thou, O Jerusalem/ for «May the tribe of Israel weep», because among the encyclopedic properties of Jerusalem must be included that of its being the holy city of the Jews).

This type of metonymic substitution is no different from the process Freud called "displacement." And just as condensation is involved with the process of displacement, so is metaphor involved (as we shall see) with these metonymic exchanges. On the basis of a representation by cases, I attempted to show (1976) the mechanism of displacement from seme to sememe (and vice versa) by analyzing a line from Virgil: *Vulnera dirigere et calamos armare veneno* (*Aeneides* 10.1.140).

The verse, which can be translated either as "to distribute wounds with poisoned arrows" or as "to smear with poison the arrows and hurl them," plays on the fact that /*vulnera dirigere*/ stands for «*dirigere tela*» (or *dirigere ictus, dirigere plagas, vulnerare*). Let us suppose that *vulnerare* is the right interpretation and imagine a semantic representation in case-grammer form like the following:

/Vulnerare/ ⊃ (Entailments)

$$
\begin{array}{cccc}
A & O & I & P \\
\text{Action} & \text{Human} & \text{Human} & \text{Weapon} & \text{Wound } (\textit{Vulnus})
\end{array}
$$

Strike
Wound
With aim

Here is where the expression /aim the wounds/ appears as a metonymy in place of «to wound», given that it takes the Goal for the whole Action or, in other words, that a seme stands for the entire sememe. Of the same type would be the Aristotelian example of /to stand/ for «to lie at anchor». Standing still would appear in the representation as the Goal of anchoring. The opposite case (sememe for seme) would be to describe a parked car as being firmly anchored. An encyclopedic representation of /to stop/ would have to include even an anchor among its various instruments.

This type of representation seems to work for verbs but poses some problems for nouns. How can an Agent, an Object, or an Instrument, in fact, be found for such linguistic entities as *house, sea, tree?* One possible suggestion would be to understand all substantives as 'reified' verbs or actions: not *house,* then, but *to build a house.* But there is one type of representation that seems to substitute for this difficult translation of substantives into verbs, which permits seeing the object expressed by the substantive as the result of a productive action entailing an agent or Cause, a Material to be manipulated, a Form to be imposed, and a Goal or Purpose to direct the object toward. It is a representation based on nothing other than the four Aristotelian causes (efficient, formal, material, and final), it being clear that these are assumed in merely operational terms and without metaphysical connotations.

Here, in the meantime, is the representation of a noun /x/, which might take the following format:

$$/x/ \supset F \quad\quad A \quad\quad\quad\quad M \quad\quad\quad\quad P$$

| F | A | M | P |
|---|---|---|---|
| Perceptual aspect of $x$ | Who or what produces $x$ | What $x$ is made of | What $x$ is supposed to do or to serve for |

Such a representation takes into account only encyclopedic properties, without distinguishing between $\Sigma$ and $\Pi$ properties. We shall see in 3.11.3 how these properties, potentially infinite, must be selected according to co-textual clues.

Each property can, however, be 'appointed' as a $\Sigma$ property. Suppose that /x/ is to be considered from the point of view of its Purpose: it will be seen as belonging to the class of all the entities having the same Purpose or function. In this case, one of the $P$ properties will become the genus of which the sememe «x» is a species; that is, one of the $P$ properties will become the upper node of a possible Porphyrian tree (Figure 3.7).

The same operation can be implemented upon $F$, $M$, or $A$ properties. A property's assumption of the $\Sigma$ mode thus depends on a contextual decision on the part of the interpreter (or the producer) of the metaphor, who is interested in singling out a given property as the one *from whose point of view* a generalizing or particularizing synecdoche in $\Sigma$ can be set

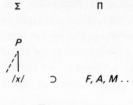

FIGURE 3.7

forth. Thus /x/ will name all the «P», or /P/ will name «x». Supposing that /x/ corresponds to /house/ and that it is represented, for the sake of economy, as

$$\text{/house/} \supset F_{\text{With roof}} \quad A_{\text{Culture}} \quad M_{\text{Bricks}} \quad P_{\text{Shelter}}$$

If one decides to consider a house from the point of view of its function, the property of being a shelter becomes a $\Sigma$ property, and it will then be possible to name a house as a shelter, or every shelter as a house. The same would happen if the house were described from the point of view of its shape: one can name a house as one's own roof, a house being a species of the genus 'artifacts with a roof'.

It is worth noticing that house for shelter (and vice versa) traditionally has been considered a case of metonymy (object for function, and vice versa), while house for roof, or vice versa, has been traditionally considered a case of synecdoche (*pars pro toto*, a synecdoche in $\Pi$).

This difference, between metonymy and synecdoche in $\Pi$, becomes absolutely irrelevant in the present framework. The only case of synecdochic movement seems to be in the $\Sigma$ mode, produced by a co-textual decision, and consisting in the transformation of a property into a genus. All the other cases of substitution of a sememe with a seme, and vice versa, can be called metonymy. Naturally, in our framework the difference between synecdoche and metonymy has nothing to do with the concrete relations between a 'thing' and its parts or other contiguous 'things': the difference lies purely within formal bases.

As a matter of fact, the traditional rhetoric has never satisfactorily explained why a substitution genus/species ($\Sigma$) and a substitution *pars/totum* ($\Pi$) are both synecdoches, whereas all the other kinds of substitution (object/purpose, container/content, cause/effect, material/object, and so on) are called metonymies. In the present framework, both a *pars pro toto* and a cause/effect substitution can work on $\Pi$ properties.

The explanation of this ambiguity in the tradition must be made in historical and phenomenological terms. According to many time-honored theories of knowledge, things are first perceived and recognized according to their formal (morphologic) characteristics: a body is round or heavy, a sound is loud or deep, a tactile sensation is hot or rough, and so on. These morphological properties in our model are recorded under $F$. Instead, always according to traditional theories of knowledge, to establish that a thing has a cause $A$, that it is made of a certain material $M$, or that it has a function $P$ seems to depend on further inferences — by a sort of shifting from a simple act of apprehension to an act of judgment. It is evident, then, why $F$ properties enjoyed a privileged status and were ranked as synecdoches along with the $\Sigma$ relations (genus/species). To perceive and to recognize the formal characteristics of a thing meant to grasp its 'universal' essence, to recognize that thing as the individual of a species related to a genus.

Obviously, such an assumption does not capture the complexity of a perceptual experience, where frequently an object, to be recognized and classified, requires a complex inferential labor, dealing with its functional, material, and causal aspects, as well. Our model eliminates the effects of all these implicit philosophical assumptions. All properties must be considered encyclopedic and must allow for metonymical substitution — except when a property is transformed into a genus (substitution in $\Sigma$) because for co-textual reasons a given semantic item has to be considerd *under a certain 'generic' description* (see also Eco 1979, 8.5.2).

### 3.11.3.  'Topic', 'frames', isotopies

Naturally, an encyclopedic representation is potentially infinite. In a given culture, a cup's functions can be many, and, of these, holding liquid is only one. (One has only to think of the liturgical functions of a chalice, or of cups in sports.) What, then, are the interpretants that will have to be registered under the aspect $P$ (purpose or function) of the cup? And which will be those grouped under $F$, $A$, $M$? If they are not infinite, they are at least indefinte. As I have written elsewhere, "a *semiotics of the code* is an operational device in the service of a *semiotics of sign production*. A semiotics of the code can be established — if only partially — when the existence of a message *postulates it* as an explanatory condition. Semiotics must proceed to isolate structures *as if* a definitive general structure existed; but to be able to do this one must assume that this global structure is a simply regulative hypothesis . . ." (1976: 128 – 29). In other words, the universe of the encyclopedia is so vast (if the hypothesis of infinite interpretation from sign to sign and thus of unlimited semiosis is valid) that, in the instance (and under the pressure) of a certain co-text, a given portion of the encyclopedia is activated and proposed to explain the metonymical substitutions and their metaphorical results (see Eco 1979, 2.6).

Where does this contextual pressure come from? Either (a) from the identification of a theme or *topic* and, consequently, from the selection of a path of interpretation or *isotopy;* or (b) from the reference to *frames,* which permit us to establish not only what is being talked about, but also under what profile, to what ends, and with what in view, it is being talked about (see Eco 1979, 0.6.3).

### 3.11.4.  Trivial metaphors and 'open' metaphors

Let us consider two elementary, even crude, examples of Icelandic riddles (*kenningar*) mentioned by Borges (1953): /The tree for sitting/ for «bench» and /The house of the birds/ for «the sky». In the former example, the first term (/tree/) contains no ambiguity. Let us construct a componential spectrum:

/Tree/ ⊃  $F$        $A$         $M$          $P$
 Trunk     Nature     *Natural*    Fruits
 Branches              *wood*       . . .
 . . .
 (Vertical)

As is clear in this first stage, we do not yet know which are the semes that must be kept in mind contextually. The encyclopedia (a potential reserve of information) would permit filling in this representation indefinitely. But the context gives as well the indication *for sitting.* The expression as a whole is ambiguous. One does not sit on trees, or, alternatively, one can sit on every branch of every tree, but then it is hard to understand why the definite article *the* is used (which, according to Brooke-Rose, is an indicator of metaphorical usage). This tree, then, is not a tree. Something must be found that has some of a tree's properties, but not others, requiring the tree to have properties that it does not have (normally). We are faced with a task of abduction (a kenning is a riddle based on a 'difficult' metaphor). A series of hypotheses leads us to single out in the tree trunk the element of 'verticality', so as to look for something that is also wooden but 'horizontal'. We try a representation of *to sit.* We look among those Objects on which an Agent sits for those that have the seme of 'horizontal.' A primitive Icelander, or someone who knows that the expression must bear a relation to the code of primitive Icelandic culture, immediately picks out the bench.

We assemble the representation of *bench:*

/Bench/ ⊃  $F$           $A$         $M$         $P$
 Horizontal     Culture     Worked      To seat
                            timber      oneself

At first glance, the two sememes have no property in common. Now we carry out a second operation: we look for those among the different

properties that can form part of the same Porphyrian tree (Figure 3.8).
Here we see tree and bench unified at a high node of the stem (both
things are vegetal) and opposed at lower nodes. This solution creates a
condensation by means of a series of displacements. Cognitively speaking, not much is learned, except for the fact that benches are made of
crafted timber.

Let us pass to the second riddle, *The house of the birds*. Here it is possible to assemble a double representation immediately.

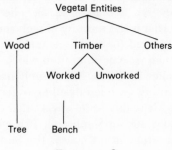

FIGURE 3.8

/House/ $\supset$ $F$             $A$       $M$          $P$

       Rectangular    Culture     Earth        Shelter

       Closed                   (Inorganic)   Resting on

       Covered                         ground

/Birds/ $\supset$ $F$ Winged,    $A$ Nature    $M$ Earth     $P$ Flying in

          etc.                    (Organic)    the sky

Obviously, certain semes have already been identified as the most pertinent here, on the basis of a series of hypotheses. The materials have
been characterized according to a logic of the elements (earth, air, water,
and fire), and an interesting difference has been found, at this point,
between the earthliness or earthbound property of houses and the air-
borne nature of birds (suggesting the seme 'sky'). These are mere
hypotheses (since many other alternatives exist); but it is a fact that this
metaphor is more 'difficult' than the other and, thus, that it requires
more daring abductions. So the interpreter can make a 'fair guess' out of
the opposition between a house (closed) and the sky (open). At this
point we can try to represent /sky/, keeping in mind, obviously, its
possible differences and similarities with house:

/Sky/ $\supset$ $F$ Formless    $A$ Nature    $M$ Air    $P$ Nonshelter

       Open

Clearly, among the ends or functions of sky, only 'nonshelter' has been identified, since the seme 'shelter' exists in *house*. At this point, though it seems as though all the semes in the comparison house/sky are in opposition. What is there that is similar? If we try a Porphyrian tree on the opposition air/earth, we discover that these two units find a common node in the property 'element'.

The interpreter is led, then, to draw inferences concerning those semes that have been singled out. One is led, in other words, to take the various semes as th starting points for new semantic representations or compositional analyses (see Eco 1976, 2.12). The domain of the encyclopedia is widened: what is the territory of men and what is the territory of birds? Men live in closed (or enclosed) territories, and birds in open territories. What for man is something from which he must shelter himself is the natural shelter for birds. New Porphyrian trees are tried out: closed dwelling or territory vs. open dwelling or territory. Birds 'live', so to speak, in the skies. It is this 'so to speak' that creates the condensation. Frames or settings are superimposed. If a man is menaced, what does he do? He takes refuge in his house. If a bird is menaced, it takes refuge in the skies. Therefore, enclosed refuge vs. open refuge. But then the skies that seemed a place of danger (producing wind, rain, storm) for some beings become a place of refuge for others. This is a case, then, of a metaphor that is 'good' or 'poetic' or 'difficult' or 'open', since it is possible here to continue the process of semiosis indefinitely and to find conjunctions or contiguities at one node of a given Porphyrian tree and dissimilarities at lower nodes, just as an entire slew of dissimilarities and oppositions are found in the encyclopedic semes. That metaphor is 'good' which does not allow the work of interpretation to grind to a halt (as occurred with the example of the bench), but which permits inspections that are diverse, complementary, and contradictory. Which does not appear to be different from the criterion of pleasure cited by Freud (1905) to define a good joke: thrift and economy, to be sure, but such that a shortcut is traced through the encyclopedic network, a labyrinth which would take away too much time if it were to be explored in all its polydimensional complexity.

The problem now is to see whether this model of metaphorical production and interpretation holds true for other metaphorical expressions, for the most exaggerated catachreses and for the most delicate poetic inventions alike. We shall start by putting ourselves in the position of someone who has to disambiguate *The leg of the table* for the first time. In the beginning, it must have been a kenning, an enigma. One must know first, though, what a table and a leg are. One finds in a (human) leg a function $P$ of sustaining or holding up a body. In the formal description $F$ of *table*, one finds the instruction that it is held up by four unnamed

elements. One hypothesizes a third term, *body*, and finds that in *F* it is
held up by two legs. The semes for verticality may be found both in leg
and in the object *x* holding up the table. One also finds differences and
oppositions between semes, such as 'nature vs. culture', 'organic vs. inorganic'. Table and body are joined under a Porphyrian tree that considers articulated structures: we find that body and table meet at the
higher node and are distinguished from each other at the lower nodes
(for example, organic articulated structures vs. inorganic articulated
structures). In the end, we might well ask if the catachresis is 'good.' We
do not know, it is too familiar, we will never again regain the innocence
of first invention. By now it is a ready-made syntagm, an element in the
code, a catachresis in the strict sense, and not an inventive metaphor.

Let us try out, then, two indisputably genuine metaphors: *She was a
rose* and, from Malherbe, *Et rose elle a vécu ce que vivent les roses, l'espace
d'un matin*.

The first metaphor right away says contextually what the metaphorizing term (or vehicle) is and who the metaphorized term (or tenor) is. *She*
cannot be anything other than a human being of the female sex. One
proceeds thus to the comparison of *woman* and *rose*. But the operation
can never be so completely ingenuous. The interpreter's intertextual
competence is already rich with ready-made expressions, with already
familiar *frames*. One already knows which semes to bring into focus and
which to drop (Figure 3.9). The comparison is of unsettling simplicity.
The greater part of the encyclopedic semes is similar; there is opposition
only on the vegetal/animal axis. The Porphyrian tree is built on that
opposition, and we find that, despite opposition at the lower nodes,
there is a conjunction at the higher node (organic). But, in order to arrive
there, it was necessary, obviously, to know already that, when a woman
is compared to a flower, it is in terms of a woman-object, which, like the
flowers, lives for its own sake, purely as an ornament to the world. And,
finally, the question of the similarity or dissimilarity between properties
becomes clear: it is neither perceptual nor ontological, but, rather,
semiotic. Language (the figurative tradition) must already have understood 'freshness' and 'color' as interpretants both of the healthy condition of a human body and of the healthy condition of a flower, even if
from a physical perspective the rosiness of a woman's cheek rarely has
the same spectral frequency as the red color of a flower. There is a
difference in millimicrons, but culture has blurred the distinction, naming two shades of color with the same word or representing them visually
with the same pigment.

This is a poor metaphor, then, scarcely cognitive, saying something
that is already known. However, no metaphor is absolutely 'closed': its
closure is pragmatic. If we imagine an ingenuous user of language who

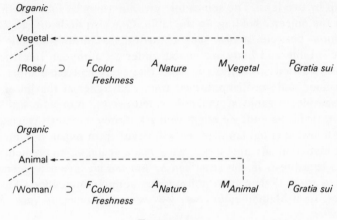

FIGURE 3.9

encounters *she is a rose* for the first time, we will see him caught in a game of trial and error, like the person who were to disambiguate for the first time *the house of the birds*. There is no metaphor that is absolutely 'unpoetic'; such metaphors exist only in particular sociocultural situations.

As for absolutely 'poetic' metaphors, it is impossible to say how much a user knows of a language (or of every other semiotic system). What, however, is known is what a language has already said, and it is possible to recognize a metaphor that demands unprecedented interpretive operations, and the identification of semes not yet identified.

Malherbe's metaphor apparently demands the same work of comparison as did the preceding example. The problem of *space* is already resolved; tradition has already made it a metaphor of the passage of time. Tradition has already secured the metaphorical use of *life* for the duration of nonanimal entities. The relation between duration, young girl, rose, and morning must be inspected, then. The seme of 'fleetingness' (already intertextually codified) will be recognized as particularly pertinent to *rose* (the rose opens at dawn and closes at sunset; it lasts for a very short time). All the other similarities between girl and rose will already have been reviewed and taken as intertextually correct. As far as morning is concerned, it has the property of being the most beautiful, delicate, and active hour of the day. Naturally, then, a maiden, fair as a rose, has lived a fleeting life, and has lived only that part of it that, albeit brief, is the best. (Aristotle, moreover, had already said: the morning of life is youth.) Thus we find identity and dissimilarity between encyclopedic markers, conjunction at a high node of the Porphyrian tree (organic, or living), and difference at the low nodes (animal vs. vegetal). Thenceforth all the condensations in this example, of maiden and flower, of vegetal life-pulse becoming carnal life-pulse, of dew turning into moist eyes, of petals assuming the shape of mouths follow; the encyclopedia allows the imagination (even the visual) to gallop ahead, and the continuous web of semiosis becomes animate with alliances and incompatibilities.

But some ambiguities remain. The rose lives one morning and it closes at night, but only to see the light again the next day. The maiden dies, instead, and is not reborn. Must one review, then, what is known about death for human beings? Is there rebirth? Or must one review what is known about the death of flowers? Is the rose that is reborn tomorrow the same as yesterday's, or is yesterday's that which was not picked? The effect of the condensation is unstable; underneath the cadaveral stiffening of the maiden, the long pulsation of the rose continues. Who wins? The life of the rose or the death of the maiden? Obviously, there is no answer; the metaphor is, in point of fact, 'open' — even if it is sustained by a play of intertextually familiar overcodings that verges on the manneristic.

### 3.11.5. Five rules
We are now in a position to sketch a series of rules for the co-textual interpretation of a metaphor (noting that the process of interpretation maps out in reverse the process of production):

(a) Try to provide a first tentative and partial componential representation of the metaphorizing sememe or sememes (the *vehicle*). This representation must single out only those semes or properties that the co-text has suggested as relevant. (For the processes of *blowing up* and *narcotizing* properties, see Eco 1979, 0.6.2). This operation represents a first *abductive* attempt.

(b) Look abductively in the encyclopedia for some other sememe that possibly shares some of the focused properties of the first sememe(s) while displaying other, *interestingly different* properties. This new sememe becomes a plausible candidate for the role of metaphorized sememe (*tenor*). If there are competing terms for this role, make further abductions based upon co-textual clues. It must be clear that by 'identical properties' we mean those representable by the same interpretant. By 'interestingly different properties' we mean those that are representable by interpretants that are not only different from each other, but that can also be opposed according to some overcoded incompatibility (such as open/closed, living/dead, and so on).

(c) Select one or more of the mutually different properties and build on them one or more Porphyrian trees such that these oppositional couples may join at one of its upper nodes.

(d) Tenor and vehicle display an interesting relationship when their mutually different properties meet at as high a node as possible in the Porphyrian tree.

Expressions such as 'interestingly different' and 'as high a node as possible' are not vague; they refer to a co-textual plausibility. Similarities and differences can be evaluated only according to the co-textual success of the metaphor, and we cannot look for a 'formal' criterion that establishes the proper degree of difference and the proper position in a Porphyrian tree. According to these rules, we start from metonymical relations (from seme to sememe) between two different sememes and by checking the possibility of a double synecdoche (which interests both vehicle and tenor); we finally accept the substitution of a sememe with another. Thus the *sememic substitution* appears as the effect of a *double metonymy* verified by a *double synecdoche*. From this point on, a fifth rule holds:

(e) Check whether, on the grounds of the 'abduced' metaphors, new relations can be implemented, so as to enrich further the cognitive power of the trope.

### 3.11.6.   From metaphors to symbolic interpretation

Once the process of unlimited semiosis has started, it is difficult to say where and when the metaphorical interpretation stops: it depends on the co-text. There are cases in which from one or more metaphors the interpreter is led to an allegorical reading, or to a symbolic interpretation, where the boundaries between metaphor, allegory, and symbol can be very imprecise. (For a distinction between these three notions, see Chapter 4.)

On this score, Weinrich (1976) has posited an interesting distinction between *micrometaphorics, metaphorics of the context* and *metaphorics of the text*. Let us briefly follow his analysis of a lengthy passage from Walter Benjamin, of which only the most salient points will be summarized here. In the text *Seagulls* (*Mǫwen*), Benjamin speaks of a trip by sea that he made, a voyage that is dense with metaphors which will not be analyzed here. Two, however, appear singular to Weinrich: the seagulls, *peoples* of winged creatures, winged *messengers*, bound in a pattern of signs, which at a moment divide into two rows, one black, vanishing westward into thin air, the other row white, pulling toward the east, still present and 'to be resolved'; and the mast of the ship, which describes in the air a *pendular movement*. Weinrich develops first a *micrometaphorics* (for example, of common and dissimilar properties between mast and pendulum) and then a *metaphorics of the context*, where he connects the various 'metaphorical fields' activated by Benjamin. In brief, something slowly emerges that begins to look increasingly like an allegorical enunciation, which in the final stage of the *metaphorics of the test* reveals its politico-ideological key (whereby the text is considered also in terms of the historical circumstances of its enunciation): the year 1929, the crisis of the Weimar Republic, the contradictory situation of the German intellectual, on one side obsessed by the extreme polarization of contrasts (friend vs. enemy), on the other uncertain about what position to take, and oscillating between neutrality and a dogmatic surrender to one of the parties. Hence the mast that becomes a metaphor for the «pendulum of historical events», and the antagonistic contrast between the seagulls.

Regardless of whether Weinrich's reading is correct or not, let us return to the metaphor of the mast-pendulum, to identify its constitutive mechanism, which must permit all the contextual inferences that the reader (in the case postulated as a Model Reader) may possibly draw. We will go right past the stage of finding those contextual pressures that lead the reader to select certain semes at the expense of others, and draw the componential spectrum of the two terms present in the context: *mast* and *pendulum*. In effect, the text does speak of a "pendular movement" (*Pendelbewegungen*), so that more than of metaphor we should speak of a simile (the mast moves as though it were a pendulum). But the specific effect of condensation is not affected by this.

The representation of mast and of pendulum is as follows:

| /Mast/ $\supset$ F | A | M | P |
|---|---|---|---|
| *Vertical* | *Culture* | *Wood* | Support |
| Fixed | | *Iron* | for sails |
| Blocked at | | | *Permits movement of ship* |
| base | | | Space |
| | | | Slight oscillation |
| | | | Ship |

| /Pendulum/ $\supset$ F | A | M | P |
|---|---|---|---|
| *Vertical* | *Culture* | *Wood* | Counterweight |
| Mobile | | *Iron* | *Permits movement of hands* |
| Blocked | | | Time |
| at top | | | Sensible oscillation |
| | | | Time-piece |

We can see immediately on which semes the identity may be established and on which the difference may be based. A hasty conjunction in a given Porphyrian tree would give disappointing results: both a mast and a pendulum are handcrafted, both are of wood or iron, or, at the very least, both belong to the class of vertical things. This is just not enough. The only oppositions worth noticing seem to be that between fixity and oscillation, and the fact that the one must be referred to intervals in *space* and the other to intervals in *time*. At a second inspection, we see that even a mast, while staying fixed, must oscillate somewhat, just as a pendulum to oscillate must be fixed at its peg. But this is still not a cognitive acquisition worth nothing. A pendulum fixed at its top end oscillates and measures time, and a mast fixed at its base oscillates and in some way is bound to the dimension of space — which we already knew.

If this metaphor had appeared in a context that dropped it immediately, without taking it any further, it would not constitute an invention worthy of emphasis. In this analysis Weinrich shows that the intertextual framework focuses the interpreter's attention on the theme of oscillation; moreover, within the same context, the insistence on the play of alternation among the seagulls and on the oppositions right/left and east/west establishes an isotopy of tension between two poles. This is the isotopy prevailing at the deepest levels, and not that which is established by the topic 'trip by sea' at the level of discursive structures (see Eco 1979). The reader is led, then, to shift the center of semiosis to the seme of oscillation — which is the primary function of a pendulum and secondary for a mast (the encyclopedia must begin to acknowledge a hierarchy of semes). Moreover, the pendulum's oscillation is functionally adapted to precise measurement, whereas that of a mast is more casual. The pendulum oscillates in an unfaltering, constant manner, without any changes of rhythm, whereas the mast is subject to changes and, at the worst, to fractures. The fact that the mast is functionally adapted to a ship (open to movement within space and to idefinite adventure) and that a pendulum is functionally adapted to being a timepiece, fixed in space and regular in its measurement of time, opens the way to successive oppositions: the certainty of a pendulum against the uncertainty of a mast, the one closed and the other open . . . ; and then, naturally, the relation of the mast (uncertain) to the two contradictory peoples of seagulls . . . ; as can be seen, our reading can go on ad infinitum. By itself, the metaphor is a poor one; set in its context it sustains other metaphors and is by them sustained.

Others have attempted to define the value of a metaphor according to the greater or lesser 'distance' between the properties of the terms brought into focus; it does not seem to me, though, that there is such a rigorous rule. It is the encyclopedic model constructed for the purposes of interpreting a given context that sets *ad hoc* the center and periphery of the relevant semes. There remains the criterion of the greater or lesser openness, that is, of how far a metaphor allows us to travel along the pathways of semiosis and to discover the labyrinths of the encyclopedia. In the course of such traverses, the terms in question are enriched with properties that the encyclopedia did not yet grant them.

These considerations do not yet definitely establish an aesthetic criterion for distinguishing 'beautiful' metaphors from those that are 'ugly'. On that score, even the strict relations between expression and content and between form and substance of expression come into play (in poetry one might speak of musicality, of the possibility of memorizing both contrast and similarity, and thus such elements as rhyme, paronomasia, and assonance enter one's consideration). But these considerations do permit us to distinguish the closed (or scarcely cognitive) metaphor from that which is open, thereby enabling us to know better the possibilities of semiosis or, in other words, precisely of that categorical index of which Tesauro spoke.

### 3.12. Conclusions

No algorithm exists for the metaphor, nor can a metaphor be produced by means of a computer's precise instructions, no matter what the volume of organized information to be fed in. The success of a metaphor is a function of the sociocultural format of the interpreting subjects' encyclopedia. In this perspective, metaphors are produced solely on the basis of a rich cultural framework, on the basis, that is, of a universe of content that is already organized into networks of interpretants, which decide (semiotically) the identities and differences of properties. At the same time, content universe, whose format postulates itself not as rigidly hierarchized but, rather, according to Model Q, alone derives from the metaphorical production and interpretation the opportunity to restructure itself into new nodes of similarity and dissimilarity.

But this situation of unlimited semiosis does not exclude the existence of *first tropes*, of 'new' metaphors, in other words, never before heard of or, at least, experienced as though they were never before heard. The conditions of occurrence for such tropes, which we might term metaphorically 'auroral' (but which in Eco 1975 are defined as instances of *invention*), are multiple:

(a) There always exists a context that is capable of reproposing as new a codified catachresis or dead metaphor. One can imagine a text of the *école du regard* in which, by means of an obsessive description of our perceptual activity, the force and vividness of such an expression as *the neck of the bottle* is rediscovered.

(b) In shifting from one semiotic system to another, a dead metaphor becomes an inventive one anew. Think of Modigliani's female portraits, which, it could be said, *visually* reinvent (but also oblige us to rethink even conceptually and, through various mediations, verbally) an expression such as *neck of a swan*. Investigations of the visual metaphor (see Bonsiepe 1965) have shown how a worn-out expression such as *flexible* (used to indicate openness of mind, lack of prejudice in decision making, sticking-to-the-facts) can reclaim a certain freshness when, instead of being uttered verbally, it is translated visually through the representation of a flexible object.

(c) The context with an aesthetic function always posits its own tropes as 'first': insofar as it obliges one to see them in a new manner and arranges a quantity of correlations between the various levels of the text so as to permit an ever new interpretation of the specific expression (which never functions alone, but which always interacts with some new aspect of the text; see the image of the mast/pendulum in Benjamin). Moreover, it is characteristic of contexts having an aesthetic function to produce *objective correlatives*, which have an extremely 'open' metaphorical function inasmuch as they give one to understand that relations of similarity or of identity may be postulated without the possibility of those relations being further clarified. At this point, one frequently speaks of symbol.

(d) The 'deadest' trope can work 'like new' for the any 'virgin' subject, approaching for the first time the complexity of the semiosis. Both restricted and elaborate codes exist. Imagine a subject who has never heard of comparing a girl to a rose, who ignores the intertextual institutionalizations, and who responds even to the most worn-out metaphors as though discovering for the first time the relations between a woman's face and a flower. The kinds of metaphorical communication may also be explained on the same basis, the cases, namely, in which the 'idiot' subject is incapable of understanding figurative language or perceives its functions in a labored manner, experiencing it only as a bothersome provocation. Situations of the kind also arise in the translating of metaphors from one language to another: there are equal chances of a translation producing puzzling obscurity or limpid intelligibility.

(e) There are privileged cases, finally, in which the subject 'sees' for the first time a rose, notices its freshness, its petals pearled with dew — because previously the rose for him had only been a word or an object espied in the windows of a florist. In such cases the subject reconstructs, so to speak, his own sememe, enriching it with properties, not all verbalized or verbalizable, some interpretable and interpreted by other visual or tactile experiences. In this process various synaesthesic phenomena compete in constituting networks of semiosic relations. These reinvented metaphors are born of the very same reason that one tells one's own symptoms to a doctor in an improper manner (*My chest is burning . . . I feel pins and needles in my arms . . .*). In this way a metaphor is reinvented through ignorance of the lexicon, as well.

And yet, these first tropes themselves arise because every time there is an underlying semiotic network. Vico would remind us that men know how to speak as heroes because they already know how to speak as men. Even the most ingenuous metaphors are made from the detritus of other metaphors — language speaking itself, then — and the line between first and last tropes is very thin, not so much a question of semantics as of the pragmatics of interpretation. At any rate, for too long it has been thought that in order to understand metaphors it is necessary to know the code (or the encyclopedia): the truth is that the metaphor is the tool that permits us to understand the encyclopedia better. This is the type of knowledge that the metaphor stakes out for us.

In order to arrive at this conclusion, we had to give up looking for a synthetic, immediate, blazing definition of the metaphor: substitution, leap, abbreviated simile, analogy. . . . Because the way in which one seems to understand a metaphor is simple, it is easy to be deluded into thinking that the metaphor is capable of being defined by means of a simple category. This simplicity, it must be noted, this felicitousness in making shortcuts within the process of semiosis, is a neurological fact. Semiotically speaking, instead, the process of metaphorical production and interpretation is long and tortuous. It is not at all a given that the explanation of the immediate physiological or psychic processes must be equally immediate. In his collection of classical *Witze*, Freud quotes this aphorism of Lichtenberg: "He marveled that cats should have two slits in their skin, just where their eyes are." And Freud comments: "The stupefaction exhibited here is only apparent; in reality this simplistic observation conceals within it the great problem of teleology in the structure of animals. That the flap of the eyelid should open where the cornea is exposed is not at all obvious, at least not until the history of evolution has made clear for us this coincidence" (1905, 3.1). Behind the 'felicitousness' of natural (physical and psychic) processes, remains hidden a long labor. I have tried here to define *some* of the phases of that labor.

# [4]
# Symbol

What is a symbol? Etymologically speaking, the word σ ύμβολον comes from συμβάλλω, to throw-with, to make something coincide with something else: a symbol was originally an identification mark made up of two halves of a coin or of a medal. Two halves of the same thing, either one standing for the other, both becoming, however, fully effective only when they matched to make up, again, the original whole. In the semiotic dialectics between signifier and signified, expression and content, or name and thing, such a rejoining is always deferred, the first half of the couple being always *interpreted* by our substitution of another first half of another couple, and so on *in infinitum,* so that the initial gap between *signans* and *signatum* grows more and more. On the contrary, in the original concept of symbol, there is the suggestion of a final recomposition. Etymologies, however, do not necessarily tell the truth — or, at least, they tell the truth, in terms of historical, not of structural, semantics. What is frequently appreciated in many so-called symbols is exactly their vagueness, their openness, their fruitful ineffectiveness to express a 'final' meaning, so that with symbols and by symbols one indicates what is always *beyond* one's reach.

Are there in the specialized lexicons more technical definitions of this category and of the corresponding term? Alas. One of the most pathetic moments in the history of philosophical terminology is when the collaborators of the *Dictionnaire de philosophie* of Lalande (1926) gather to discuss the definition of /symbol/. This page of a 'technical' lexicon is pure Ionesco.

After a first definition, according to which a symbol is something representing something else by virtue of an analogical correspondence (for example, the sceptre, symbol of regality — where it is not clear where the analogy lies, because this is a paramount case of metonymic

*continguity*), a second definition is proposed, namely, that symbols concern a continued system of terms, each of which represent an element of
another system. It is a good definition for the Morse code; unfortunately, the following definition speaks of a system of uninterrupted
metaphors, and the Morse code seems hardly definable as a metaphorical
system. At this point, Lalande adds that a symbol is also a "formulary of
orthodoxy" and quotes the *Credo*. A discussion follows: Delacroix insists
on the analogy; Lalande asserts to have received by O. Karmin the proposal of defining as a symbol every conventional representation;
Brunschvicq speaks of an "internal" representational power and mentions the archetypical circular image of the serpent biting its own tail;
van Biéma reminds the party that the fish was the symbol of Christ only
for acronymic reasons; Lalande wonders how a piece of paper can become the symbol for a given amount of gold, while a mathematician
speaks of symbols for the signs of the square root; Delacroix is caught by
the suspicion that there is no relation between the sign for square root
and the fox as a symbol for cunning; someone else distinguishes between intellectual and emotional symbols, and the entry fortunately
stops at this point. The effort of Lalande has not been fruitless; it has
suggested that a symbol can be everything and nothing. What a shame.

There are undoubtedly among all the definitions above some family
resemblances. But family resemblances have a curious property (see, for
instance, Bambrough 1961). Let us consider three concepts $A$, $B$, and $C$
analyzable in terms of component properties $a \ldots g$ (Figure 4.1). It is
clear that every concept possesses some of the properties of the others,
but not all of them. But let us now broaden the series according to the
same criterion (Figure 4.2).

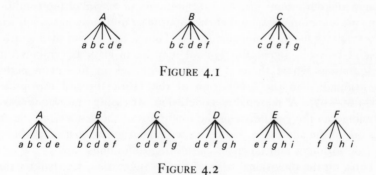

FIGURE 4.1

FIGURE 4.2

At the end no common property will unite $A$ with $F$, but one; they
belong to the same network of family resemblance. . . .

When speaking apropos of the concept of sign, it seems that it is possible to outline a unique definition that can take into account the various

senses attributed to this expression, thus establishing a proper, abstract object for a general semiotics. On the contrary, it seems that, when facing the various occurrences of a term such as symbol, such an univocity is impossible.

*Symbol* is not an expression of everyday language. A word such as *sign* occurs in many ready-made syntagms, and, when one is unable to give a univocal definition of the isolated term, one is still able to give a certain interpretation of these syntagms. It is, on the contrary, the pseudo-everyday language of the press or of literary criticism that says that certain merchandises are the symbol of the productivity of a given country, that Marilyn Monroe was a sex symbol, that the terrorists attempted to assassinate the American ambassador in Rome for symbolic reasons, that a certain word, description, or episode has to be read symbolically. A common speaker would have some difficulty in explaining the 'right' sense of these and of other similar expressions.

In his exhaustive survey of all the possible uses of *symbol*, Firth (1973) remarks that this term is used in the place of *sign* when there is a certain *ineffectuality:* a 'symbolic' gesture does not attempt to get immediate concrete effects. He notices that there is a web of contrasting relationships, from concrete to abstract (fox for cunning), from abstract to concrete (logical symbols), of vague metaphors (darkness for mystery); at its first level a symbol can also be conventional (the keys of Saint Peter for the power of the church), but, as soon as the symbol is considered in transparence, one finds in it new and less conventional meanings (since it is unclear what the gesture of Jesus, when he gives the keys to Peter, means exactly — moreover, why Jesus does give the keys, not materially, but 'symbolically').

At the end of his survey, Firth shows a propensity for a provisional and 'pragmatic' definition: "In the interpretation of a symbol the conditions of its presentation are such that the interpreter ordinarily has much scope for exercising his own judgement. . . . Hence one way of distinguishing broadly between signal and symbol may be to class as symbols those presentations where there is much greater lack of fit — even perhaps intentionally — in the attribution of the fabricator and interpreter" (1973:66 – 67). A reasonable conclusion, stressing the vagueness of meaning and the gap between the intentions of the sender and the conclusions of the addressee. However, we cannot ignore that other theories provide different and far more contrasting definitions.

Thus, on the provisional basis of Firth's suggestion, we shall try three complementary critical moves:

(a) We must first isolate these cases in which /symbol/ is plainly equivalent to «sign» as defined above in chapter one. This first decision is certainly a terminologically biased one. It would not be forbidden to decide that it is better to call symbols what we have called signs, therefore considering signs a subclass of symbols. Why decide that signs will be a genus of which symbols (if any) are a species? There is, however, a reason for our choice: there are many people who call symbols what we call signs, but fewer people who call signs what other people call symbols. It seems, in other words, that, in the couple sign/symbol, only the second term is the *marked* one; if there are theories where *symbol* is unmarked, there are no theories where *sign* is marked).

(b) Provided that *sign* expresses a genus, we shall then isolate many species of it that do not display the properties that, according to Firth, we have tentatively assigned to the symbolic experience.

(c) At this point we shall look for a 'hard core' sense of *symbol*, that is, for a specific semantico-pragmatic phenomenon that we decide to label as *symbolic mode*.

The diagram in Figure 4.3 tries thus to outline the series of semiotic phenomena labeled as symbolic by many theories and that in the following sections (4.1 – 4.3) will be excluded from the rank of symbols. We shall see that many of them can provide polysemous interpretations, but that these interpretations are always controlled by certain rules (be they lexical, rhetorical, and so on). Once having eliminated all these improper senses, we shall be in the position to give a survey of many instances of a properly called symbolic mode (see 4.4) as well as to provide a tentative description of the textual strategies implemented in order to produce interpretations in the symbolic mode (see 4.5).

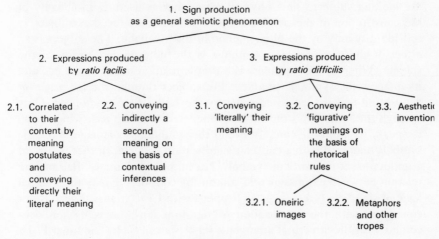

FIGURE 4.3

## 4.1.  Genus and species

There are, first of all, theories that identify the symbolic with semiotic activity in its entirety. In these perspectives symbolic activity is that by which man organizes his own experience into a system of contents conveyed by an expression system. The symbolic is the activity by which experience is not only coordinated but also communicated.

Goux (1973) has shown that such a notion of symbolic activity underlied Marx's theory, thus permitting the dialectic between structures and superstructures (see also Rossi-Landi 1974). Semiotic and symbolic activities are identical in Lévi-Strauss structuralism: culture is an ensemble of "symbolic systems" such as language, marriage rules, economical relationships, art, science, and religion (1950). The possibility of the mutual transformation among structures is permitted by the existence of a more profound symbolic ability of the human mind, which organizes the whole of our experience according to the same modalities.

The symbolic and the semiotic also coincide in Lacan's thought. The registers of the psychoanalytic field are the *imaginary,* the *real,* and the *symbolic.* The imaginary is characterized by the relation between an image and a similar object, but the similarity of which Lacan speaks is not the one of so-called iconic signs; it is a phenomenon that takes place within the very perceptual mechanism. Men experience a mere relationship of similarity (an imaginary one) in the mirror stage, in the erotic dual relationship, in many cases of isomorphism. In "Seminar I" (1953), Lacan considers these images that in catoptrics are called 'real' images, produced by curved mirrors (as opposed to the 'virtual' images of the plane mirrors) and that appear and disappear according to the position of the looking subject. This physical experience is used as an allegory of the constitution of the psychic subject, which is produced as subjective self-identity only by the phenomenon of the symbolic. The subject is an effect of the symbolic; the symbolic is the determining 'order' of the subject. Whereas the imaginary is a simple relation between the ego and its images, the symbolic produces the subject through the language (*la parole*) and realizes its closed order by the Law (the *Nom-du-père*). Only through the symbolic is the subject connected with the real, which is, so to speak, its umbilical cord. In Freud the symbolic is a storage of oneiric symbols endowed with a constant signification (see 4.2.4); that is, Freud attempts to set up a *code* of symbols. Lacan, on the contrary, flattens the relation between expression and content by considering only the internal logic of signifiers (see 1.5.4). As happens with Lévi-Strauss, Lacan is not concerned with the organization of sign-functions; he is, rather, concerned with the structural arrangements of signifiers. In "Seminar I" he says that thinking means to substitute elephants with the word *elephant,* and the sun with a circle. But the sun, insofar as it is designated by a circle, is nothing if this circle is not inserted within a system of other formalizations that, in their entirety, set up the symbolic order. A symbol becomes a signifying entity when it is inserted within a world of symbols (undoubtedly for Lacan the symbolic order is an *s-code*). In this sense Lacan speaks of symbols both for a word as *elephant* and for a visual sign as the sun-circle, even though the symbolic model he is more interested in is undoubtedly the verbal one. Lacan is not so interested in a typology of signs as he is in the general category of symbolic. It is, however, clear that for Lacan the symbolic order is what we can call the semiotic one. It is true that, in his interpretive practice, he introduces elements of what we shall call the symbolic mode. But this happens at the level of the interpretation of oneiric-verbal *texts*. From the point of view of a general definition, Lacan identifies the symbolic with the semiotic in general.

Symbolic and semiotic are the same also for Cassirer (*The Philosophy of Symbolic Forms*, 1923). Science does not mirror the structure of being (considered as the unattainable Kantian thing-in-itself): "The fundamental concepts of each science, the instruments with which it propounds its questions and formulates its solutions, are regarded no longer as passive images of something but as *symbols* created by the intellect itself." (ibid.; Eng. tr. p. 75) Cassirer mentions Hertz and Helmholtz's theory of scientific objects as 'inner fictions' or symbols of outward objects: "These symbols are so constituted that the necessary logical consequences of the image are always images of the necessary natural consequences of the imagined objects" (ibid.). Cassirer does not identify symbols only with those *models* or *diagram* rules by *ratio difficilis* (see 4.2.3 below); his purpose is a wider one. He deals with the Kantian theory of knowledge as if it were a semiotic theory (even though Cassirer's a priori is more similar to a cultural product than to a transcendental structure of human mind): the symbolic activity does not 'name' an already known world, but establishes the very conditions for knowing it. Symbols are not translations of our thought; they are *its organs*:

The logic of things, i.e., of the material concepts and relations on which the structure of a science rests, cannot be separated by the logic of signs. For the sign is no mere accidental cloak of the idea, but its necessary and essential organ. It serves not merely to communicate a complete and given thought content, but is an instrument, by means of which this content develops and fully defines itself. . . . Consequently, all truly strict and exact thought is sustained by the *symbolic* and *semiotics* on which it is based. (Ibid., pp. 85 – 86)

## 4.2.   Expression by *ratio facilis*

### 4.2.1.   Symbols as conventional expressions

Peirce defines an icon as "a sign which refers to the Object that it denotes merely by virtue ot characters of its own," an index as "a sign which refers to the Object that it denotes by virtue of being really affected by that Object," and a symbol as "a sign which refers to the Object that it denotes by virtue of a Law, usually an association of general ideas. . . . It is thus itself a general type" (*C. P.* 2.249).

As such, a symbol is correlated to its Object by an arbitrary and conventional decision. In this sense words are symbols insofar as their lexical content depends on a cultural decision. Since Peirce had decided to use the term *sign* for the *genus generalissimum* of semiotics, he had to decide whether to reserve *symbol* for iconic signs (as Saussure and Hjelmslev did; see 4.3.1) or for the category of arbitrary signs. He made his choice following a rather frequent scientific usage, by which symbols are conventional signs standing for chemical, physical, or mathematical entities. It is true that Peirce knew very well that these scientific symbols display many 'iconic' qualities (as we shall see when speaking in 4.3.1 of expression produced by *ratio difficilis* and conveying a 'literal' meaning), but it is also true that Peirce never identified something as a mere symbol or as a mere icon. In any case, his decision contrasts with the most common terminological usage, and he certainly never thought that symbols convey a vague meaning. On the contrary, he speaks of symbols for those expressions that mean directly and univocally what they are designed to mean.

Curiously enough, many call symbols in the Peircean sense those *stylizations* (such as flags, emblems, astrological and chemical symbols) that Peirce would have recognized as abundantly endowed with iconic qualities. Probably at their very beginning, the alchemical symbol for the Balneum Mariae and the astrological symbol for Lion displayed some more or less evident 'analogy' with their content, but nowadays they function as conventional devices. Emblems, coats of arms, and other heraldic devices do have a second sense: an image represents in first instance a tree, a hill, a city while its heraldic meaning is another one. But they are visual allegories whose meanings — even though multiple and difficult to guess — are already coded. Thus either they are symbols in the Peircean sense or they are 'literal' expressions ruled by *ratio difficilis;* in both cases they must be excluded from the rank of the instances of a symbolic mode.

### 4.2.2.   Symbols as expressions conveying an indirect meaning

The full content of a sign can be actualized only by progressive interpretations. But the notion of interpretation (rooted in the one of inference) is not sufficient to characterize the symbolic mode. It characterizes every semiotic phenomenon at large.

There are, however, many expressions (usually sentences or texts) that suggest, beyond their *prima facie* interpretable 'conventional' or 'lexical' meaning, an additional 'intended meaning' (see Grice 1957). If I tell a lady that I saw her husband at a cozy restaurant with a beautiful girl, I undoubtedly try to convey along with the literal meaning the intended meaning that the lady's husband is unfaithful to her. This second meaning is certainly 'indirect', and, as such, it must be actualized by an inferential labor on the part of the addressee; nevertheless, it is neither vague nor ambiguous.

Todorov (1978), aware of the difficulty of assigning a univocal sense to the term *symbol*, decides to provide a framework within which all its contrasting definitions can find a place, and wants to keep as "plural" what is in fact irreducible to a unique definition. In doing so, however, he accepts the line of thought criticized above; he identifies symbols with the whole gamut of indirect and even of direct meanings: connotations, presuppositions, implications, implicatures, figures of speech, intended meaning, and so on. Once again the symbolic is identified with the semiotic in general, since it is impossible to think of discourses that do not elicit some inferential response.

Many of the devices people call *symbols* have something to do with these phenomena of 'indirect' meaning, but not every device conveying an indirect meaning can be called symbolic. Every semiotic device can be used, if not from the point of view of the sender, at least from the point of view of the interpreter, in order to actualize further meanings.

All these instances of indirect meaning say what they are intended to say on the basis of contextual inferences governed by semantic or pragmatic rules. What the sender intends to express, what he wishes to be understood, is so precise that the sender would be irritated if the addressee did not understand it. On the contrary, the genuine instances of a symbolic mode seem to be those where neither the sender nor the addressee really wants or is able to outline a definite interpretation.

## 4.3. Expressions produced by *ratio difficilis*

### 4.3.1. Symbols as diagrams
Saussure called symbols what Peirce called icons, and Hjelmslev ranked diagrams and games among the 'symbolic systems', meaning by symbolic systems those which are *interpretable* but not *biplanar*. Thus Hjelmslev listed among symbols those signs that are *isomorphic* with their interpretation, such as in

the case of pure games, in the interpretation of which there is an entity of content corresponding to each entity of expression (chesspiece or the like), so that if two planes are tentatively posited the functional net will be entirely the same in both. . . . *Symbol* should be used only for entities that are isomorphic with their interpretation, entities that are depictions or emblems, like Thorvaldsen's Christ as a symbol for compassion, the hammer and the sickle as a symbol for Communism. . . . There seems to be an essential affinity between the interpretable pieces of a game and isomorphic symbols, in that neither permits the further analysis into figures. . . . (1943:113–114)

Saussure and Hjelmslev spoke in fact of signs ruled by *ratio difficilis* (Eco 1976, 3.4.9) where the expression maps, according to preestablished projection rules, some features of the corresponding content. In this sense one can call symbols those used by algebra and formal logic, at least insofar as their syntactic structure is concerned. They are such because every transformation performed upon the syntactical arrangement of the expression mirrors a possible rearrangement in the structure of their content. If, on a geographical map, one alters the borderline between France and Germany, one can forecast what would happen if in a possible world (the new content corresponding to the manipulated expression) the geopolitical definition of both countries were different. An algebraic formula and a map are *diagrams*. That is why in electrotechnics Seinmetz and Kennelly (following Helmholtz) called 'symbolic' the method postulating biunivocal correspondence between the emsemble of sinusoidal functions of the same frequency (which incidentally are expressed by mere conventional and by no means 'analogical' devices) and the ensemble of points upon an Arnauld-Gauss plane of rotating vectors. The rotation of a vector is a diagram that implies different sinusoidal functions.

It is, however, clear that there is a difference between diagrams and other phenomena labeled as symbols. Diagrams are based on precisely coded transformational and projective rules, in the same way in which in a musical score the 'symbolic' relation between rising points on the stave (spatial height) and frequency increments (phonic height) are ruled by a precise proportional criterion. On the contrary, many so-called symbols are characterized by the vagueness of their content and by the fact that the correlation is not precoded but invented at the same moment in which the expression is produced. In Hjelmslev's definition the category of symbols encompasses both phenomena, without acknowledging the radical difference between the way in which the Christ of Thorwaldsen is a symbol for compassion and the way in which a move on the chessboard has a symbolic nature. A different chess move would imply different interpretations of the further course of the game, whereas we do not know how many manipulations the Christ of Thorwaldsen should undertake in order to stand for something other than compassion.

Moreover, a diagram such as the map of a subway is certainly ruled by *ratio difficilis*, but it is neither vague nor indirect: its meaning is a 'literal' one; one can extrapolate from one's operations upon the map a precise possible state of affairs. It could not be said that this possible state of affairs is a sort of 'second' sense that the map conveys. In the same way as one can interpret the word *father* by inferring that if there is a father there should be either a son or a daughter, thus, if one detects on the map that, for reaching the node *C* from the node *A*, one must pass through the node *B*, one can infer that, if *A* and *C* were tied by a direct connection, the *B* would be avoided. In both cases the word and the map tell what they tell as soon as they are correctly interpreted according to given cultural criteria.

Rather different, on the contrary, is the image of the serpent biting its own tail. It is defined as a symbol because there is the strong feeling that it not only represents a snake in an unusual position but that it also aims at communicating something more.

### 4.3.2.  Symbols as tropes

**4.3.2.1.**  *Oneiric symbols.* In *The Interpretation of Dreams* (1899), Freud speaks of oneiric symbols. Dreams convey images which stand for something else, and Freud is interested in establishing how a "latent content" is organized by the oneiric labor into the form of a "manifest content." The latent content is transformed by the dream distortion (ibid., 4), and the dream is the disguised fulfillment of repressed wishes. Freud does not interpret (as the ancient oneiromancy used to do) dreams as organic allegories. Allegories do have a logic, whereas dreams do not. The psychoanalytic interpretation does not work upon organic oneiric discourses but upon fragments and their idiosyncratic mechanisms of substitution. Dreams work through condensation and displacement, and (even though Freud does not say it explicitly), since they do not have a logic, they have a rhetoric. Condensation and displacement are modalities of tropic substitution.

In the dream of the botanical monography (1899, 6a) the botanic symbol *condenses* Gärtner, Flora, the forgotten flowers, the flowers loved by the author's wife, a university exam: "Each of the elements of the dream's content turns out to have been 'overdetermined' — to have been represented in the dream-thoughts many times over" (1899; Eng. tr., 4, p. 283).

Freud knows that the oneiric image is correlated to its content by a sort of *ratio difficilis*, since it displays certain features that in some way map equivalent features of the latent content. But, as happens in all cases of *ratio difficilis*, the mapping relationship takes place between *selected features* of the expression and *selected feature* of the content. To decide which properties have to be selected, that is, which properties are co-textually pertinent, is exactly the typical labor performed by dreams, according to certain requirements of plasticity, immediacy, representability (1899, 6d).

Freud knows that oneiric symbols are not 'stenographic' signs endowed with a preestablished meaning; however, he tries to anchor these expressions to an interpretable content. To find such an anchorage, Freud distinguishes between those oneiric symbols produced by idiosyncratic reasons, which must be interpreted by using the patient's associations as their idiolectal encyclopedia, and those whose symbolism "is not peculiar to dreams, but is characteristic of unconscious ideation, in particular among the people, and it is to be found in folklore, and in popular myths, legends, linguistic idioms, proverbial wisdom, and current jokes" (1899; Eng. tr., 5, p. 351). It is true that every dreamer shows a remarkable plasticity in employing the most disparate images for symbolic purposes, but Freud tries repeatedly (see the various editions of the book, 1909, 1911, 1919) to find out a *symbolic code* so as to explain the intersubjective (or cultural) meaning of umbrellas, sticks, railway travels, staircases, and so on.

To look for an oneiric code means to touch on the hypothesis of a collective unconscious, as Jung will do; but Freud understands that in doing so one risks going backward, to the very sources of human mental activity, where there will no longer be *a code*. On the other hand, a code is indispensable in order to speak intersubjectively of a semantics of dreams beyond the idiosyncratic attitudes of the dreaming subjects. Thus Freud links the decoding of oneiric symbols to verbal puns, and in doing so he suggests that the knowledge of linguistic mechanisms can help one to understand the oneiric strategies of condensation and displacement. (The Lacanian decision to anchor the order of the imaginary to the order of the symbolic must be understood in this sense.) Freud suggests that the code can be reconstructed and that it is neither universal nor innate, but is historical, semiotic, and depends on the cultural encyclopedia of the dreamer.

This assumption is not, however, so unambiguous. The dream must be interpreted according to a linguistic and cultural competence (that is, according to a competence which is external to the world of dreams); nevertheless, every oneiric image can be polysemous, as Freud explicitly says, and must be referred to the idiolect of the dreamer as well as to the whole dream as its co-text. Notwithstanding these perplexities and contradictions, Freud is undoubtedly looking for 'correct' interpretations of dreams, and in this sense his oneiric symbols are not constitutively vague.

Freud has thus elaborated on oneiric rhetoric, with its own rules for generating and for interpreting images.

**4.3.2.2.** *Metaphors and other tropes*. Must we also exclude, from the rank of properly called symbols, metaphors, allegories, and other tropes? This is not to be taken for granted, because in many theories of literary criticism this distinction is not at all clear. However, even though they are 'open' to various interpretations, metaphors are always governed by rhetorical rules and controlled by their co-texts.

In any case, there is a clear-cut test for distinguishing a metaphor from a symbol: a trope cannot be taken 'literally' without violating a pragmatic maxim according to which a discourse is supposed to tell the truth; it must be interpreted as a figure of speech, since otherwise it would appear senseless or blatantly false. On the contrary, the instances of the symbolic mode do suggest a second sense, but could also be taken literally without jeopardizing the communicational intercourse. (I shall elaborate on this point in 4.5.)

More evident is the coded nature of allegories. They can be interpreted according to complementary senses (see in 4.4.3 the medieval theory of the four senses of the Scriptures), but these senses are never vague or indefinite.

A radical difference between symbol and allegory has been definitely established by Romantic theorists, who have, however, dangerously identified the symbolic with the aesthetic.

### 4.3.3. The Romantic symbol as an aesthetic text
Originally, a symbol was produced by the mutual relationship of two pieces of a coin destined to acquire their full purport through their actual or potential rejoining. In other sorts of signs, the *signans* becomes irrelevant at the moment at which its *signatum* is caught (the *signans* is thrown away, so to speak); instead, in the signs that Romantic philosophers and poets called symbols, the *signatum* acquires its full purport only insofar as it is continually compared to the physical presence of its *signans*.

This idea suggests that there should be some resemblances between symbolic activity and the aesthetic function of a language, where the message is self-focusing and speaks mainly of itself or of the relation between *signans* and *signatum*. The aesthetics of Romanticism has particularly insisted on this parenthood between symbolism and art. The work of art is conceived as an absolutely coherent organism where expression and content are inseparable. A work of art is thus an untranslatable and unspeakable message (its 'meaning' cannot be separated from what conveys it), and art is symbolic by definition because its discourse cannot be but undefinable or infinitely definable. Schelling identifies works of art with symbols because they are hypotyposes, self-presentations, and, instead of signifying an artistic idea, they are that idea *in themselves*. There is no 'semantic' interpretation of a work of art.

Schelling distinguishes schemes, where the general provide us with the understanding of the particular, from allegories, where the particular provides us with the knowledge of the general; in the aesthetic symbols, both procedures are at work simultaneously.

In the same line of thought, Goethe says that allegories designate directly, whereas symbols designate indirectly (1797; 1902–12:94). Allegories are transitive, whereas symbols are intransitive. Allegories speak to the intelligence, whereas symbols speak to perception. Allegories are arbitrary and conventional, whereas symbols are immediate and motivated. A symbol is an image which is natural and universally understandable. Allegories employ the particular as an example of the general; symbols embody the general in the particular. Moreover, symbols are polysemous, indefinitely interpretable; they realize the coincidence of the contraries; they express the unexpressible, since their content excedes the capability of our reason:

> Symbolisms transform the experience into an idea, and an idea into an image, so that the idea expressed by the image remains always active and unattainable and, even though expressed in all languages, remains unexpressible. Allegory transforms an experience into a concept and a concept into an image, but so that the concept remains always defined and expressible by the image. (1809–32; 1926, n. 1112–13)

In this sense the aesthetic and the symbolic come to definitely coincide, but they define themselves with each other, in a circular way.

As a matter of fact, Romantic aesthetics does not explain the semiotic strategy by which, in the poetic use of languages, particular meanings are conveyed; it only describes the effect that a work of art can produce. By doing so, Romantic aesthetics flattens the concept of semiosic interpretation (which undoubtedly acquires a particular status in aesthetic texts) into the one of aesthetic enjoyment. On the other hand, semiotics can explain the phenomenon of symbolic mode, but it cannot fully explain the aesthetic enjoyment, which depends on many extrasemiotic elements. In a work of art, the expression is indefinitely interpretable, because the interpreter can continually compare it with its content and with the whole of his encyclopedic competence, but such a *semiosic* interpretation represents only one among the various aspects of aesthetic openness. A work of art can be aesthetically interpreted in many ways, because we compare its meanings (*interpreted* in the semiosic sense) with the individual structure of the token expression that conveys them. By displaying further and further new and uncoded possible relationships between these two planes, the work of art elicits also nonsemiosic reactions, such as synesthesiae, idiosyncratic associations, more and more refined perceptions of the material texture of the conveying expression.

To interpret semiosically means to know better and better the possibilities of the encyclopedia; to interpret aesthetically also means to know more and more *intus et in cute* the details of an individual object. In Hjelmslev's terms, the semiosic interpretation has to do with *forms;* the aesthetic one has to do with *substances.* Thus if one uses the term *symbol* to describe the aesthetic experience, one has then to avoid the same term for other forms of 'symbolic' understanding, as, for instance, those that take place in mystical experience (where the mystic gets something beyond his own visionary experience).

The Romantic tradition is, instead, very ambiguous in this regard. Influential theorists of symbolism such as Creuzer (1810–12) speak of symbols as "epiphanies of the Sacred." The basic ideas of the established religious doctrines spring from symbols that act as a light beam coming from the depths of the Being (ibid., vol. 1, p. 35). However, the same Creuzer says that a Greek sculpture is a plastic symbol, thus showing an oscillation between the idea of symbols as unattainable and transcendent revelations and symbols as the self-evident presence of the artistic value embodied in a physical form. Is the Romantic symbol the instance of an *immanence* or of a *transcendence?*

## 4.4. The symbolic mode

### 4.4.1. The Hegelian symbol

A radical attempt to distinguish the symbolic experience from the aesthetic one was performed by Hegel (1817) in his philosophy of the fine arts.

The Hegelian symbol represents the first stage of artistic creativity (which dialectically progresses from symbolic to classical and to romantic art). "Generally speaking, symbol is some form of external existence immediately present to the senses, which, however, is not accepted for its own worth, as it lies before us in its immediacy, but for the wider and more general significance which it offers to our reflection. We may consequently distinguish between two points of view equally applicable to the term: first, the *significance*, and, second, the mode in which such a significance is *expressed*. The *first* is a conception of the mind, or an object which stands wholly indifferent to any particular content; the *latter* is a form of sensuous existence or a representation of some kind or other" (ibid., vol. 2; Eng. tr. p. 8). In symbols the correlation between signifier (expression) and signified (significance) is not a conventional one (the lion is a symbol for strength because it is strong); nevertheless, the motivation determining the correlation is in some way undetermined. The lion, for example, possesses qualities other than mere strength, and these qualities do not become relevant to the symbolic

purpose. It is exactly this selection or reduction of the relevant qualities
that provides for the ambiguity of symbols. Hegel refuses the idea of
aesthetic symbolism as expressed by Creuzer: "In this sense the gods of
Greece, insofar, that is to say, as the art of Greece was able to represent
them as free, self-subsistent, and unique types of personality, are to be
accepted from no symbolical point of view, but as self-sufficient in their
own persons" (ibid., p. 21). The symbolic mode arises as a form of
pre-art only when men look at natural objects as if they suggest something universal and essential, without a strict and absolute identity between expression and significance. In these first stages of the artistic
activity, when men try to spiritualize nature and to naturalize the universal, fantastic and confused results are produced; symbolic art experiences the inadequacy of its images and reacts to the sentiment of their
limits by deforming them so to realize an excessive and merely quantita-
tive "sublimity."

Hegel outlines carefully these phases of symbolic activity (unconscious
symbolism, symbolism of the sublime, conscious symbolism of the comparative type of art); through which mankind progresses from the symbols of Eastern art and religion to Western fables, parables, and
apologues, to the allegory, the metaphor, the simile and the didactic
poems. What is important, however, in Hegelian perspective, is the re-
fusal to put together the symbolic and the artistic. The symbol always
displays a certain disproportion, a tension, an ambiguity, an analogical
precariousness. In "genuine symbolism," the forms do not signify themselves; rather, they "allude to," hint at a wider meaning. Any symbol is
an enigma, and "the Sphinx stands as a symbol for symbolism itself"
(ibid., p. 83). In primeval symbolism a symbol has a meaning but it is
unable to express it completely. The meaning of a symbol will be fully
expressed only by the comparative mode of art, but at this point one is
witnessing the dialectic "death" of the symbolic mode which transforms
itself into higher and more mature forms of rhetorical expression.
Hegel's whole argument is extraordinarily lucid, at least in distinguishing
the symbolic from the aesthetic at large as well as from the rhetoric.
Hegel helps us in outlining a symbolic mode as a specific semiotic phenomenon in which a given expression is correlated to a *content nebula* (see
Eco 1976, 3.6.10).

### 4.4.2. Archetypes and the Sacred

Jung's theory of symbols as archetypes clearly outlines a notion of the
symbolic mode as characterized by an analogy between expression and
content and by a fundamental *vagueness* of the expressed content.

Jung (1934) opposes the personal unconscious to the collective one,
which represents a deeper, innate layer of human psyche and which has

contents and modes of behavior that are more or less the same everywhere and in all individuals. The contents of the collective unconscious are the archetypes, archaic types, universal images, *representations collectives:* lunar, solar, vegetal, metereological representations, more comprehensible in myths, more evident in dreams and visions. Jung is explicit in saying that these symbols are neither mere signs (he uses the Greek technical word *semeîa*) nor allegories. They are genuine symbols precisely because they are ambiguous, full of half-glimpsed meanings, and in the last resort inexhaustible. They are paradoxical because they are contradictory, just as for the alchemists the spirit was conceived as *senex at iuvenis simul,* an old man and a youth at once. If the archetypes are indescribable and infinitely interpretable, their experience cannot be but amorphous, undetermined, and unarticulated. Symbols are empty and full of meaning at the same time, and in this sense the experience of the mystics, which is strictly concerned with symbolic visions, is a paradoxical one. As also Scholem (1960) remarks apropos of Jewish mysticism, mystical thought lives on a continual threshold between tradition and revolution: on one side the mystic is nourished by the tradition, but on the other side the visions he has can be interpreted so to perturb the traditional truths. Usually the mystic uses old symbols, but fills them up with new senses and, in doing this, always challenges the authority, that is, the thought of the tradition he is supposed to follow and to reinforce. This kind of nihilistic experience is very well illustrated by the story of Brother Klaus von der Flue, mentioned by Jung. Brother Klaus has the vision of a mandala divided into six parts, within its center the "crowned countenance of God." His experience was defined as "terrifying," and the humanist Woelflin (fifteenth century) describes it by saying that "all who came to him were filled with terror at the first glance." Jung remarks that visions such as the mandala are the usual and traditional antidote for chaotic states of mind.

Brother Klaus has to choose between a free interpretation of the symbol and a traditional one. He relies on a devotional booklet by a German mystic and assumes that what he has seen was the image of the Trinity. In this way the mystic 'tamed', so to speak, his unbearable experience:

> This vision, undoubtedly fearful and highly perturbing, which burst like a volcano upon his religious view of the world, without any dogmatic prelude, and without exegetical comment, naturally needed a long labor of assimilation in order to fit it into the total structure of the psyche and thus restore the disturbed psychic balance. Brother Klaus came to terms with his experience on the basis of dogma, then firm as a rock, and the dogma proved his powers of assimilation by turning something horribly alive into the beautiful abstraction of the Trinity idea. But the reconciliation might have taken place on a quite different basis provided by the vision itself and its unearthly

actuality — much to the disadvantage of the Christian conception of God and
no doubt to the still greater disadvantage of Brother Klaus himself, who
would then have become not a saint but a heretic (if not a lunatic). (Jung
1934; Eng. tr., p. 11)

In the mystical experience, symbols must be tamed exactly because
they are exaggeratedly 'open' — and their force must be controlled. It
depends obviously on one's religious and philosophical beliefs to decide
whether this force springs from a Sacred Source, or is nothing other than
the way in which an interpreter, idiosyncratically, fills up the empty
container of the symbolic expression. Firth (1973) observes that the
mystical symbol is a private one; the mystic is the "detonator" of the
symbol, but immediately afterward a public "elaborator," who establishes certain collective and understandable meanings of the original
expression, is needed. In the story of Brother Klaus, both detonator and
elaborator coincided. Firth mentions, in contrast, the case of Saint Margaret Mary Alacoque, who, as detonator, experiences the vision of the
Sacred Heart of Jesus, while her Jesuit confessor interprets and elabo-
rates her symbolic material, providing the Catholic community with a
new cult.

Incidentally, the case of this vision is interesting insofar as the pertinence of the so-called analogous properties is concerned: Saint Margaret
Mary had her vision when both science and common opinion were definitely convinced that, physiologically speaking, the heart was not the
seat of human feelings; nevertheless, in the first half of this century,
Pope Pius XII still spoke of the Sacred Heart as a "natural symbol" of
the Divine Love. A symbol that was 'natural' only for those who, with an
unconscious semiotic sensitivity, identified nature with encyclopedia.
Pius XII knew certainly that the human heart was not the seat of emotions, but he also knew that, according to a nonspecialized competence
(such as is expressed and supported by many ready-made syntagms and
by love songs), it still was considered so. What counts, in the symbolism
of the Sacred Heart, is not the weakness of the analogical correlation but
the vagueness of the correlated content. The content of the expression
/Sacred Heart/ (be it uttered by words or visually represented) is not a
series of theological propositions but an uncontrollable ensemble of mental and affective associations that every believer can project into the cardiac symbol. On the other hand, the symbol is the device by which a
given authority controls these associations, as well as the profound drives
that elicit them — in the same way in which the saint herself had probably projected into the mystical symbol a series of obsessions that, without the symbolic discipline, could have driven her to insanity.

But this is a positivist interpretation of a mystic experience. Usually,

in the symbolic line of thought, symbols are considered as the vehicle of
a transcendent Voice who speaks through them. Such is the perspective
of Ricoeur's hermeneutics (1962). Symbols are opaque because they are
analogic; they are bound to the diversity of languages and cultures, and
their interpretation is always problematic: "There is no myth without
exegesis, no exegesis without confrontation," but, if there are recognizable symbols, there must be a Truth that symbols express, and symbols
are the voices of Being: "The implicit philosophy of any phenomenology
of religion is the renewal of a theory of reminiscence" (1962:22). Ricoeur
knows very well that, along the Freudian line of thought, religious symbols do not speak of the Sacred but of what has been removed; but in his
hermeneutic perspective these two possibilities remain as complementary, and symbols can be interpreted in either way. They tell us about
the unconscious that *we were* and the Sacred that *we ought to become*.
Freud and Heidegger are reread in a Hegelian mood. The eschatology of
human consciousness is a continual creative repetition of its archaeology.
In this way, naturally, nobody can assign to symbols a final truth or a
coded meaning.

### 4.4.3. The symbolic interpretation of the Holy Scriptures

The symbolic mode is a recurrent tendency in many cultures and can
coexist with other ways of producing or interpreting texts. Since it appears in many historical stages, it would be sufficient to isolate some of
its instantiations: one of its characteristics is to reproduce itself in different epochs with the same features, so that a historical survey need not
be exhaustive and can procede through examples.

We can start from one of the most influential instances of the symbolic
mode, the one developed by late Antiquity and the Middle Ages, not
only because it has represented one of the most impressive and long-
lasting cases of the symbolic mind, but also because our civilization is
still dependent in many respects on that historical experience.

Pagan poets believed, more or less, in the gods of which they were
speaking. But, since the century B.C., Theagenes of Regium tried to
read these poets allegorically, and so did the Stoics many centuries afterward. This allegorical reading had secular purposes: it aimed at discovering some 'natural' truths beneath the mythical surface. However,
once this way of reading was outlined, why not turn the method, and its
purposes, the other way around? Thus, while in the first century A.D.
Philo of Alexandria was still attempting a secular intepretation of the Old
Testament, Clement of Alexandria and Origenes attempted the opposite, that is, a nonsecular and, if possible, more mystical reading of religious texts. At the moment in which the newborn Christian theology
dared to speak of God, the Church Fathers realized that, in order to

speak of Him, they could only rely on what He had told them: the Holy Scriptures.

The Holy Scriptures were two, the Old Testament and the New Testament. At that time the Gnostics assumed that only the New Testament was true. Origenes wanted to keep the continuity between the two Testaments, but he had to decide in what way they were saying the same thing, since apparently they were speaking differently. Thus he made the decision of reading them in a parallel way: the Old Testament is the signifier, or the 'letter', of which the New Testament is the signified, or the spirit. At the same time, the New Testament was also speaking of something concerning the Incarnation, salvation, and moral duties. The semiosic process was thus rather complicated: a first book speaking allegorically of the second one, and the second one speaking — sometimes by parables, sometimes directly — of something else. Moreover, in this beautiful case of unlimited semiosis, there was a curious identification between sender, message as signifier or expression, and signified or content and referent, *interpretandum*, and interpretant — a puzzling web of identities and differences that can be hardly represented by a bidimensional diagram such as in Figure 4.4. (For a splendid discussion on these points, see Compagnon 1979).

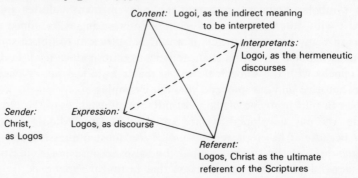

FIGURE 4.4

This semiosic web was encouraged by the ambiguous status of the term *logos*, which is at the same time *verbum mentis* and *verbum vocis*, as well as the name and the nature of the second person of the Trinity. Moreover, the first interpreter of the ancient law was still Christ as *Logos*, and every commentary of the Holy Texts was an *imitatio Christi*, so that in the light of the *Logos* all faithful interpreters can become *Logikoi*. To make the web even more inextricable, Christ, insofar as He was the *Logos*, that is, the knowledge that the Father had of Himself, was the ensemble of all the divine archetypes; therefore he was fundamentally polysemous.

Thus both Testaments speak of their sender and of their own polysemous nature, and their content is the nebula of all the possible archetypes.

What the first exegetes understood was that, at that point, the Scriptures were in the position of saying everything, and everything was too much, for any exegesis looks for a translatable Truth. The Church is the divine institution supposed to explain the truth, to make it understandable, even to the illiterate. The symbolic nature of the Books had thus to be tamed and reduced, in the same way in which the mystic vision of the detonator has to be tamed by its elaborator. The *symbolic* mode had to be transformed into the *allegorical* one. The Scriptures potentially had every possible meaning, but in fact their reading was susceptible to being governed by a code, and the senses of the text had to be reduced to a manageable format. That is why the first Fathers proposed the theory of the allegorical senses. In the beginning the senses were three: literal, moral or psychic, mystic or pneumatic. According to Origenes, the moral sense held also for the unfaithful and was thus immediately dependent on the literal one. Later, the senses became four (literal, allegorical, moral, and anagogical). As Dante explained in the *Epistula XIII* (but the theory is already fully elaborated by Bede in the seventh century), given a verse such as *in exitu Israel de Aegypto,* "if we look at the letter it means the exodus of the sons of Israel from Egypt at the time of Moses; if we look to the allegory it means our redemption through Christ; if we look at the moral sense it means the conversion of the soul from the misery of sin to the state of grace; if we look at the mystical sense it means the departure of the sanctified spirit from the servitude of this corruption to the freedom of eternal glory."

With this further elaboration, the moral sense can be understood only through the mediation of the allegorical one, and is attainable only by the faithful ones. The whole medieval tradition was elaborating upon this theme, which can be summarized through the line of Nicholas of Lyra: *Littera gesta docet, quid credas allegoria, moralis quid agas, quo tendas anagogia.* (But the same formulation appears in many other authors; for an impressive survey of all these theories, see De Lubac 1959.)

The theory of the four senses provided a sort of guarantee for the correct decoding of the Books. But the Patristic and Scholastic mind could never avoid the feeling of the inexhaustible profundity of the Scriptures, frequently compared to a forest or to an ocean. According to Saint Jerome they are an *infinita sensuum sylva* (*Ep.* 64.21) and an *"oceanum mysteriosum Dei, ut sic loquar labyrinthum"* (*In Gen.* 9.1). Origenes speaks of a *"latissima sylva"* (*In Ez.* 4) or of a sea where, if we enter with a small boat, our mind is caught by fear and we are submerged by its whirls (*In Gen.* 9.1).

Gilbert of Stanford tries to show how many senses can be found in the rapids of the divine discourse:

> Scriptura Sacra, morem rapidissimi fluminis tenens, sic humanarum mentium profunda replet, ut semper exundet; sic haurientes satiat, ut inhexausta permaneat. Profluunt ex ea spiritualium sensuum gurgites abundantes, et transeuntibus aliis, alia surgunt: immo, non transeuntibus, quia sapientia immortalis est; sed, emergentibus et decorem suum ostendentibus aliis, alii non deficientibus succedunt sed manentes subsequuntur; ut unusquisque pro modo capacitatis suae in ea reperiat unde se copiose reficiat et aliis unde se fortiter exercent derelinquat. (*In Cant.* 20.225)

Which is to say that, even though the senses of the Scriptures are infinite, none of them annuls the others, each increasingly enriching this immense storage of meanings, where everybody can find what he is able to find according to his interpretive capabilities.

The metaphor of the ocean or of the forest alluded to the symbolic structure of the Books, and this symbolic structure was the continual challenge to their allegorical interpretability. Either the Books had infinite readings (therefore they were ambiguous expression correlated to the content nebula of all possible archetypes) or they had only the four canonical ones. But, if the four senses were coded, there was no further possibility of interpreting the Books, therefore of exploiting their admirable profundity. The problem was how to reconcile these two trends, so that it was possible to read them, continually discovering in their pages, if not new things, at least the same and everlasting truth rephrased in ever new ways: *non nova sed nove*, no new things but the same things increasingly retold in a new way.

The early Christian theology had then to find a way of controlling (by an allegorical code) the free interpretation of the (symbolic and uncoded) nature of the Books. A rather oxymoric situation, indeed. At this point the topological model able to represent this situation should be even more complex (perhaps a Moebius' Ring), since the only authority that could establish the right way of interpreting the Books was the Church, founded upon the Tradition; but the Tradition was represented exactly by the series of the 'good' interpretation of the Holy Scriptures. In other words, the Tradition draws its right to control the interpretation of the Books from the interpretation of the Books. *Quis custodiet custodes?* How can the authority legitimate the interpretation, since the authority itself is legitimated by the interpretation?

This question had no answer; no theory of types or of metalanguage was elaborated to legitimate the circle of hermeneutic legitimation (no theory of hermeneutic legitimation can be indeed legitimate if not by the very process of hermeneutic reading). At the origins of the hermeneutic practice, there is a circle; it does not matter how holy or how vicious.

The only possible answer to this question was a practical one: the rules for good interpretation were provided by the gatekeepers of the orthodoxy, and the gatekeepers of the orthodoxy were the winners (in terms of political and cultural power) of the struggle to impose their own interpretation. Such a rule also holds for a more secular hermeneutics: the text will tell the truth insofar as the reader has the rhetorical power to make it speak. And the reader will be sure to have seen right insofar as he has seen — in the text — his own image. The same, albeit less secular, procedure held for the interpretive practice in the Jewish mysticism: "The literal meaning is preserved, but merely as the gate through which the mystic passes, a gate, however, which he opens up to himself over and over again. The Zohar expresses this attitude of the mystic very succinctly when, in a memorable exegesis of Genesis 12:12., God's words to Abraham, *Lekh lekha*, are taken not only in their literal meaning, 'Get thee out', that is, they are not interpreted as referring only to God's command to Abraham to go out into the world, but are also read with mystical literalness as 'Go to thee', that is, to thine own self" (Scholem 1960; Eng. tr., p. 15). We feel here, preechoed, the Freudian maxim, as reread by Lacan: *Wo Es war, soll Ich werden.*

The whole history of medieval exegesis is the story of the establishing and, at the same time, of the fair challenging of exegetical *auctoritates.* First of all, and from the time of Augustine, it was discovered that, if the Books always tell something Other, they do it not only by the *words* they use but also through the *facts* they tell about. The allegory is not only *in verbis* but also *in factis.* The problem was how to assign an allegorical value to facts, that is, to the furniture of the existing world, to animals, to plants, to stones, to actions, to gestures, and so on. In *De Doctrina Christiana* Augustine decides that, in order to understand the Scriptures, the exegete must know physics, geography, botany, mineralogy. Thus the new Christian civilization accepts and introduces (by further and further reelaborations) into the interpretive circle, that is, into its own growing encyclopedia, all the knowledge of classic civilization, as it was inherited by the late Roman culture, under the form of a syncretistic encyclopedia. This is the origin of the acceptance of the Hellenistic *Physiologus* and of the successive production of herbaries, bestiaries, lapidaries, *Imagines*, and *Specula Mundi.*

The main characteristics of these texts are the following: (a) Since every visible entity has an allegorical meaning, the world creatures are not described according to their empirical properties, but according to those properties that display some analogy with the content they are supposed to represent. So the lion is described as an animal which cancels with its tail the traces of its passage in order to deceive its hunters, simply because he *must* possess this property to function as the image of Christ deleting the traces of human sin by His incarnation. (b) Whether because of the growth of a hallucinatory imagination or because of a symbolic temptation challenging the rights of the allegorical coding, the properties of these creatures are frequently contradictory, so that every item of the medieval encyclopedia can acquire alternative meanings: the lion is at the same time the figure of Christ and the figure of the Devil because of its hideous jaws. How can an interpreter be sure that in a given context the lion stands for Christ and not for the Devil? The allegorical code is open, so as to become a symbolic matrix where the meanings are, if not nebulous, at least manifold. The medieval solution is that a preceding *auctoritas* should have already established the 'good' contextual selections: once again the vicious hermeneutic circle. The medieval interpreter looks continually for good authorities, knowing at the same time that any authority has a wax nose that can be moulded as the interpreter wants. With humble and hypocrital flexibility, the medieval interpreter knows that he is a dwarf in respect to the *auctoritates*, but a dwarf mounted upon the shoulders of giants, and therefore is able to look a little further ahead: perhaps he does not see new things (*nova*), but he sees them in a new way (*nove*).

In this way the allegorical mode is inextricably and ambiguously intertwined with the symbolic one: the medieval mind is a divided one, rent by the conflict between confidence in an indisputable truth (repeated by every word and every fact) and the feeling that words and facts must be continually reinterpreted in order to go further and further, beyond their acknowledged sense, since the whole universe is *quasi liber scriptus digito Dei*, but in this book *aliud dicitur, aliud demonstratur*.

Once again, as in the case of mysticism, the gathering of the community around the ever speaking voices of the Scriptures and of the world, has a function of social control. It does not matter what both the Book and the world say; it matters that they *speak* and that there is a center of elaboration of their speech. When people gather around a flag, it does not matter what exactly the flag symbolically means, since it can have multiple senses; what matters is that the flag undoubtedly *means something to them*. The power consists in possessing the key for the right interpretation or (which is the same) in being acknowledged by the community as the one who possesses the key. Not only in the Middle Ages does every community (be it a church, a country, a political regime, a scientific school) in which the symbolic mode holds need an *auctoritas* (the Pope, the Big Brother, the Master). The *auctoritas* is indispensable when there is not a code; where there is a code — as a system of preestablished rules — there is no need for a central *auctoritas*, and the power is distributed through the nodes of organized competence. Either power eliminates the other one. Civilizations and cultural groups have to make a choice.

The medieval symbolic mode collapses when, with the theology of Aquinas, *a* code wins (the *Summae* are a sort of institutional code; they do not allow for a vague interpretation of the reality and of the Scriptures). Aquinas definitely destroys with cogent argumentations the medieval tendency to the allegorical and symbolic reading of the reality and reserves a strictly coded allegorical reading only for the facts narrated by the Old Testament.

The language of the Scriptures is purely literal: the Old Testament tells us about facts that, insofar as they have been predisposed by God in order to teach us, are to be interpreted allegorically. But these facts are only the facts narrated by the Old Testament. After the Incarnation the possibility of looking at facts as meaning something else no longer exists.

As far as language (be it poetic or scriptural) is concerned, every rhetorical strategy represents an instance of *modus parabolicus,* but this *non supergreditur modum litterale (Quodlibetales* 8.6.16.*ob*1, *ad* 1). This means that, since there are rhetorical rules, tropes and allegories can be interpreted univocally as if they were literal expressions. Rhetoric is a natural language.

If the symbolic mode collapses, for a while, in Western throught, it, however, survives and grows in different directions in other forms of mysticism. A paramount example of a different symbolic mode is the Jewish mysticism of the Kabala, where the Book, which the Christian tradition tried desperately to anchor to a fixed allegorical reading, blows up, so to speak, in a really unlimited semiosis, even losing the linear consistency of its material expressive level.

### 4.4.4. The Kabalistic drift
Scholem (1960) says that Jewish mystics have always tried to project their own thought into the biblical texts; as a matter of fact, every unexpressible reading of a symbolic machinery depends on such a projective attitude. In the reading of the Holy Text according to the symbolic mode, "letters and names are not conventional means of communication. They are far more. Each one of them represents a concentration of energy and expresses a wealth of meaning which cannot be translated, or not fully at least, into human language" (1960; Eng. tr., p. 36). For the Kabalist, the fact that God expresses Himself, even though His utterances are beyond any human insight, is more important than any specific and coded meaning His words can convey.

The *Zohar* says that "in any word shine a thousand lights" (3.202a). The unlimitedness of the sense of a text is due to the free combinations of its signifiers, which in that text are linked together as they are only accidentally but which could be combined differently. In a manuscript of Rabbi Eli-yaku Kohen Ittamari of Smyrna, we read why the scrolls of the Torah, according to Rabbinic law, must be written without vowels and punctuation:

> This is a reference to the state of the Torah as it existed in the sight of God before it was transmitted to the lower spheres. For He had before Him numerous letters that were not printed into words as is the case today, because the actual arrangement of the words would depend on the way in which this lower world conducted itself. . . . The divine purpose will be revealed in the Torah at the coming of the Messiah, who will engulf death forever. . . . For the God will annul the present combination of letters that form the words of our present Torah and will compose the letters into other words, which will form new sentences, speaking of other things. (Scholem 1960; Eng. tr., pp. 74–75)

Thus, when a man utters the words of the Torah, he hever ceases to create spiritual potencies and new lights: "If therefore he spends the whole day reading just this one verse, he attains eternal beatitude, for at all times, indeed, in every moment, the composition [of the inner linguistic elements] changes in accordance with the names that flare up within him at this moment" (ibid., p. 76). Such a disposition to interrogate a text according to a symbolic mode still rules many contemporary hermeneutic practices. They can take two alternative (though profoundly connected at their source) routes. Language can be the place where things come authentically to begin: in Heidegger's hermeneutics the word is not 'sign' (*Zeichen*) but 'to show' (*Zeigen*), and what is shown is the true voice of Being. In such a line of throught, texts can be indefinitely questioned, but they do not speak only of themselves; they reveal something else and something more.

On the other hand, there is a radically secularized hermeneutics where the text is no longer transparent and symptomatic, since it only speaks of its possibility of eliciting a semiosic 'drift'. More than 'auscultate', the text must be (with a more radically Kabalistic option) *deconstructed*, until fracturing its own expressive texture. Thus the text does not speak any longer of its own 'outside'; it does not even speak of itself; it speaks of our own experience in reading (deconstructively) it. There is no more a dialectics of *here* and *there*, of *signans* and *signatum*. Everything happens *here* — and the dialectics takes place, at most, as a *further-and-further* movement, from *signans* to *signans*.

Only in this way, even in epistemological frameworks devoid of a traditional notion of truth, is it possible that the very act of reading provide a certain approach to what a text truly (even though never definitely) says. From this point of view, it is interesting to reread the fascinating discussion that took place between John Searle (unwillingly playing the role of the 'literal' man, who believed that the word *copyright* conventionally means that the excerpt of a given paper cannot be reproduced without permission) and Jacques Derrida who, in a true kabalistic mood, from the unstable combination *copyright* draws infinite inferences on the instability and fragility of Searle's language and on the deconstructibility of every linguistic utterance. Focused as a new and unfaithful Torah, the text of Searle allows Derrida to read in it something else, other than what his adversary believed it to mean, and by and through which he in fact has been meant:

> The questioning initiated by the logic and the graphics of *Sec* does not stop at the security of the code, nor at its concept. I cannot pursue this problem too far, since that would only add new complications to a discussion that is already too slow, overdetermined, and overcoded in all respects. I shall simply observe that this line of questioning is opened in the first of *Sec's* three parts, and to be exact by the following phrase: "The perhaps paradoxical consequence of my here having recourse to iteration and to code: the disruption, in the last analysis, of the authority of the code as a finite system of rules, at the same time, the radical destruction of any context as the protocol of code" (p. 180). The same direction, that of an iterability that can only be what it is in the *impurity* of its self-identity (repetition altering and alteration identifying), is charted by the following propositions: "As far as the internal semiotic context is concerned, the force of the rupture is no less important: by virtue of its essential iterability, a written syntagm can always be detached from the chain in which it is inserted or given without causing it to lose all possibility of functioning, if not all possibility of 'communicating', precisely. One can perhaps come to recognize other possibilities in it by inscribing it or *grafting* it onto other chains. No context can entirely enclose it. Nor any code, the code here being both the possibility and impossibility of writing, of its essential iterability (repetition/alterity)" (p. 182). And: ". . . in so doing [i.e., by the iterability *or* the citationality that it permits] it [the sign] can break with every given context, engendering an infinity of new contexts in a manner which is absolutely illimitable. This does not imply that the mark is valid outside of a context, but on the contrary that there are only contexts without any center or absolute anchoring [*ancrage*]" (pp. 185–6). (Derrida 1977:203–4)

In this ultimate epiphany of the symbolic mode, the text as symbol is no longer read in order to find in it a truth that lies *outside:* the only truth (that is, the old Kabalistic God) is the very play of deconstruction. The ultimate truth is that the text is a mere play of differences and displacements. Rabbi Levi Isaac said that "also the white, the spaces in the scroll of the Torah, consist of letters, only that we are not able to read them as we read black letters. But, in the Messianic Age, God will also reveal to us the white of the Torah, whose letters have become invisible to us, and that is what is meant by the statement about the 'new Torah'" (Scholem 1960; Eng. tr., p. 82). The Lacanian acknowledgment of the autonomy of the symbolic as the chain of the signifiers, by inspiring the new deconstructionist practices, has now allowed the new and atheistic mystics of the godless drift, to rewrite indefinitely, at every new reading, the new Torah.

## 4.5. Semiotics of the symbolic mode

Our quest for the specific symbolic mode is seriously challenged by the deconstructive practice. If in a text everything can be read beyond its conventional (and delusory) meaning, then *every* text is a reserve of symbols. Once again, the symbolic mode is equated with the semiotic one: each human discourse always speaks indirectly. A fascinating but unsatisfactory conclusion. Symbols looked so mysterious, they promised such a privileged way of knowing, and now we are left with two equally irritating alternatives: either every utterance provides for this privileged knowledge (but where everything is privileged, there is no longer a privilege) or language is always symbolic but only a happy few can deal with it as such. It will be then unclear what the others really understand; they probably misunderstand, but why despise them, since misunderstanding is the only way of interpreting? Or is there a difference between 'correct' and 'incorrect' misunderstanding?

There is, however, a fully secularized way of conceiving of the symbolic mode, as limited to specific forms of communication, and it is the one proposed by many modern aesthetic theories springing from the experience of French Symbolism. Even though the cultural roots of artists such as Baudelaire go back to many currents of mystical throught, in the modern aesthetic perspective the artist is a free detonator of a vision that he himself produces: an expression purposefully endowed with vague meanings and that cannot be anchored to a preestablished code (there is no fixed elaboration). The poetic work remains *open*. It is still the Romantic ideal, but definitely dominated by the ideal of poetic ambiguity. It is true that when Baudelaire (in "Correspondances") speaks of Nature as a temple whose living pillars whisper a cryptic speech, so that man wanders among them as in a wood of symbols where colors, perfumes, and sounds echo each other, this picture reminds us of the medieval world as a book written by the hand of God. But Baudelairean symbols (be they albatrosses, cats, or serpents) are *private;* they do not need a *Physiologus* to explain their possible meanings. They acquire their full significance only within their poetic context. It is true that Mallarmé's idea of a context made up by empty and white spaces can recall the rabbinic idea of a scroll where even the white spaces are to be read as letters — but this time there is no God to warrant (and to be named by) the combinatory game: the Book is not conceived by God to speak of Himself; on the contrary, it is the whole world which exists in order to give birth to the Book (*Le Livre*), and the Book only speaks of its infinite combinatorial possibilities.

More radically, the symbolic mode is poetically secularized in Joyce's theory of epiphanies and in Eliot's notion of objective correlative. Here events, gestures, things suddenly appear as a strange, inexplicable, intrusive evidence within a context which is too weak to justify their presence. So they reveal that they are there to reveal something else; it is up to the reader to decide what else.

In this line of thought, *not everything can be a symbol*. A symbol has to be textually produced; it requires a specific semiotic strategy. It is exactly such a strategy that should now be in some way outlined — at least under the form of an abstract model. A symbolic strategy can produce aesthetic enjoyment, but it is first of all semiotic machinery.

Let us start from the normal conversational implicatures as described by Grice (1967). They are instances of indirect signification (see 4.2.2 above), but not necessarily of the symbolic mode: the additional meaning transmitted by an implicature is not a vague one, at least as far as the intentions of the speaker are concerned (it can become vague only because of a lack of cooperation by the hearer).

In a text, the device of flouting the conversational maxims can be used rhetorically. Metaphors, irony, hyperboles violate the maxim of quality, since they do not tell (literally) the truth. If I say that a hero is a lion, literally speaking I lie; my addressee, by recognizing such a blatant case of lying, must infer that I probably intend to say something else. But, since the correct interpretation of the metaphor is that this hero is a courageous or ferocious man, the metaphorical expression does not necessarily convey a content nebula (even though it could). Many metaphors (and all catachreses) can be disambiguated without vagueness.

More interesting are the violations of the maxims of quantity, relation, and manner. Not every rhetorical violation of these maxims produces the symbolic mode: figures such as periphrasis or laconism violate the maxim of quantity without conveying vague meanings, and certain synecdoches and metonymies violate the maxim of manner without referring to nebulous contents.

Nevertheless, we can say that, even though not all the violations of these maxims result in producing the symbolic mode, the symbolic mode springs from certain violations of them and represents a case of *textual implicature*.

Naturally, a text can *narrate* a case of conversational implicature, thus encouraging the interpreter to implement the appropriate inferences. If a narrative text reports a conversation in which the first speaker asks the second one about his love affairs, and the second speaker answers by some meteorological remarks, the reader has to infer that the second speaker was making a conversational implicature, meaning "I am not supposed to tell you about my private life," and, by means of other co-textual inference, some additional information about this character can be extrapolated. But all these inferences follow rhetorical or psychological laws, more or less coded, and rely on preestablished frames. This will not be considered an instance of textual implicature but, rather, a case of mere reported conversational implicature.

On the contrary, when in a Zen story the Master, asked about the meaning of life, answers by raising his stick, the interpreter smells an abnormal implicature, whose interpretant keys lie outside preexisting frames. This gesture means not only that the Master refuses to answer but also that his (gestural) answer has a still uncoded meaning, and maybe more than one. The textual implicature signaling the appearance of the symbolic mode depends on the presentation of a sentence, of a word, of an object, of an action that, according to the precoded narrative or discursive frames, to the acknowledged rhetorical rules, to the most common linguistic usages, *should not* have the relevance it acquires within that context.

The standard reaction to the instantiation of the symbolic mode should be a sort of uneasiness felt by the interpreter when witnessing an inexplicable move on the part of the text, the sentiment that a certain word, sentence, fact, or object should not have been introduced in the discourse or at least not have acquired such an importance. The interpreter feels a *surplus* of signification since he guesses that the maxims of relevance, manner, or quantity have not been violated by chance or by mistake. On the contrary, they are not only flouted, but — so to speak — flouted dramatically.

"By an epiphany [Stephen] meant a sudden spiritual manifestation, whether in the vulgarity of speech or of gesture or in a memorable phase of the mind itself. He believed that it was for the man of letters to record these epiphanies with extreme care, seeing that they themselves are the most *delicate* and *evanescent* of moments" (*Stephen Hero*). In producing most of his epiphanies, Joyce puts them within a co-text that explicitly introduces and stresses their strangeness and their revealing intrusiveness. Other authors — see, for example, the objective correlatives in Eliot — present the irrelevant apparitions without justifying their presence. What signals their role is the fact that they *should not be there*. Incidentally, the feeling that something should not be there is the one that accompanies, in the early theory of textual symbolism, the interpretation of an event, of an object, of a precept in the Holy Scriptures. See how Augustine, in the *Doctrina Christiana*, explains when an expression of the Bible has to be taken figuratively and not literally (naturally, as we have seen in 4.4.3, the problem of Augustine and of the Middle Ages will be to reduce the symbolic power of the expression by interpreting it allegorically):

> To this warning that we must beware not to take figurative or transferred expressions as though they were literal, a further warning must be added lest we wish to take literal expressions as though they were figurative. Therefore a method of determining whether a locution is literal or figurative must be established. And generally this method consists in this: that what-ever appears in the divine Word that does not literally pertain to virtuous behavior or to the truth of faith you must take to be figurative. (3.14; Eng. tr. D. W. Robertson, *On Christian Doctrine* [Indianapolis: Bobbs-Merrill, 1977] p. 87)

The symbolic mode, as theorized by Decadent and contemporary aesthetics has also been, and can also be, implemented in different cultural frameworks. In Gerard de Nerval's *Sylvie,* the narrator, in the first chapter, lives a conflict between his actual love for an actress (seen as an unattainable ideal woman) and the crude everyday reality. A piece of news read by chance plunges him (at the beginning of the second chapter) into a state of half-sleep, in which he recollects the events of an imprecise past — presumably his childhood, in the village of Loisy. The temporal contours of this reverie are blurred and misty: he remembers the apparition of a mysterious and ethereal beauty, Adrienne, destined for the convent.

In the third chapter, when awakening from his state of half-sleep, the narrator compares the image of Adrienne with the actress and is caught by the suspicion that they are the same person, an unreasonable hypothesis, indeed, but he still suspects having overlapped the two images, loving the disappeared girl of his childhood in the shape of the actress of his adult age. Suddenly, he decides to set foot into reality again. Incidentally, at this point the narration abruptly shifts to the present tense; previously it had been carried on by the imperfect (a tense that in French stresses the intemporal vagueness much more than the supposedly equivalent English tenses can do). Returning to the reality, the narrator decides to go back to Loisy, not to see the girl of his dreams, but to see Sylvie, who in the second chapter appeared as the representative of the humble reality as opposed to the enchanted Adrienne. He wonders what time it can be, realizing that he has no watch. He steps back to ask the doorman, and with this concrete information he takes a cab to go back in space and, ideally, in time.

However, between the first question about the right time and his visit to the concierge, the narrative sequence is interrupted by the following description:

> Among all the bric-à-brac splendours which it was cutomary to collect at that period to give local colour to an old apartment, shone the restored brilliance of one of those Renaissance clocks, whose gilded dome surmounted by the figure of Time is supported by caratides in the Medici style, resting in their turn on semi-plunging horses. The historical Diana, with her arm round her stag, is in low relief on the face, where the enamelled numbers of the hours are marked on an inlaid background. The works, excellent no doubt, had not been wound up for two centuries. I had not bought that clock in Touraine to learn the time from it. (Nerval 1853; Eng. tr., pp. 80–81)

What is the narrative function of this description? None. The reader already knows that the narrator had no reliable watch. At the discursive level, this long digression does not add much to the knowledge of the habits of the character. The presence of that clock sounds strange and strangely delays the action. Thus the clock must be there to mean something else.

What it could mean will be inferred throughout the further course of the story. In the fourth chapter, Nerval does not narrate the present trip to Loisy. Just at the end of the third chapter, the author abandons the narrator sitting in the cab and follows his new memories. The narrator muses on another time, different from the one of the second chapter. It is some temporal state between the remote childhood and the time of the narration, an imprecise moment of the narrator's adolescence, which lasts from chapter four until chapter six. At the beginning of the seventh chapter, there is a very short return to the present (time and tense); then the narrator starts a new reverie about a bewitched voyage to the Abbey of Chaalis — where he *believes* he saw Adrienne for a second time. The temporal contours of this experience are absolutely gloomy: was he there before or after the experiences remembered in the previous three chapters? Moreover, did he really meet Adrienne, or was it a hallucination? This chapter is a revealing clue that impels the reader to consider the following, as well as the preceding, chapters in the light of an unsuccessful quest for the things of the past. Nerval is not Proust; he does not come to terms with his past. Sylvie is the story of the failure of memory as well as of the failure of identity: the narrator is unable to distinguish not only the present from the bygone times but also the imaginary from the real. Sylvie, Adrienne, and the actress are three 'actorial' embodiments of the same *actant* — each woman becoming in her turn the instance of a forgotten and lost ideal, as opposed to the crude presence (or absence and death) of the others. The narrator fails to understand which one he really loves and which one he really loved. At this point the reader catches the *possible* symbolic meanings of the Renaissance clock. It was a symbol standing for a nebula of alternative and nevertheless complementary contents, namely, the vagueness of remembrance, the incumbence of the past, the transiency of time, the longing for the remnants of an idealized heroic era — perhaps the clock is the symbol for *Sylvie* as a whole, a story within a story — and so on *in infinitum*. The novel encourages as many interpretations as there are readings. This symbol is *open*; it is, however, *overdetermined* by the co-text. It is *undoubtedly* a symbol, since its interpretation is *doubtful*, and there were only *doubtful* reasons for its textual appearance.

The episode is interpreted as symbolic exactly insofar as it cannot be definitely interpreted. The content of the symbol is a *nebula* of possible interpretations; open to a semiosic displacement from interpretant to interpretant, the symbol has no authorized interpretant. The symbol says that there is something that it could say, but this something cannot be definitely spelled out once and for all; otherwise the symbol would stop saying it. The symbol says clearly only that it is a semiotic machine devised to function according to the symbolic mode.

In this sense, a symbol is different from a metaphor. When facing a metaphor, the interpreter, in discovering that the metaphoric expression does not tell the truth, is obliged to interpret it metaphorically. In the same way, when facing the flouting of a conversational maxim, one is obliged to assume that the expression should express something else.

On the contrary, when meeting an allegory, the interpreter could also decide to interpret it in its literal sense. The fact that, at the beginning of the *Divine Comedy*, Dante is in a gloomy wood can be taken as a report of a literal event, disregarding the possibility of seeing it as the adventure of a human soul lost in the wood of sin.

Both symbol and allegory are signaled, at least, by a feeling of literal waste, by the suspicion that spending such a textual energy for saying *only this*, is pragmatically 'uneconomic'.

The further difference between symbol and allegory stands in this: that the allegory is more insisted upon than the symbol and, furthermore, that the allegory is a piece of extended narrativity, whereas usually a symbol is the sudden apparition of something that disturbs the course of a previous narration. Moreover, an allegory should immediately suggest its own key; it should point toward a portion of encyclopedia which already hosts the right frames for interpreting it (it represents an explicit intertextual reminder), whereas a symbol leaves the interpreter face to face with the uncoded. Thus a symbol cannot send back to a previously coded cultural competence; it is idiolectal because it holds only for the textual environment where it appears (otherwise it is only the 'quotation' of a previously catachresized symbol). In this sense, aesthetic symbols are subtracted from every 'political' control; they *detonate*, but they cannot be *elaborated* from the outside. The aesthetic experience cannot by a mystical one, because it cannot be interpreted and tamed by an external authority. No critical achievement has the force to establish an interpretive tradition; when this happens, the aesthetic symbol has provisionally (perhaps definitely) lost its appeal — it has become something that can be quoted as 'shibboleth' by the members of a critical clique, the 'gesture' of a frozen ritual, the mere mention of a previous symbolic experience. The living symbol is then substituted with a Kitsch label.

## 4.6.  Conclusions

If one then makes an abstraction from any possible underlying metaphysics or mystical assumption, the symbol is not a particular sort of sign, endowed with mysterious qualities, nor is it a particular modality of sign production. It is a *textual modality*, a way of producing and of interpreting the aspects of a text. According to a typology of sign production (see Eco 1976, 3.6) there is an actualization of the symbolic mode when, through a process of *invention*, a textual element which could be interpreted as a mere *imprint*, or a *replica*, or a *stylization* is produced. But it can also be identified, by a sudden process of recognition, as the *projection*, by *ratio difficilis*, of a content nebula.

Put the wheel of a carriage at the door of a country house. It can be the sign for the workshop of a carriage maker (and in this sense it is an *example* of the whole class of object there produced); it can be the sign for a restaurant (thus being a *sample, pars pro toto,* of that rural world of which it announces and promises the culinary delights); it can be the *stylization* of a stylization for the local seat of the Rotary Club. One *can also* decide to recognize it as a manifestation of the symbolic mode: one can focus its circularity as suggesting the ability of proceding ad infinitum, the equal distance of the hub from every point of the circle, the radiant symmetry that links the hub to the rim through its spokes. . . . One can disregard as symbolically irrelevant other properties (namely, its wooden material, its artificial origin, its metonymic link to oxen and horses . . .). Starting from the selected properties, one can discover, in one's encyclopedic competence, that these pertinent properties map the properties of something else, even though this something else is a nebula of many things, let us say, time with its forward progress, the perfect symmetry of God, the creative energy that produces from a unique center the circular perfection of every being, the progression of the divine lightbeams throughout the fall of Neoplatonic emanations. . . . That wheel can send us back to all these properties of all these entities, and in its content nebula it conveys all of them, and all of them can coexist at the same time, irrespective of their mutual contradictoriness. The symbolic mode neither cancels the wheel as a physical presence (all the suggested content seems *to live within the wheel* and *because of the wheel*) nor cancels the *token* wheel as a vehicle of a 'literal' conventionalized meaning. For the profane it could still remain the sign for the carriage maker's workshop. In the same way, the profane only sees a cobbler at work where the Kabalist recognizes in his operation the symbolic action of who "at every stitch of his awl . . . not only joined the upper leather with the sole, but all the upper things with all lower things," drawing at every step "the steam of emanation down from the upper to the lower (so transforming profane action into ritual action), until he himself was transfigured from the earthly Enoch into the transcendent Metatron, who had been the object of his meditation" (Scholem 1960; Eng. tr., p. 132).

The symbolic mode is thus not only a mode of producing a text, but also a mode for interpreting every text — through a pragmatic decision: "I want to interpret this text symbolically." It is a modality of textual *use*.

This pragmatic decision produces at the semantic level a new sign-function, by associating new content — so far as it is possible, undetermined and vague — to expression already correlated to a coded content. The main characteristic of the symbolic mode is that the text, when this mode is not realized interpretively, remains endowed with sense — at its literal or figurative level.

In the mystical experience, the symbolic contents are in some way suggested by a preceding tradition, and the interpreter is convinced (he must be convinced) that they are not cultural unit but *referents*, aspects of an extrasubjective and extracultural reality.

In the modern aesthetic experience, the possible contents are suggested by the co-text and by the intertextual tradition: the interpreter knows that he is not discovering an external truth but that, rather, he makes the encyclopedia work at its best. Modern poetic symbolism is a secularized symbolism where languages speak about their possibilities. In any case, behind every strategy of the symbolic mode, be it religious or aesthetic, there is a legitimating theology, even though it is the atheistic theology of unlimited semiosis or of hermeneutics as deconstruction. A positive way to approach every instance of the symbolic mode would be to ask: which theology legitimates it?

# [5]
# CODE

## 5.1. The rise of a new category

### 5.1.1. A metaphor?

In the second half of this century, semiotics and related disciplines have largely diffused the usage of the term *code*. The meaning of this term seems to have become exaggeratedly generous, covering many semantic areas, at least all those that philosophers of language would label as linguistics competence, a language, a system of rules, world knowledge or encyclopedic competence, a set of pragmatic norms, and so on; as everyone realizes, these areas, albeit frequently overlapping each other, are by no means co-extensive.

The notion of encyclopedia has been proposed in order to explain how signs work according to an inferential model and in what way their meaning can be interpreted as a set of co-textually oriented instructions. If one now compares such a flexible notion with the one of code, such as it has been worked out in the first linguistic, semiotic, anthropological writings of the 1950s and 1960s, one wonders whether these two notions still have something in common.

The idea of encyclopedia attempts to take into account a process of interpretation which takes the form of an inference $(p \supset q)$, whereas codes, according to common opinion, are sets of point-to-point equivalences $(p \equiv q)$.

It would be sufficient to assume that the concept of encyclopedia improves and better articulates the 'old' concept of code, so that it would be advisable to get rid of such an outdated category. However, if it is wise to try new coinages when a concept becomes more elaborate and more comprehensive, it is always imprudent to dispose of the old ones

[164]

without exploring, along with their history, the reasons for which they enjoyed consensus and popularity, as well as their perhaps still undiscovered fruitfulness. We can easily start from the assumption that, as it appeared and as it was so voraciously employed, the expression *code* is a mere metaphor. But as it is shown in Chapter 3, metaphors reveal the underlying structure of an encyclopedia; that is, they show (when interpreted) many 'family resemblances' among different concepts. Thus they should never be discarded as merely 'poetic' devices. To understand *why* they have been coined will reveal *what* they aimed at suggesting. What was suggested is never an idiosyncratic connection; it has something to do with the semantic interconnections provided by a given historical encyclopedia.

### 5.1.2. Dictionaries

Until the second half of this century, *code* was used as dictionaries suggest, that is, in three senses: paleographic, institutional, and correlational.

The *paleographic sense* provides a clue for understanding the other two: the *codex* was in Latin the stock or the stem of a tree from which wooden writing tablets, smeared over with wax, were made; thus the term came to designate parchment or paper books. Thus a code is something which tells something else; it has had to do with communication or signification since its most remote origins.

There is a book and a communicational purpose in *correlational codes:* the Morse code is a *code book* or a *dictionary* which provides a set of correlations between a series or a system of electric signals (written down as dots and dashes) and a series of alphabetic letters. As we shall see, speaking of the difference between ciphers and cloaks, there are codes correlating expressions to expressions and codes correlating expressions to contents.

Also, *institutional codes* are books, insofar as they are a "systematic collection of statutes, a body of laws arranged as to avoid inconsistency and overlapping . . . a set of rules of any subject," and in this sense also "the prevalent morality of a society or class" (*Oxford English Dictionary*). Legal codes, codes of etiquette, chivalric codes, and so on, are systems of instructions.

At first glance, correlational codes seem to obey the equivalence model, whereas institutional codes seem to obey the inferential one. The difference is not, however, so clear-cut. For instance, the Roman Law (as opposed to the Anglo-Saxon Common Law, which is rather a body of examples endowed with instructional or implicative power) looks like a system of correlations: the Italian Codice Penale (penal law code) does not say explicitly that murder is bad and does not forbid it as such but, rather, correlates various forms of homicide with various forms of punishment. On the other hand, the Italian Codice Civile (civil law code) is a set of directions as to how one should act, and at the same time a set of sanctions correlated with violations of the norm.

Our question is, however, the following: did the notion of code, such as it appeared in the structuralistic milieu in the mid-century have something to do with one or more of the notions above? And why?

### 5.2.   The landslide effect

Saussure speaks vaguely (in *Cours de linguistique générale*) of *le code de la langue*. The expression betrays embarrassment: Saussure does not say that a language is a code, but that there is a code of a language. We can say that this first hint remained unexploited until the 1950s. This date has been chosen for several reasons: 1949 is the year of Shannon and Weaver's *Mathematical Theory of Communication;* and 1956 is the year of a book which had been influenced by research in the theory of information, Jakobson and Halle's *Fundamentals of Language.*

After these two scientific events, the code wave crested, and the landslide effect of the new category did not allow enough time to make subtle formal distinctions. Thus one can record such expressions as phonological code, linguistic codes, semantic codes, kinship codes, codes of myths, literary and artistic codes, cultural codes, genetic code, discrete vs. analogical coding, coded vs. uncoded communication, behavioral codes, gestural kinesic, paralinguistic, proxemic, physiognomic, perceptual codes — to give only some prudent examples.

Even though a suspicion of indulgent metaphorization was authorized, it was impossible to avoid the question as to whether this code boom represented a sort of epistemological trend, something similar to the common 'formative will' that, in the domain of arts, Panofsky called *Kunstwollen*. Was the code boom an instance of *Wissenschaftwollen*, the proof of the active, underlying presence in human affairs of the Hegelian *Zeitgeist?* Cultures know such kinds of terminological pollution: a given term, extrapolated from a precise disciplinary framework, quickly becomes a password, a shibboleth, and, not only for cliquish reasons, comes to designate a cultural atmosphere, an era. 'Barocco' was the medieval name of a syllogism and became the *precise* designation of a way of making art and poetry, of thinking, of behaving, of acting politically, of believing in God (as happened also with the term 'mannerism', coming from painter's jargon). In such cases these metaphors have a cognitive power and frequently announce a sudden switch from one scientific paradigm to another, a scientific revolution.

## 5.3.  Codes and communication

I have said that, underlying the three canonical definitions of code (paleographic, correlational, and institutional) there is a communicational purpose. What is rather curious in our story is that, from its very beginning, this purpose is more concealed or alluded to than asserted. As we shall see in 5.4.2, the communicational purpose is implied, by no means focused, in the mathematical theory and in Jakobsonian phonology, and the same happens with the early proposal of Lévi-Strauss. I insist particularly on Lévi-Strauss because the code boom starts, in the French structuralist milieu, with Lévi-Strauss' cultural anthropology, even though Lévi-Strauss elaborated the idea of a code because of his former contacts, through Jakobson, with the information theorists.

*Les structures élémentaires de la parenté* was written in 1947, but there the word *code* only turns up incidentally, never as a technical term (for example, "many contemporary codes" are vaguely mentioned; Lévi-Strauss 1947, 1.1.3). The basic categories of Lévi-Strauss are those of *rule, system,* and *structure.* Even when the same author in 1945 proposed his comparison between linguistics and anthropology (Lévi-Strauss 1945), he spoke of phonological "systems" (not of phonological codes). Code appears as a category only with the analysis of myths in "La geste d'Asdival" (Lévi-Strauss 1958– 59).

In the concluding chapter of *Les structures élémentaires,* an equivalence is posited among rule, communication, and sociality: "Linguists and sociologists not only utilize the same methods, but they apply themselves to the study of the same object. From this point of view, in effect, 'exogamy and language have the same fundamental function: communication with others and the integration of the group'" (1947, ch. 29). Lévi-Strauss, however, is not saying that both kinship and language represent cases of communication; he suggests that society communicates also at the kinship level because there is a more general code (I am interpreting, since the word is not yet used here) which rules kinship, language, architectonic forms, and other phenomena.

The point is: where there is rule and institution, there is society and a deconstructible mechanism. Culture, art, language, manufactured objects are phenomena of collective interactions governed by the same laws. Cultural life is not a spontaneous spiritual creation but, rather, is rule-governed. These rules represent an object of investigation, since they probably are something deeper and more universal than their transitory and superficial instantiations.

As confirmation that the concept of code serves not so much to suggest that everything is language and communication as to establish that every cultural production is rule-governed, there is the first text in which (as far as I know) Lévi-Strauss introduces explicitly the term 'code': his essay "Language and the Analysis of Social Laws" (1951), in which he takes up again the thesis of *Les structures élémentaires*, dwelling in particular on the analogies between kinship and language. Conscious of the daring of his hypothesis, he points out that it is not sufficient to limit investigation to one society alone, or even to many, unless one identifies a level at which a *transition* is possible from one phenomenon to another. Thus the problem is how to devise a 'universal code' capable of expressing the properties common to different phenomena: a code whose use would be legitimated both in the study of an isolated system and in the comparison between systems. The final aim is to find "unconscious similar structures . . . a truly fundamental expression . . . a formal correspondence" (pp. 155 – 63).

Therefore, as in Jakobsonian phonology, the code is not so much a mechanism which allows communication as a mechanism which allows transformations between two systems. It is irrelevant whether these are systems of communication or something else; what matters is that they are systems which communicate *among one another*.

Thus, at its very birth, the idea of code appears wrapped in ambiguity: bound to a pancommunicative hypothesis, it is not a guarantee of communicability but, rather, of structural coherence and of access between different systems. An ambiguity rooted in the twofold meaning of communication: communication as a *transfer* of information between two poles, and as *accessibility* or *passage* between spaces. The two concepts imply one another. Their confusion can be fruitful: maybe there are common rules for two distinct operations and these rules are not ineffable but can be expressed (maybe) by an algorithm. In other words, they are *coded*. Most of the resistance against the notion of code was due to this fear of hyperrationalization as if these code-oriented theories wanted to put human minds into a computer. On the other hand, the popularity of the new category had all the characteristics of an exorcism: it constituted an attempt to force order upon movement, structure upon events, organization upon earth tremors. Speaking of codes meant for many to identify 'scripts' where, previously, only random, blind impulses, unspeakable creativity, dialectic contradictions were recognized. It was perhaps a short 'rationalistic' season; as soon as it was possible, poststructuralism replaced codes with drives, *désirs*, pulsions, drifts.

However, we are not interested in this new instantiation of the eternal struggle between Apollo and Dionysus. Let us, rather, follow the technical history of our concept: the present problem is that the early *avatars* of the notion of code were closer to the semantic field 'rule' than to the semantic field 'communication and/or signification'.

## 5.4.  Codes as s-codes

### 5.4.1.  Codes and information

In the texts of the theoreticians of information, there is a sharp distinction between information, as the statistical measure of the equiprobability of events at the source, and meaning. Shannon (1948) distinguishes the meaning of a message, irrelevant to an information theory, from the measure of information that one can receive when a given message (which can also be a single electrical signal) is selected among a set of equiprobable messages.

*Prima facie* the problem of information theorists seems to be how to encode a message according to a rule of this type:

$$A \rightarrow 00$$
$$B \rightarrow 01$$
$$C \rightarrow 10$$
$$D \rightarrow 11$$

On the contrary, the true concern of the information theorist is not the correlation between signals (as if they were expressions of something) and their *correlated* content. The specific concern of the theory is the most economic way of sending a message so that it does not produce ambiguity. For instance, the problem can be solved by inventing a code that allows for more redundant messages, for example:

$$A \rightarrow 0001$$
$$B \rightarrow 1000$$
$$C \rightarrow 0110$$
$$D \rightarrow 1001$$

It must be clear that the real problem of the theory is the internal *syntax* of the system of 1's and 0's, not the fact that the strings generated by this syntax can be associated to another sequence (for instance of alphabetic letters) so to correlate them (as expressions) to a 'meaning'.

Thus the code of which information theorists speak is a *monoplanar* system, a noncorrelational device, and as such I defined it (Eco 1976) as an *s-code*.

### 5.4.2.  Phonological code

Phonological code is also an s-code. The distinctive features which make up phonemes are elements of a mere system of mutual positions and oppositions, pure paradigm. They make up a structure, in the sense defined by Lalande as "an ensemble of elements, be they material or not, reciprocally dependent on each other, that form an organized system" (1926, "Structure"). A phoneme is distinguished from another by the presence or absence of one or more among the features that form the phonological system. A phonological system is governed by a structural rule, but this rule does not correlate anything to anything else.

It was Saussure who spoke of "code de la langue," but it has undoubtedly been Jakobson who extrapolated from information theory the notion of code, and the like, and extended them to linguistics and semiotics at large. At first glance, Jakobson seems to be responsible for a confusing generalization by which the term *code* indicates both a syntactic system of purely differential units devoid of any meaning and a correlation of two series of elements systematically arranged term to term or string to string, the items of the first standing for the item of the second. As a matter of fact, just when proposing the acceptance of this notion, Jakobson (1961) appeared clearly conscious of this difference: there is a code only when there is an ensemble of forecasted possibilities based on the correlation of a given signifier to a given signified. But "the exceptionally rich repertoire of definitely coded meaningful units (morphemes and words) is made possible through the diaphanous system of their merely differential components devoid of proper meaning (distinctive features, phonemes, and the rules of their combinability). These components are semiotic entities sui generis. The signatum of these entities is bare otherness, namely, a presumably semantic difference between the meaningful units to which it pertains and those which ceteris paribus do not contain the same entity" (1968:15). It would then be more fruitful to call those systems sui generis simply systems, reserving the name code for the correlations between the elements of two different systems. But frequently Jakobson speaks of codes in both cases (see, for instance, Jakobson 1970). The reason is, I think, rooted in the basic concrete attitude that Jakobson (faithful to his phenomenological inspiration) has always showed. The notion of a purely distinctive and differential system is a rather abstract one and could be considered in isolation only from the standpoint of an 'algebraic view' such as that of Hjelmslev. The main object of all of Jakobson's research is, on the contrary, language in action. The *langue* is a theoretical tool useful for explaining why and how *langage* works. Therefore Jakobson cannot think of a phonological system (or of any semiotic analogue of it) as anything other than something designed for signification. People do not invent phonemes in order to utter them without any intention of signifying (nor in order to contemplate the system without using it); a phonological system takes its form in order to compose words (endowed with meanings and therefore ruled by a code in the full sense of the term).

A l'origine du langage phonique ne se trouvent pas des associations d'élements dépourvus de sens qui présentent par la suite un sens ou sont chargés de sens. A l'origine se trouvent bien au contraire des associations de sons qui reçoivent leur forme spécifiquement linguistique précisément en vue d'une fonction de signification et qui ne peuvent être définies sans recours à cette fonction de signification. . . . Un phonème est défini par sa fonction de signe. (Holenstein 1974:96, 202)

Thus, playing on this double sense of code, Jakobson has renounced an emphasis on a sharp methodological distinction in order to preserve the unity of language in action. In many authors who have been inspired by Jakobson, this sense of concreteness has been lost, and there has remained only a sort of imprecise oscillation between two linguistic usages of the word.

### 5.4.3. Semantic s-codes

Structural semantics studies the way in which the content of one or many languages is segmented according to certain criteria of pertinence. In this sense, many of the codes studied by cultural anthropology (kinship, culinary, myths) are semantic structures made up with oppositions such as raw vs. cooked, nature vs. culture, male partner vs. female partner, and so on. The organization of the content of a given culture and the organization of a portion of the content common to many cultures are s-codes. Let us consider the system of kinship and take into account a triple set of properties: (a) generation hierarchy ($G_0$ being the Ego-parameter, $G + 1$ the individual who generated Ego, and $G - 1$ the individual generated by Ego); (b) sex (with the opposition male vs. female); (c) lineage. We shall obtain a matrix that can be further expanded (Figure 5.1). Such a matrix can analyze all the relationships within the system of kinship even though we have no means for expressing certain positions, that is, certain content units made up with combined features of the system.

It happens that English has a linguistic expression for each of the above positions (from 1 to 9, Grandfather, Grandmother, Father, Mother, Brother, Sister, Son, Daughter, and Uncle), but there can be a civilization where for two items from the matrix there is a unique term (by the way, English too is able to designate both positions 7 and 9 by the unique term *sibling*) and a civilization which has either no names, or more names, for one position. Different linguistic codes can correlate different expressions to each of the positions above; however, the system, the s-code of the kinship positions, remains unchanged through different cultures.

At this point, the difference between a language (as a code) and an s-code is clear: a language correlates the units of an s-code taken as the expression plane to the units of another s-code or more taken as the content plane.

A language is a code because it is, in the first instance, a correlational

|                 | 1 | 2 | 3 | 4 | 5 | 6 | 7 | 8 | 9 | et cetera |
|-----------------|---|---|---|---|---|---|---|---|---|-----------|
| **(a) Generation** |   |   |   |   |   |   |   |   |   |           |
| $G+2$           | + | + |   |   |   |   |   |   |   |           |
| $G+1$           |   |   | + | + |   |   |   | + |   |           |
| $G_0$           |   |   |   |   | + | + |   |   |   |           |
| $G-1$           |   |   |   |   |   |   | + | + |   |           |
| $G-2$           |   |   |   |   |   |   |   |   |   |           |
| **(b) Sex**     |   |   |   |   |   |   |   |   |   |           |
| $m$             |   | + |   | + |   | + |   | + |   | +         |
| $f$             |   |   | + |   | + |   | + |   | + |           |
| **(c) Lineage** |   |   |   |   |   |   |   |   |   |           |
| $L_1$           |   | + | + | + | + |   | + | + |   |           |
| $L_2$           |   |   |   |   | + | + |   |   | + |           |
| $L_3$           |   |   |   |   |   |   |   |   |   |           |

FIGURE 5.1

device. Is every correlational device a language? Is a language only a correlational device? What is the difference between correlational and institutional codes? Are there correlational codes which are different from a language? What is the difference between an institutional code and an s-code? Such are the questions which should be answered in the following sections.

## 5.5. Cryptography and natural languages

### 5.5.1. Codes, ciphers, cloaks

The most elementary example of a correlational code is a cryptographic one. In cryptography a code is a set of rules which transcribe a *plaintext* (in theory a conceptual content, in practice a sequence expressed in some semiotic system, be it linguistic or else) into an *encoded message* so that the receiver knowing the transcriptional rule can map backward from the encoded message to the plaintext.

Transcriptions can be realized either by transposition or substitution. *Transposition* does not require specific rules, except a sort of meta-instruction warning that the encoded sequence has to be worked out in order to find again the original order of the expression; typical examples of transposition are anagrams and palindromes. *Substitution* is allowed either by ciphers or by cloaks.

A *cipher* substitutes every minimal element of the plaintext with the element of another set of expressions; for instance, every letter of the Latin alphabet with a number, or with a letter of the Greek alphabet, and so on. Ciphers are clearly working upon the expression-planes of two different semiotic systems. The Morse code is a cipher.

A *cloak* makes entire strings of a given content correspond to the strings or to the units of another semiotic system. A cloak can work from content to content; for example, a cloak establishing that the encoded message /the sun also rises/ means «the D-day will be tomorrow» could work very well even though the expressions were written or spelled out in Chinese or in French. There are, on the other hand, cloaks working from expressions to content: an English dictionary is a cloak of this type (/bachelor/ «unmarried male adult», where the definition could also be expressed in French without changing the correlational rule); a bilingual dictionary makes the expression of a given language correspond to a content expressed in a second language (definition) or to another expression of the same second language taken as absolutely synonymous (if any).

The boundaries between ciphers and cloaks are frequently imprecise. To which category belongs, for instance, the following code invented in 1499 by Thritemius?

$$A \rightarrow \text{In the Heavens}$$
$$B \rightarrow \text{Forever and Ever}$$
$$C \rightarrow \text{World without End}$$
$$D \rightarrow \text{In an Infinity . . . (and so on)}$$

With such a code /bad/ can be translated as «Forever and Ever, In the Heavens, In an Infinity». It represents an expression-to-expression cipher, but it works also if the sentences are translated into another language (as a matter of fact, the original code was in Latin); therefore it seems to permit also an expression-to-content mechanism.

In any case, so far we can say that there is only a category of codes which are blatant instances of pure correlation, that is, ciphers matching an expression to another expression, as the Morse code. We can call these ciphers *substitutional tables*. Being uniquely correlational, they do not imply any interpretation, and they instantiate a case of minimal semiotic level. We shall see, however, in the following section, that, except for the Morse code, certain codes used by secret agents, and alphabets (where a given graphic signs correspond to a given sound), substitutional tables have a very restricted and nearly theoretical domain of usage. Every true code always correlates an expression to a series of contextual instructions and triggers inferential processes (interpretation).

### 5.5.2. From correlation to inference
One can say that even substitutional tables involve some inference. In a minimal cipher, $p$ is equivalent to $q$, but only if $p$ is considered the token

of a type belonging to the expressive plane of a given code α. If by chance the code were β, then *p* would be the token of another expressive type and would represent the expression of a different sign-function (see Eco 1976, 2.1.). Such an introductory choice represents a case of *overcoded abduction*. In the same way, to recognize the written letter /e/ as the equivalent of one sound (or more!) in English implies a certain abductive labor; in Italian the same letter would correspond to a different sound.

Beyond this unavoidable inferential character of any communicational approach, there are cases in which a seemingly correlational cipher is in fact intermingled with inferential instructions. Consider, for instance, the case of a computer receiving instructions in a binary language according to the following cipher α:

| Character | Zone | Numeric |
|-----------|------|---------|
| 0 | 00 | 0000 |
| 1 | 00 | 0001 |
| 2 | 00 | 0010 |
| 3 | 00 | 0011 |
| 4 | 00 | 0100 |
| 5 | 00 | 0101 |
| 6 | 00 | 0110 |
| 7 | 00 | 0111 |
| 8 | 00 | 1000 |
| 9 | 00 | 1001 |

The operator programs instructions in a 'numeric operation code system' that we shall call code β:

$$00 \rightarrow \text{Unconditional Jump}$$
$$01 \rightarrow \text{Read}$$
$$02 \rightarrow \text{Print}$$
$$03 \rightarrow \text{Multiply}$$

Suppose that now the machine must receive the instruction MULTIPLY 03 15 87, that is, multiply the content of the cell 03 by the content of the cell 15 and place the product in cell 87. Assuming that a three-addresses instruction has the format as represented in Figure 5.2, the instruction will be as represented in Figure 5.3 or, in binary digits, as in Figure 5.4.

| digit 1 | digit 2 | digit 3 | digit 4 | digit 5 | digit 6 | digit 7 | digit 8 |
|---------|---------|---------|---------|---------|---------|---------|---------|
| operation code | | address 1 | | address 2 | | address 3 | |

FIGURE 5.2

| 03 | 03 | 15 | 87 |
|----|----|----|----|

FIGURE 5.3

| 000000 | 000011 | 000000 | 000011 | 000001 | 000101 | 01000 | 000111 |
|--------|--------|--------|--------|--------|--------|-------|--------|

FIGURE 5.4

One realizes that both in the first and in the second position of the sequence there are two binary digits that, insofar as they are a numerical manifestation or a series of impulses, appear to be the same semiotic expression. In fact, it is not so. The expression /03/ in the first position must be referred to the operation code and must be read as MULTIPLY, whereas the expression /03/ in the second position must be referred to the address I – code and must be read as CELL 03. Likewise, it is the fact of being respectively in the second and the third position that 'means' that 03 and 15 are the cells whose content must be multiplied by each other, whereas being in the fourth position means that the corresponding cell is the one where the product must be placed. So it is the position which establishes of which sign-function a given numerical manifestation is the expression. In this sense, we are witnessing here three different levels of conventions: (a) a cipher $\alpha$ which correlates every decimal expression to a binary one, (b) a cloak $\beta$ which correlates numeric expressions to operations to be performed, and (c) a cloak $\gamma$ which correlates a different address to each position in the sequence.

Such a language, composed of many simple correlational codes, is no more based upon mere equivalences. Its way of functioning is as follows: if — according to $\gamma$ — the digit $x$ is found in the position $a$, then the equivalence system is $\beta_1$, but if it is found in the position $b$, then the quivalence system is $\beta_2$, and so on. Such a complex code implies *contextual selections* (see Eco 1976, 2.11). Let us disregard the objection that the machine does not make inferences; we are not interested in the 'psychology' of the machine but, rather, in the semiotics of the code — a code that, theoretically speaking, could also be 'spoken' by human beings and that undoubtedly complicated the equivalence model with the inferential one.

### 5.5.3. Codes and grammars

Let us consider now a code clearly conceivable for human beings but not structurally dissimilar to the previous one. Let us invent a way of label-

ing the books of a library in order to find them with a certain ease and to
know in advance where they can be found.

Let us suppose that every book is designated by four numeric expressions based on positional or vectorial rules (for *vectors* as modes of
sign production, see Eco 1976, 3.6). From left to right, every position in
the linear manifestation of the encoded message has a different meaning, according to the conventions as shown in Figure 5.5. Therefore, the
expression /1.2.5.33/ will mean the thirty-third book on the fifth shelf of
the second wall of the first room. According to Eco (1976, 3.4.9) this
mode of sign production is ruled by *ratio difficilis,* and the form of the
expression maps (or is determined by) the spatial organization of the
content. Such a code has a lexicon (a semantics) as well as positional
values (a syntax) and works, at a very primitive level, as a grammar.

| Positions in the linear manifestation of the encoded message | System of architectural positions | Reciprocal positions of each element of the system of architectural positions |
|---|---|---|
| Leftmost position | room | 1 = first room at left immediately after main door<br>2 = second room . . . and so on |
| Center-left position | wall | 1 = first wall at left when entering room<br>2 = second wall . . . and so on |
| Center-right position | shelf | 1 = first shelf from floor, and so on, upward |
| Rightmost position | book | 1 = first leftmost book on shelf, and so on, rightward |

FIGURE 5.5

It is 'a language' because, with it, it is possible to generate infinite
messages. One can conceive of the expression
/3,000.15,000.10,000.4,000/ which means: «the four thousandth book of
the ten thousandth shelf of the fifteen thousandth wall of the three
thousandth room». The only problem would be whether or not such a
description has a referent in some possible world. There are no fictional
difficulties in imagining a Borges-like library with thousands and
thousands of enormous rooms, each structured as a bugeye megahedron
with thousands and thousands of walls hosting billions of shelves, the
whole construction free from gravitational laws. Whether such a universe
exists or not is a metaphysical problem; whether it can physically exist or
not is a cosmological question; whether our imagination can conceive of
it or not is an interesting psychological puzzle; what matters for the pre-

sent purposes is that the structural logic of this code permits descriptions of this type. This code can only generate true or false sentences (such as *there is a book so and so in a place so and so*) and could hardly generate texts, except in a 'me-Tarzan-you-Jane-jargon'. It provides a grammar for a very primitive holophrastic language, but it does not seem so handicapped as compared with more respectable formal grammars. Our library-language not only is a system of correlation, it also involves inferential movements and provides sets of instruction.

It has been repeatedly said that a natural language is not a code because it not only correlates expressions with contents but it also provides discursive rules. Cherry remarked that "we distinguish sharply between *language*, which is developed organically over a long period of time, and *codes*, which are invented for some specific purposes and follow explicit rules" (1957:7). If the difference is only in terms of historical growth, it is uninteresting for our present purposes. If the complexity of historical growth implies a greater organicity and flexibility, there is indeed a difference, let us say, between English and the library-code above. But the difference lies in the complexity of inferential instructions displayed by the English language in comparison with the library-code, in the maze-like effect produced by this complexity, and in the fact that English changes faster than the library-code (a difference that could be eliminated if we decide to complicate the library-code day by day). However, from the point of view of their elementary logic, both codes display the same mechanism, where equivalences are complicated by instructions and where the principle of interpretability holds for both. Even the library-code can elicit many interpretations of its expression, except that, being rather stiff, it allows interpretations only through other semiotic systems and is not self-interpretable as a natural language. This is by no means a minor difference, but here we are not looking for differences (which are, besides, rather intuitive); we are looking for basic identities.

## 5.6.  S-codes and signification

### 5.6.1.  S-codes cannot lie

So far we have understood why the notion of code was used to designate many and variously complex systems of semiotic conventions. But, as we have seen, there was also a general tendency to consider s-codes and codes as fundamentally similar. What we must now do is to ascertain in what sense this apparent confusion took place and why. Codes as semiotic constructions can be used to produce propositions designating or mentioning states of the world. Therefore, with codes true or false, assertions can be generated.

This does not hold for syntactic systems or s-codes. With systems one cannot lie. Provided arithmetic is a system, one who says that $2 + 2$ makes 5 does not lie; it is simply *wrong*, and one is wrong because one does not obey the tautological laws of the system. Obviously, there can be a teacher cheating his students and communicating to them false notions about basic arithmetical operations; but this is not a case of lying *with* arithmetic, it is an instance of lying *about* arithmetic by using a verbal or graphic language. This teacher in fact lies about the arithmetic we are used to recognizing as the true one in our 'real' world, but is building up an alternative system, no matter how internally coherent it may be.

In the same vein, one who says that fatherhood in the kinship system is expressed by the position $G + 1, f, L_1$ is wrong. If, on the contrary, one says that the English word /father/ corresponds to that kinship position, one lies *about* the English code.

One can lie by using the verbal or graphic *names* of the numbers (as when one says that there are three apples on the table when in fact there are four). But numbers as names are not numbers as elements of a mathematical system: the former can be used to mention quantities that are not the case; the latter only allows for tautological assertions.

Nevertheless, s-codes, even though they do not permit acts of reference or descriptions of possible situations but only tautological operations, can produce strings of expressions that, by virtue of the internal logic of the system, make one expect a further course of systematic events. In other words, there is a sort of elementary signifying power in an s-code, since the sequence $5,10,15$ makes one expect $20$ as the following event.

This leads us to the problem of the signifying power of monoplanar systems (see, against this point, Hjelmslev 1943:111 – 14; and, for the opposite view, Eco 1976, 2.9.2). A monopolanar system can produce signification, not insofar as it provides correlations, but insofar as it permits or elicits interpretations.

A given position on the chessboard can be right or wrong in respect to the further course of the game (the game aiming at creating, inside the system of chess positions, cases of incompatibility and compatibility). But a given position upon a given (token) chessboard not only becomes the expression whose content is the type position on a type of chessboard (case of sheer monoplanarity); it also becomes the expression whose content is the set of possible forecasting and therefore of acceptable instructions as to how go on in the game.

Thus systems and codes are different, but codes host institutional and instructional elements, and systems display the possibility of a correlational use of their elements, since a given syntactical event 'means' (or can be correlated to) one or more further events — and there are handbooks recording the most plausible (or correct) among the possible correlations.

In 1919, speaking of futurism, cubism, and nonrepresentational painting, Jakobson substantially anticipates (without making recourse to
semiotic terminology) what is better defined in *Coup d'oeil sur le
développement de la sémiotique* (1974), that is, the function of internal and
mutual *referral*, or *renvoi*, performed by all the elements of a purely syntactic sequence: "Significance underlies all the manifestations of the 'artifice'" (1980:25). In 1932, speaking of musicology and linguistics,
Jakobson assigns the musical sounds to the kingdom of signs by a sort of
Husserlian definition: the elements of music are not simple sounds
(sonic substances) but count insofar as they are the goal of an *intentional*
act. Sounds in music work as elements of a system and acquire a value
according to specific criteria of pertinence: a primitive who makes pertinent timbre instead of pitch perceives as the same melody what a
European feels as two different melodies played on two different instruments. In this essay (Jakobson 1932), the phonological concept of
opposition is presented as a capital tool for the study of musical systems.
It is from this essay, as well as from the investigations of the phonemic
entities (Jakobson 1949), that a quarter of century later there springs the
first significant interests in a linguistics approach to music.

For this reason Jakobson, even though admitting that there are purely
syntactic systems such as chess (what Hjelmslev called *symbolic* systems,
as opposed to the semiotic ones), immediately tries to find within them
the possibility of an internal signification, or "the referral of a semiotic
fact to an equivalent fact inside the same context. . . . The musical
referral which leads us from the present tone to the anticipated or remembered tone is replaced in abstract painting by a reciprocal referral of
the factors in question" (1980:23 – 25). When there is, as in music, a
language signifying itself, "diversely built and ranked parallelisms of
structure enable the interpreter of any immediately perceived musical
signals to infer and anticipate a further corresponding constituent (e.g.,
series) and the coherent ensemble of these constituents. . . . The code
of recognized equivalences between parts and their correlation with the
whole is to a great degree a learned, imputed set of parallelisms which
are accepted as such in the framework of a given epoch, culture, or
musical school" (1968:12).

### 5.6.2. S-codes and institutional codes

From this point of view, there is a difference between tautological
s-codes (the system of numbers, the phonological code, and so on) and
those s-codes that we have called institutional codes. Institutional codes
(such as a body of laws) are s-codes, but of a specific kind. They do not
follow an *aletic* logic but a *deontic* one, or a logic of preference.

Given the numerical sequence *5,10,15,* the expected result is *20* if the
sequence is a simple progression, *30* if its members are the addenda of

an addition, 750 if its members are the multiplicands of a multiplication, and so on. Once the 'topic' (so to speak) of the series has been found, its expected further course will be as it *must* be.

Our expectations elicited by a given musical course, by the move of a chess game, and by the display of a given narrative function in the course of a fairy tale are of a different sort: they are open to failure. They can be more or less plausible but never mathematically sure.

Institutional codes as deontic system certainly imply a sort of calculus, but different from a logico-mathematical one. A system of behavioral instructions, such as a moral or etiquette code, involves acceptations and rejections, considers the possibility of violations, introduces imperatives, law reinforcements, and concessions, is open to *possibility*; it is a calculus of a modal order.

In this sense, institutional codes such as the Italian Codice Civile (see 5.1.2 above), which seemed to display certain correlational features, display a further difference even in comparison with strictly correlational codes. If we assume that a lexicon is a correlational code matching expressions with definitions, so that *definiens* and *definiendum* are absolutely reciprocable (but we have seen in chapter one of this book that such a conception betrays the very nature of linguistic signs), then the Penal Code does not provide *definientia* reciprocable with the *definienda*. When paragraph 580 prescribes that whoever leads someone to commit suicide deserves from one to five years of prison, this does not entail that whoever deserves from one to five years has led someone to commit suicide. The reason is not that such a code is a correlational one endowed with many synonymous expressions (of which a certain penalty is the constant 'meaning'); it is that in such a code there is not a correlation between crime and punishment, but between a given crime and a given set of instructions. These instructions are open to circumstantial and contextual choices (the judge must evaluate whether the culprit deserves one or more years), but what is more relevant is that giving instructions means to prescribe the obligation (or the suggestion) to perform something. As in other s-codes, if the judge does not respect the dictatum of the Penal Code, one does not say that he is lying but that be behaves improperly.

Nevertheless, institutional codes can be used in order to produce signification and to communicate something to somebody else. Let us consider four examples:

A. Given a certain institutional code, my obedience to its rules stands for my decision to appear faithful to the institution. Let us suppose that I wish to pretend to be a Knight of the Holy Grail. I could do this by setting up an appropriate coat of arms (but in this case I lie by using an emblem-code) or by rescuing an unprotected virgin, even though I am not usually eager to defend the oppressed. The possibility of lying with the s-code is due to the fact that the rules of the chivalric code are not mandatory but are proairetic, based on a logic or preference, and consequently allow for their own rejection. Since the rules of chivalry are not obligatory for all, by following at least one of them I make believe that I accept them all. The noncompulsoriness of the acceptance of an s-code makes the acceptance of some of its instructions significant.

B. Let us now suppose that, in telephoning John in the presence of Charles, I want Charles to think that John asked me a question. I therefore utter the statement *No, I do not think so* or *Certainly, I'll do it*. In cheating Charles I refer to a conversational rule that he too shares, namely, that usually answers are reponses to questions, so that an answer is the sign (in the sense of the Stoic *sēmeîon*) that there was a previous question. By the consequent I have artificially and falsely produced, Charles is led to think of the most presumable antecedent. I am using in this case Charles' presupposition that conversational rules are strictly normative for everybody, in order to make the consequents significant of the antecedents. In the case A I *pretend* to accept a system of nonobligatory rules (but a constrictive system once one has accepted it), and, in order to pretend, I observe one of its rules; in the case B I presuppose that everybody is bound to a system of quasi-obligatory rules and I pretend to observe one of them (while in fact I violate it). Case A is an example of lying *about* the rules, whereas case B is an example of lying *with* the rules.

C. One can also lie by using improperly the modalities of a literary genre (which is an institutional system): one can begin a poem in an epic style and then betray the reader's expectation by a sudden anticlimax, shifting thus from heroic to grotesque. One can put into play, in a fairy tale, an actor who apparently covers the position of the Helper and then reveals that he was the Adversary. One can supply a hero with the characteristics of the villain (hardboiled novel) or the villain with the characteristics of the hero (gothic novel). All C cases will be mixtures of A and B because, on the one hand, the noncompulsoriness of the rule permits one to pretend to accept it; on the other hand, the restrictiveness of the rules (once the genre has been blatantly selected) permits one to make the violation significant.

D. Besides all these cases of malicious or artistic lie, I can also make significant the blatant violation of the rules. I do not observe the rules of chivalric etiquette in order to make clear not only that I am not a knight but also that I do not recognize the validity of these rules. I do not shake hands with a person I despise, in a situation in which the good manners would make it compulsory, to signify that this person is outside the realm of civil greeting.

This is how institutional s-codes can act as correlational codes.

So far, in our examination of the internal logic of both correlational and institutional codes, we have ascertained the difficulty of clearly separating equivalences from inferences. It seems as if there were neither pure correlational codes nor pure institutional codes — except the rare and blatant cases of transciption tables, such as the Morse code and the most elementary ciphers equating expression with expression. In every other case, we have met an inextricable web of pseudocorrelations that involve instructions and inferences on one hand and, on the other hand, sets of instructions that can generate relationships of signification and processes of communication. We can say that, every time the word *code* has been pronounced in the semiotic milieu to indicate both s-codes and semiotic codes, it was this 'strong' sense of the term which was really in play.

To find perhaps more reason to justify this attitude, we should now consider a case where the term *code* seems to have been used in a naive metaphorical way, as referred to a process or to a series of processes that by no means can be called 'communicative', since they represent cases of sheer physical stimulation.

## 5.7.  The genetic code

Signs always request an interpretation. Stimuli, on the contrary, produce or elicit a blind reaction (see Eco 1976, 0.7.1). However, the expression *genetic code* has been largely used in the biological milieu, since the discoveries of Crick and Watson (in the 1950s) and at the time when Jacob and Monod discovered the transcriptional process from DNA to RNA, in 1961.

Obviously, we should first distinguish between what happens in the cell and the metalanguage used by a scientist in order to describe it. The equivalences reproduced below, insofar as they are used by a scientist in order to know or to say what happens when RNA reproduces the message conveyed by DNA, sound like ciphers. In this sense, we could speak of a genetic code only apropos of the metagenetic device used by geneticists when they speak to each other about genetic phenomena. But once again one is compelled to ask why that 'metaphor' and not another one has been so successfully used.

As is known, proteins are defined by a sequence of amino acid residues in the polypeptide, and this sequence is determined by a sequence of nucleotides in a fragment of DNA. Since the fragment of DNA is in the cell while the protein synthesis takes place in the ribosome, then the information conveyed by DNA must be brought to the ribosome, and this transfer requires a series of 'translations'. Thus the message of DNA is translated in terms of messenger-RNA, this one in terms of transfer-RNA, where special enzymes catalyze the covalent association of the amino acid with the RNA molecule. 'Translation' and 'transcription' are metaphors; as a matter of fact, the elements in play are coupled together because of a *stereochemical complementarity*, for the same reasons (so to speak) for which a given key fits a given keyhole.

In any case, in order to show which keys fits which keyhole, one can express this phenomenon by a sort of cipher. The nucleotides of DNA being adenine, guanine, cytosine, and thymine (A, G, C, T), whereas in the messenger RNA thymine is substituted by uracil (U), the code ruling the transcription from DNA to messenger-RNA can be expressed as follows:

$$A \rightarrow U$$
$$T \rightarrow A$$
$$G \rightarrow C$$
$$C \rightarrow G$$

In order to determine an amino acid, a triplet of nucleotides is needed; four nucleotides being in the position of producing 64 three-letter 'words', and the amino acid residues to be specified being only 20, then many different triplets can specify the same amino acid residue (thus realizing a sort of synonymy). Certain triplets, which do not designate any amino acid, play the role of punctuation signals to establish the beginning and the end of a given sequence of nucleotides.

We have now a second code, where the expression (for the sake of simplicity) is written in the 'language' of the messenger-RNA and where the corresponding 'content' (or result) is the amino acid residues:

| GCU | GCC | GCA | GCG | | | $\rightarrow$ | Alanyl |
| GCU | CGC | CGA | CGG | AGA | AGG | $\rightarrow$ | Arginyl |
| AUU | AAC | | | | | $\rightarrow$ | Asparagyl |

(and so on)

As it is written, this code looks like a system of equivalences (though between a unique content and synonymous expressions). But since the transcription takes place through a process of steric stimuli, one could describe the process as an instructional one. The protagonists of the whole process 'know' (by a sort of blind material wisdom) that, *if* a given series of stimuli is provided, *then* a given insertion must be performed.

Prodi (1977) maintains that such a basic phenomenon represents an elementary, but by no means metaphorical, example of *interpretation* in Peirce's sense. Every element in the process interprets a previous one and, in doing so, makes the process grow. A case of semiosis, even though not unlimited.

Thus the genetic code (but this time we can speak of the one of the organism, not only of the one of geneticists) seems to be an s-code made up with minor s-codes, in which every element is definable in terms of its (steric) position and opposition to other elements, but also a code in the strong sense of the term, both correlational and institutional, where not only *x* correponds to *y*, but where also *if x then y* must be realized. More similar to a mathematical system than to a judicial deontic code, ruled by necessity, susceptible obviously to errors (mutations, cancer), but not optional.

The fruitfulness of the genetic metaphor is not due to the fact that it can say whether the genetic processes are semiotic or not. What the metaphor reveals is that, even at the elementary level of these biological phenomena, there is no sensible difference (a) between s-codes and codes and (b) between correlation and instruction — that is, there is no sensible difference between equivalence and inference, each equivalence being a quasi-automatic inference.

Maybe it is too hard to assume (as Prodi suggests; see 1983) that the bio-logic represents the model, the source, and the materialistic foundation of the 'cultural' logic, and therefore of every semiotics. It is certain, however, that when studying both bio-logic and conceptual logic we are in trouble when we try to distinguish correlation from instruction, s-codes from codes. Or, to put it in more reasonable terms, we can outline theoretical distinctions, by elaborating different abstract models, but we are obliged to recognize that in the actual semiosis these models are instantiated all together at the same time. Which explains (even though maybe it does not completely legitimate) the 'generous' use of *code* made by so many disciplines in the last decades.

Undoubtedly, the notion of encyclopedia is more flexible and describes better than the one of code the kind of competence needed to express and to interpret texts in a natural (not necessarily verbal) language. But, from the point of view of their internal structures, codes and encyclopedias are not radically different. Both are complex networks of complex pseudo-equivalences and of more or less cogent and constrictive instructions. The notion of encyclopedia may differ from the one of code insofar as it also comprehends, among other instructions, systems of *frames* and *scripts*. But, structurally speaking, a code in the strong sense of the term does not exclude this kind of instruction. Institutional codes do exactly this.

## 5.8. Toward a provisional conclusion

We are now in a position to disentangle a lot of apparent inconsistencies and contradictions in the current literature on codes. Many of the usages that looked rather metaphorical, self-contradictory even within the same theoretical framework, can now reveal a more profound coherence.

In *The Raw and the Cooked* (1964) Lévi-Strauss gives the impression of speaking both of s-codes and of correlational codes. For instance, he says that he is interested in "the system of axioms and postulates defining the best possible code, capable of conferring a common significance on unconscious formulations which are the work of minds, societies, and civilizations chosen from among those most remote from each other" and that "as the myths themselves are based on secondary codes (the primary codes being those that provide the substance of language)" his book "is put forward as a tentative draft of a tertiary code, which is intended to ensure the reciprocal translatability of several myths" (1964; Eng. tr., p. 12). Here he clearly means an s-code as a system of transformations. He is pursuing the same project later outlined in *The Naked Man:* the mistake of other mythologists was

> to try to understand the myths by means of a single and exclusive code, when in fact several codes are always in operation simultaneously. It is impossible to reduce the myth to any one code, nor can it be explained as the sum of several codes. It would be truer to say that a group of myths constitutes in itself a code, the power of which is superior to each individual code it uses to decipher manifold messages. It is tantamount to an 'intercode' — if I may be pardoned the neologism — which makes possible the reciprocal conversion of messages in accordance with rules, the range of which remains immanent in the different systems which, through its operation, allow the emergence of an overall significance distinct from their particular meanings. (1971; Eng. tr., pp. 44–45)

But, as is clear from this last quotation, even in the machineries of such an intercode, significations emerge — in the sense in which I have demonstrated that also institutional codes, being in themselves s-codes, permit the recognition of an immanent strategy of internal signification.

In the same work (*The Raw and the Cooked*, at the beginning of the chapter "Three-Part Inventions"), Lévi-Strauss seems to change his mind, and calls "armature" a combination of properties that remain invariant in two or several myths (the intercode?), and "code" the pattern of functions ascribed by each myth to these properties. Here the code seems closer to a notion of correlation. On the contrary, the many culinary, astronomical, vestimental, geographical codes that Lévi-Strauss quotes so frequently in his works, look more similar to content-structures, semantic s-codes, systems of values, as well as systems of prescriptions. When, however, he speaks of the "conversion of the culinary code into a vestimental one" (in *The Naked Man*, but with a reference to a more comprehensive analysis in *The Raw and the Cooked*, Eng. tr., p. 334*ff*), he seems to speak of a correlation of mutual signification between the elements of two content systems.

Thus Lévi-Strauss' codes look at the same time like syntactic systems, like institutions prescribing norms that can be either obeyed or disregarded, as bodies of textual functions eliciting forecasts about their possible transformations and as systems of signs, since in the parental code, for instance, the choice of a given partner becomes significant of the obligations to be entertained with his or her relatives. Codes made up with codes, a flexible web of codes, an inextricable texture of internal and external significations, in which it is impossible to distinguish what is semantic from what is syntactic.

Even larger and more complex is the notion of code in the typology of cultures (Lotman and Uspenskij 1971). A code is a way of modeling the world: verbal languages are primary modeling systems, whereas secondary modeling systems are all the other cultural structures, from mythology to art. For these authors there is a clear difference (even though the term *code* seems to cover it) between equivalences (gemination of two or more chains of elements belonging to different semiotic systems) and pragmatic codes, whereas in their notion of text, as opposed to grammar, there appears a clear idea of the internal signification of instructional devices. Lotman studied abundantly different institutional codes (Lotman 1969) which are systems of norms or of values, and once again the opposition 'grammar vs. text' mirrors the difference between cogent institutions and textual models which suggest or prescribe by means of examples (a given behavior is proposed as an *emblem*, a *sample*, a specimen, so that the instruction might sound like this: if you recognize the charismatic power of this text, then you should act in the same way). In Lotman's semiotics, correlational and institutional aspects are hardly distinguishable precisely because in this line of thought every social activity reveals its profound communicative purpose.

Roland Barthes frequently uses the word 'code' (and indeed he was one of those responsible for the code boom at the beginning of the 1960s). The fashion code (Barthes 1967) is an s-code, a correlational and an institutional code at the same time. There are systematic links among vestimental units, correlations between types of clothes and social attitudes, between words and clothes, and so on.

In *S/Z* (1970) Barthes lists five so-called codes: semic, cultural, symbolic, hermeneutic, and proairetic. It is difficult to avoid the suspicion of full metaphorization, and, as compared with more traditional definitions, Barthes' codes seem to overlap each other.

Through the *semic* code the reader detects that the name Sarrasine has a connotation of femininity (because of the final /e/), and in this sense the semic code does not look so different from so-called linguistic codes. It is through the *hermeneutic* code that the same name, put forth as the title of the story, articulates a question, its possible response, the variety of chance events which can delay the answer; this title is an enigma and the reader is led to ask: *"What is Sarrasine?* A noun? A name? A thing? A man? A woman?"* (Barthes 1970; Eng. tr., p. 19). The *symbolic* code seems to be an imprecise set of intertextual evocations suggested by the opening sentence ("I was deep in one of those daydreams") and by the following antitheses (garden vs. salon, life vs. death, outside vs. interior). The *proairetic* code suggests a logic of actions, of possible narrative developments, and elicits forecasts about the further course of events. The *cultural* or reference code organizes a body of world knowledge referred to by the text.

In this sense, stresses Barthes, a code is not a mere list of equivalences:

> The code is a perspective of quotations, a mirage of structures; we know only its departures and returns; the units which have resulted from it (those we inventory) are themselves, always, ventures out of the text, the mark, the sign of a virtual digression toward the reminder of a catalogue (*The Kidnapping* refers to every kidnapping even written): there are so many fragments of something that has been already read, seen, done, experienced; the code is the wake of this *already*. Referring to what has been written, i.e., the Book (of culture, of life, of life as culture), it makes the text into a prospectus of this Book. . . . Each code is . . . one of the voices of which the text is woven. (Ibid.; Eng. tr., pp. 20– 21)

*Prima facie* here Barthes mistakes codes for the infinite process of semiosis, or with what later will be called intertextuality. But, wrong from the point of view of the weak sense of *code*, Barthes is right from the point of view of the strong one. What he calls here code is the whole of the encyclopedic competence as the storage of that which is already known and already organized by a culture. It is the encyclopedia, and therefore the Rule, but as a Labyrynth. A Rule which controls but which at the same time allows, gives the possibility of inventing beyond itself, by finding new paths, new combinations within the network. If the code is not only a strict gemination of systems, or a correlation, but also a system of inference, its fate is exactly this.

A code is not only a rule which *closes* but also a rule which *opens*. It not only says 'you must' but says also 'you may' or 'it would also be possible to do that'. If it is a matrix, it is a matrix allowing for infinite occurrences, some of them still unpredictable, the source of a game. It is not by chance or by a deliberate unfaithfulness that, in the 1960s, so-called poststructuralist simply started from the model of the code and of the linguistic sign to find out, beyond or beneath the rule and the organization, the 'whirl', the difference, the *béance*. Since its very beginning, the idea of code was not necessarily a guarantee of armistice and peace, of law and order: it also signaled the coming of a new war.

Codes were introduced to put events under the control of structures, but very soon (maybe already with Lévi-Strauss; see Eco 1968) the ultimate nature of the ultimate codes (or the Ur-Code) was looked for so deeply as to turn over as the concept of an unshaped 'origin'. At this point the code became unmanageable, because it was suspected that we do not *posit* it; on the contrary, we — as thinking cultural subjects — *are posited by it.*

So the acknowledgement of codes (or of the Code) meant that we are not gods and that we are moved by rules. What was at stake, however, was the question as to whether we are not gods because we are determined by rules socially produced in the course of human history or because God is the Rule which stands behind us and our social history. In other words (and the story is a rather old one), the code can be either *nomos* or *phusis* either the Law of the Polis or the Epicurean *clinamen*. For many poststructuralists, if it was *phusis* and *clinamen*, it was not therefore structure, but the absence of every structure.

This conclusion was unnecessary and was determined by previous metaphysical assumptions. It is possible to think of an open matrix, of an unlimited rule, without assuming that it cannot be culturally produced. It is possible to think of the encyclopedia as a labyrinth without assuming necessarily that we cannot describe it, and explain its modes of birth and development.

Under the metaphoric usages of *code* there was at least a unifying obsession, and the eternal dialectics between law and creativity or, in the words of Appollinaire, the constant fight between *l'ordre et l'aventure*.

# [6]
# ISOTOPY

In *The Role of the Reader* I devoted several pages to the notion of topic, defined as a cooperative device activated by the reader (usually in the form of a question) for the purpose of identifying the isotopy for interpreting the text (Eco 1979, 0.6.3).[1] I wrote: " . . . topic as question is an abductive schema that helps the reader to decide which semantic properties have to be actualized, whereas isotopies are the actual textual verification of that tentative hypothesis" (ibid., p. 27), by which I meant to say that the topic as such is not expressed by the text, whereas the isotopy is a verifiable semantic property of it. In other words, the topic is a pragmatic device, whereas the isotopy is a level of possible semantic actualization of the text. Yet, in order to analyze that semantic property or indeed that level of meaning that a text manifests, it is necessary to specify more exactly what is meant by isotopy. My hypothesis is that the term, variously defined by Greimas and by his school, is an umbrella term, a rather general notion that can allow for various more specific ones defining different textual phenomena. Only the clarification of these differences will make it possible to throw light on the positive theoretical aspects of the notion.

Greimas defines isotopy as "a complex of manifold semantic categories making possible the uniform reading of a story" (1970:188). The category would then have the function of textual disambiguation,

1. For the convenience of the reader, I reproduce in this chapter the table of levels of textual cooperation published in *The Role of the Reader* (Eco 1979: 14). In the box on discursive structures, I did not sufficiently develop the voice 'chosen of the isotopies', since there the concept of isotopy was there understood as used in Greimas' semiotics. As to the deeper intensional levels, in *The Role of the Reader* I developed only a few aspects of the question, since my major interest was in the interpretation of the narrative level (*fabula*) and in the extensional inferences (possible worlds).

but on various occasions Greimas furnishes examples dealing with sentences and outright noun phrases. For instance, in order to explain in what sense the amalgam on a single classeme (either semantic category or repeated contextual seme) makes possible a uniform reading, he gives the example of the two expressions *le chien aboye* (the dog barks) and *le commissaire aboye* (the commissioner barks). Given that *bark* has two classemes, human and canine, it is the presence of the dog or the commissioner that reiterates one of the two that decides whether *bark* is taken in a literal or a figurative sense. It should be obvious that what are called classemes here are our *contextual* selections (see Eco 1976, 2.12.2). The human presence of the commissioner introduces a 'human' context and makes it possible to make the appropriate selection out of the compositional spectrum of *bark*.[2]

But can we say that an isotopy obtains always and only under such conditions? Aside from the fact that, if so, it would not differ from normal semantic coherence or from the notion of amalgamation, the lists made of the various meanings of the term by either Greimas or his disciples (see Kerbrat-Orecchioni 1976) do say that at various times there are isotopies that are semantic, phonetic, prosodic, stylistic, enunciative, rhetorical, presuppositional, syntactic, or narrative. It is, therefore, fair to assume that isotopy has become an umbrella term covering diverse semiotic phenomena generically definable as *coherence* at the various textual levels. (See Figure 6.1.) But is that coherence obtained at the various textual levels by applying the same rules?

In the most recent developments of Greimas' theory (see Greimas and Courtés 1979:197), there is a distinction between a first and a second stage of the theory of isotopies. The term *isotopy* designated *d'abord*, a phenomenon of semic iterativity throughout a syntagmatic chain; thus any syntagm (be it a phrase, a sentence, a sequence of sentences composing a narrative text) comprehending at least two content *figurae* (in Hjelmslev's sense) is to be considered as the minimal contest for a possible isotopy. In this first stage, the theory considered (a) syntactical isotopies; (b) semantic isotopies; (c) actorial isotopies; (d) partial isotopies of a text (or 'isosémies') that disappear when the smaller units of a text are summarized by macropropositions (Greimas calls this process "condensation"; see ibid., p. 58); (e) global isotopies, as the result of the final actualization of the isotopies listed in (d).

In a second stage of the theory, the concept has been broadened in its scope. It now designates not only the iterativity of classemes but also the

---

2. Cf. Greimas (1966:52–53). Cf. also Van Dijk, "Aspects d'une théorie générative du texte poétique" in Greimas, ed., *Essais de sémiotique poétique* (Paris: Larousse, 1972): "It can be said that the central isotopy of a text is made up of the lowest seme or classeme dominating the greatest number of lexemes of the text" (pp. 180–206).

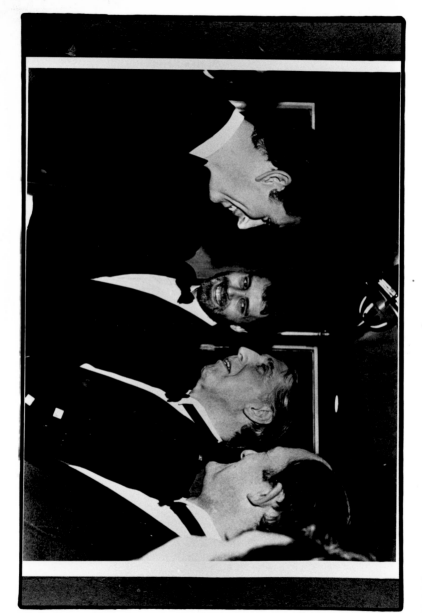

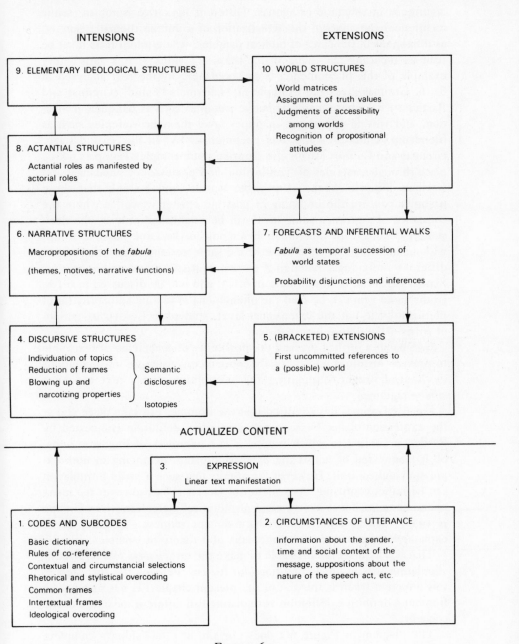

INTENSIONS                                              EXTENSIONS

9. ELEMENTARY IDEOLOGICAL STRUCTURES

10 WORLD STRUCTURES

World matrices
Assignment of truth values
Judgments of accessibility
   among worlds
Recognition of propositional
   attitudes

8. ACTANTIAL STRUCTURES

Actantial roles as manifested by
actorial roles

6. NARRATIVE STRUCTURES

Macropropositions of the *fabula*

(themes, motives, narrative functions)

7. FORECASTS AND INFERENTIAL WALKS

*Fabula* as temporal succession of
   world states

Probability disjunctions and inferences

4. DISCURSIVE STRUCTURES

Individuation of topics
Reduction of frames          } Semantic
Blowing up and                  disclosures
   narcotizing properties  }

Isotopies

5. (BRACKETED) EXTENSIONS

First uncommitted references to
a (possible) world

ACTUALIZED CONTENT

3.          EXPRESSION
      Linear text manifestation

1. CODES AND SUBCODES

Basic dictionary
Rules of co-reference
Contextual and circumstancial selections
Rhetorical and stylistical overcoding
Common frames
Intertextual frames
Ideological overcoding

2. CIRCUMSTANCES OF UTTERANCE

Information about the sender,
time and social context of the
message, suppositions about the
nature of the speech act, etc.

FIGURE 6.1

recurrence of thematic categories. Different figurative isotopies (semic recurrence) can concern the actualization of a unique thematic isotopy, as it happens in the cases of biblical parables, where minor facts must be read as meaning the same major theme. I think that a satisfactory example of this phenomenon is provided here by the text analyzed in 6.1.6. Greimas gives the example of Mallarmé's "Salut" (Greimas and Rastier 1968), where many figurative isotopies such as banquet, navigation, and writing express at an upper level thematic isotopies such as friendship, solitude/escape, and poetic creativity. In this second stage, Greimas and Courtès (1979) also mention more complex isotopies taking place through strategies of 'verification' and processes of 'modalization'. Greimas himself speaks of possible worlds, and I think that these isotopies concern the outlining of possible epistemic worlds where the constance of a given reading level can be established only by the decision of dealing with individuals belonging to the same possible world, without referring the same name or the same definite description to two different individuals belonging to. two mutually inaccessible worlds. Similar cases can be found here in 6.1.3. and will be discussed in 6.1.8. In the same vein can be read the phenomena of textual ambiguity (or of pluri-isotopicity) at the extensional level, studied in Eco 1979, apropos of Allais' "Un drame bien parisien."

Greimas has further stressed the possibility of conceiving of texts able to provide manifold and mutually contradictory isotopic interpretations (without, however, supporting the assumption that a text can have *infinite* readings).

Finally, Greimas has admitted that the isotopies can take place also at the expression-plane, by accepting a minimal definition (suggested by Rastier) according to which isotopy is the iterativity of linguistic units, be it manifested or not at the expression-plane, belonging to both expression and content. However, he admits that such a broad formulation can be rather confusing. As a matter of fact, it comes to cover too many phenomena, as, for instance, cases of rhetorical metaplasms (see Groupe $\mu$ 1970) such as alliteration, which do not request — in order to be explained — the complex paraphernalia of a theory of isotopies.

That is why it seems advisable to make the term *isotopy* less equivocal, stipulating the minimal conditions for its use. Perhaps the first step in this direction (such is the aim of the present chapter) is not so much to find out a definitive definition as to distinguish different meanings of the concept.

The diagram in Figure 6.2 does not aim at establishing a complete isotopic system but at showing that the category can assume various forms, according to the representation of the levels of actualization of a text outlined in Figure 6.1.

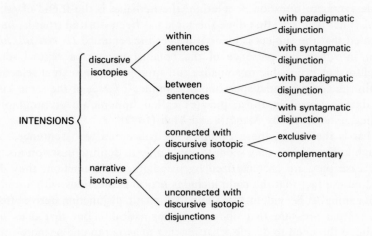

FIGURE 6.2

## 6.1. Discursive isotopies within sentences with paradigmatic disjunction

In his essay on crossword puzzles, Greimas (1970) examines this definition with its definiendum:

(1) *l'ami des simples* = herbalist

in which the clever definition arises from the fact that /simples/ has two contextual selections, one common (context 'human') and one specialized (context 'vegetal'). Only after it is decided that the term is understood in the second sense is it established that it counts as a substantive, not an adjective, and therefore it is decided to decode */ami/* as «lover» or «fan» and not as «friend». The topic has intervened as a reading hypothesis (speaking of plants and not of ethical attitudes), has pointed toward the appropriate contextual selection and has imposed a rule of interpretive coherence affecting all the lexemes involved. We can apply the term isotopy to the semantic result of that coherent interpretation and recognize the actualized isotopy as the 'objective' content of the expression (objective in the sense that it is supported by the code. Naturally, in the case of this expression, which is deliberately ambiguous, or, if we like, bi-isotopic, the objective contents are two, both actualizable). It should be noted, too, that in this case the isotopy does not depend on any redundance of semantic type, since *ami* and *simples* do not seem to have semes in common. In truth, the final isotopy is realized by the whole syntagm, question + solution: the herbalist is the friend of /simples/. That is to say, that once the topic has been isolated (that is, once assumed that the subject is plants), we get the sentence *The herbalist likes herbs,* in which the presence of the botanist imposes a vegetal seme which makes it possible to actualize the appropriate contextual selection within the componential spectrum of «simples». Cases of the same kind are demonstrated in those puzzles called 'mnemonic cryptographs' studied extensively by Manetti and Violi (1977).

That is the reason these isotopies are concerned with sentences, although at first glance they seem to apply only to definite descriptions. In each case they are characterized by paradigmatic disjunction: they depend on the fact that the code includes lexical expressions with a multiple meaning. It is evident that the paradigmatic disjunction derives from a co-textual pressure that operates syntagmatically, but that does not eliminate the need to decide what reading to assign to one or more componential spectrums.

Moreover, these isotopies are *denotatively exclusive:* the subject is either the evangelical in spirit, or it is herbs. The topic intervenes as a concurrent, cooperative hypothesis to individuate contextual selections.[3]

## 6.2. Discursive isotopies within sentences with syntagmatic disjunction

Transformational grammar has accustomed us to ambiguous sentences such as the following:

(2) They are flying planes

which can generate two different deep structures. In disambiguating the sentence, paradigmatic disjunctions undoubtedly apply (it is necessary, for instance, to decide whether the verb should be understood as active or as passive), but the fundamental decision (always deriving from the prior selection of a topic) is whether the subject is humans doing something with the airplanes or airplanes doing something. At that point, it is necessary to actuate a co-reference and establish to whom or to what *they* refers. We could say that the co-referential (syntagmatic) decision determines the paradigmatic choice concerning the meaning of the verb.

These isotopies, too, are *denotatively exclusive:* either the subject is a human action or it is mechanical objects.

---

3. The distinction between isotopies with paradigmatic disjunction and those with syntagmatic disjunction corresponds to the one between vertical and horizontal isotopies proposed by Rastier and discussed in Kerbrat-Orecchioni (1976:24–25).

Here the topic intervenes as a concurrent hypothesis to actualize both co-references and contextual selections.

## 6.3. Discursive isotopies between sentences with paradigmatic disjunction

Let us examine in this connection the little story of two fellows conversing during a party, cited by Greimas (1966). The first praises the food, the service, the hospitality, the beauty of the women, and finally the excellence of the "toilettes." The second replies that he has not yet been there. The second speaker, in interpreting the text uttered by the first, blunders because he superimposes two frames (cf. Eco 1979). The frame 'party' undoubtedly includes the host's garments, but cannot include the condition of the sanitary facilities, or it would have to consider also the electrical system, the water supply, the solidity of the walls, and the layout of the rooms. These elements are considered at most as belonging, say, to a frame such as 'interior architecture and furnishing'. The party refers to a frame that is social in nature, furnishings to one that is technological. The individuation of the topic in this case is the individuation of the semantic field, so as to enable contextual selections to be effected. The French term /toilettes/ is undoubtedly polysemic and acquires two meanings according to the disjunction between the selection «fashion» (which in turn belongs to a seme of social nature) and the selection «architecture». In this case, we can certainly speak of the presence of a classeme or a dominant semantic category, since the text of the first speaker in fact abounded in key terms containing references to the party and to the social nature of the situation. There were no misunderstandings possible, and the story makes us laugh precisely because it constitutes a case of awkward textual cooperation.

These isotopies have paradigmatic disjunction because, if only on the basis of co-textual (syntagmatic) pressure, they concern contextual selections in lexemes with multiple meaning. These isotopies, too, are *denotatively exclusive:* the subject is either clothing or it is bathrooms. The topic intervenes as a concurrent cooperative hypothesis, to individuate contextual selections that hypothesize frames.

## 6.4. Discursive isotopies between sentences with syntagmatic disjunction

This is the case of the ambiguous sentence

(3) Charles makes love with his wife twice a week. So does John.

The point is whether this short text should be read as the story of two couples or as the story of a triangle. In this case, too, we have discursive isotopies with alternative denotations. In extensional terms, it is a matter of deciding whether there are three people involved or four (see 6.1.8.). In order to do so, it is necessary to decide how *so* should be interpreted, but then it is a matter of establishing a co-reference. The choice concerns the syntactic structure of the sentence, and only through a syntactic decision is the one or the other semantic result obtained. As already seen, it is through the selection of the topic that the decision is made as to whether the subject is two couples or a triangle: in the first case the logical structure of the text would be $A:B = C:D$, whereas in the second it would be $A:B = B:C$. It is a problem of interpretive coherence; if four individuals are concerned and if $A$ and $B$ are compared in the first sentence, *so* means that in the second sentence $C$ and $D$ should be compared; if, on the other hand, three people are involved and if $A$ and $B$ are compared in the first sentence, *so* means that in the second $B$ and $C$ should be compared. But it is not obvious how the two interpretive decisions derive from the redundance of semantic categories. Here the connection is between the topic and coreferential decisions, without the mediation of contextual selections. At the most, as already seen, presuppositions of frames are involved.

The two isotopies are characterized by syntagmatic disjunction. They are mutually exclusive (the subject is either the Kinsey report or it is the story of adultery), but they are by no means denotatively alternative: some of the individuals remain the same in each case, only they are ascribed different actions and intentions.

The topic intervenes as a cooperative concurrent hypothesis to establish the co-references, thus orienting the structuralization of different narrative worlds.

## 6.5. Narrative isotopies connected with isotopic discursive disjunctions generating mutually exclusive stories

The following text is the French translation of an extract from Machiavelli.[4] It is irrelevant whether the original Italian text shows the same ambiguity as the French; the French text will be examined as if it were an anonymous original:

(4) Domitian surveillait l'âge des senateurs, et tous ceux qu'il voyait en position favorable pour lui succéder il les abattait. Il voulut ainsi abattre Nerva qui devait lui succéder. Il se trouva qu'un calculateur de ses amis l'en dissuada, va que *lui même* [my italics] était arrivé à un âge trop

4. The text was proposed by Alain Cohen in the course of a colloquium of modalities held at Urbino at the International Semiotics Center in July 1978. Cohen's analysis, however, aimed at goals different from ours and concerned only the discourse on Power referred to below.

avancé pour que sa mort ne fût toute proche; et c'est ainsi que Nerva put lui succéder.

It is immediately evident that here we have, first of all, a choice between two discursive isotopies with syntagmatic disjunction: *lui-même* can refer to either Domitian or Nerva. If it refers to Domitian, the death referred to later (*sa* mort) is the imminent death of Domitian; otherwise, it is Nerva's death. It is therefore necessary to decide on the co-reference on the basis of the choice of a topic: is the subject Domitian's age or Nerva's? Once the co-reference is decided, there is a denotatively alternative discursive sequence in respect to the other. In effect, in one case, the advisor tells Domitian not to kill Nerva because he — Domitian — will soon die and it is therefore useless to eliminate his possible successors; in the other, the advisor tells Domitian that Nerva will probably die soon and therefore does not present a danger for Domitian.

But it is clear that two different stories can be derived on the basis of the two discursive isotopies. The two discursive isotopies generate two possible narrative recapitulations. In one case, it is the story of a friend of Domitian's giving him an argument about Power: "In dying you risk losing Power, but by sparing Nerva and implicitly designating him your successor, though dying you retain control of the Power, you generate the new Power." In the other case, it is the story of a friend of Nerva's making Domitian the victim of a courtier's wiles: "O Domitian, why do you want to kill Nerva? He's so old that he'll soon die by himself!" — and thus the courtier puts Nerva on the throne.

Thus two mutually exclusive stories emerge, whose individuation depends on the discursive actualization. Not only that, but at a deeper level (see Figure 6.1), there emerge different *actantial structures* and different ideological structures. According to Greimas' categories, the advisor can be seen as the Opponent of Domitian and Helper of Nerva, or as the Helper of Power and the Opponent of Domitian as a mortal, or as a Helper of Domitian and neutral in regard to Nerva. And it can be decided that what is defined here is an ideological opposition of Power vs. Death (in which Power overcomes even Death) or Power vs. Shrewdness, where the courtier's wiles overcome the brutality of Power. It can also legitimately be asked whether it is the choice of co-references that generates the different deep structures or a preliminary hypothesis regarding the deep structures that, in suggesting a specific topic, controls the actualization of the co-references at the discursive level. The interpretive cooperation is made of leaps and short circuits at the different textual levels where it is impossible to establish logically ordered sequences.

In each case, we have seen that here the narrative isotopies are connected to these discourses (or vice versa).

The two narrative isotopies are mutually exclusive, but they are not at all denotatively alternative: in both cases, the narration is about Nerva and Domitian, except that different actions and intentions are attributed to them. The individuals remain extensionally the same but change some of their intensional features. Different possible worlds are developed.

The topic intervenes to orient the structuralization of these narrative worlds.

### 6.6. Narrative isotopies connected with isotopic discursive disjunctions that generate complementary stories

That is the case of the medieval theory of the four senses of the Scriptural verses, also cited by Dante (*Epistula XIII*). Given the text

(5) In exitu Israel de Aegypto — domus Jacob de populo barbaro — facta est Judea sanctificatio ejus — Israel potestas ejus

Dante says that "if we look only at the *letter* it means the exodus of the sons of Israel from Egypt in Moses' time; if we look at the *allegory* it means our redemption through Christ; if we look at the *moral sense* it means the conversion of the soul from the struggle and misery of sin to the state of grace; and if we look at the *mystical sense* it means the departure of the Holy Spirit from the servitude of this corruption to the freedom of eternal glory." Let us consider, in order to simplify matters, just the literal and moral senses. Once again, everything depends on the topic hypothesis: is the statement about Israel or about the human soul? The decision on this affects the discursive actualization: in the first case, Israel will be understood as a proper name of a people, and Egypt as a proper name of an African country; in the second case, Israel will be the human spirit, but then, by interpretive coherence, Egypt will have to be sin (the reading levels cannot be mixed).

Here, however, alternative senses of a componential spectrum will not be chosen, because we must foresee that, in as rich an encyclopedia as the medieval one, Israel *denoted* the Chosen People and *connoted* the soul. Thus it is not like the case of /toilette/, which has the sense of either «x» or «y»; here the expression connotes the sense «y» precisely because it denotes «x». The relationship and implication is not one of disjunction. Consequently, isotopic disjunction exists; however, it is not based on disjunction but, rather, on implication.

Once the preferred reading at the discursive level is decided, various stories can be inferred from the actualized discursive structures; the moral story will derive from the moral discursive actualization just as the literal one will from the literal discursive actualization. But the two stories (and we know in reality there are four) *are not mutually exclusive;*

they are, rather, complementary, in the sense that the text can be read simultaneously in two or more ways, and one way reinforces the other rather than eliminates it.

Thus narrative isotopies are connected with discursive isotopies but are not mutually exclusive. On the contrary, they are denotatively alternative; the subject is either the Chosen People, or it is the soul (and, in fact, the option is between various denotations and connotations). By virtue of this choice, various possible worlds developed.

The topic (both the discursive and the narrative) intervenes to choose between denotative and connotative semes and to orient the structure of the narrative worlds.

## 6.7. Narrative isotopies connected with discursive isotopic disjunctions that generate complementary stories in each case

In his analysis of the Bororo myth of the *aras*, Greimas (1970) speaks of another type of narrative isotopy. The myth in effect contains two stories, one about the search for water, and the other about the problem of diet. So we have a 'natural' isotopy vs. an 'alimentary' one. But in both cases we perceive that whatever the story (or the *fabula*) we actualize, *there is no change on the discursive level*. The stories always tell of certain people and certain events. At the most, according to the narrative isotopy, we select certain actions as more pertinent than others, but the actions and people doing them remain the same, even if there is a change in the value we attribute to them in the narrative arrangement. It is a matter of elaborating a hypothesis with a narrative theme and relying on key terms or sentences without, however, paradigmatic disjunctions as to the sense of the lexemes or syntagmatic disjunctions as to the sense of the co-references.

The persistence of a single discursive coherence results in this case in the two narrative isotopies' not annulling each other, *the relation between them not being exclusive or alternative, but complementary*. Although Greimas chooses the alimentary isotopy as best, this does not mean that the story cannot be read through the natural isotopy as well. In fact, the two isotopies reinforce each other.

The *toilettes* story is characterized by two opposing readings, of which one is clearly inferior, and, if the first speaker had really wanted to speak of bathrooms, his utterance would have been conversationally inept because it violated the rule of relevance. That cannot be said about the myth of the *aras*. Thus we have here narrative isotopies unconnected with discursive disjunctions.

The two or more narrative isotopies are not mutually exclusive. They are not even denotatively alternative; at most, different features are attributed to different individuals (cf. Eco 1979), 8.7).

The topic intervenes only to orient the evaluation of the narratively pertinent features.

## 6.8.   Extensional isotopies

Some of the isotopies examined in the preceding sections also deal with the choice between possible worlds. Typical is the case of the text (3) in 6.1.3, where, in order to actualize the anaphoric power of *so*, the interpreter has to decide whether he is considering a world furnished with four individuals (characterized as performing a 'legal' sexual activity) or a world furnished with three individuals (who have the property of behaving as adulterers). Nevertheless, these two worlds are mutually accessible, and there is no difficulty in imagining the individuals of the first world as changing some of their accidental properties, thus behaving as the individuals of the second one.

There are, on the contrary, cases where the choice between two or more worlds involves a radical characterization of the individuals, irrespective of the fact that they can bear the same name. Such is the case of Allais' "Un drame bien parisien" analyzed in Eco 1979.

Let us consider the following well known paradoxical dialogue;

(6) A: I believed that your boat was bigger than it really is. . . . 
    B: Oh no. My boat is not bigger than it really is.

The conversation is certainly comic and the second speaker is certainly a fool. Like the second speaker of the *toilettes* dialogue, he is a fool because he shifts from one isotopy to another, without realizing it. In the case of the *toilettes*, the shift took place at the semic level. Here the mistake is ontologically more puzzling.

The first speaker, A, is putting into play two worlds, one $(w_j t_{,1})$ which is the epistemic world of his beliefs at a previous time, and the other $(w_o t_o)$ which is the world of his actual experience at the time of the utterance. He is saying: "In $w_j t_{,1}$ there was an individual $x$, which I supposed to be your boat and which was endowed with the property of being big; in $w_o t_o$ I am experiencing the actual existence of an individual $y$, your real boat, endowed with the property of being small. Since in the present universe of discourse the only properties that $x$ and $y$ have are to be your boat and to have a certain size, if I compare these two individuals of two different worlds, I notice that they have different properties. Maybe these properties are only accidental (in the sense outlined in Eco 1979, 8.6.2), so that $x$ and $y$ are potential variants of the same individual in two different possible worlds; however, they are certainly not the same individual in the same world." Speaker A is avoiding such a complicated metalinguistic series of precisions, since he thinks that B will understand very well what he is in fact doing. On the contrary, B is devoided of metalinguistical ability, so that his answers sound as "The $y$ which is the only individual of the world of my experience (the only one I can conceive of) has not the property of being different from itself." Such a remark is so tautological as to result in being silly. Moreover, B does not accept the implicit request of A, that is, of comparing A's former beliefs with A's subsequent knowledge. Thus B refuses to acknowledge that in A's discourse there were two extensional isotopies, to be kept carefully separated one from another, and that A requests, at a certain moment, to make a comparison between them.

## 6.9. Provisional conclusions

According to what has been said, it is permissible to assert that isotopy is an umbrella term covering various phenomena. Like all umbrella terms (such as iconism, presupposition, code), this one shows that the diversity conceals some unity. Indeed, isotopy refers almost always to constancy in going in a direction that a text exhibits when submitted to rules of interpretive coherence, even if the rules of coherence change according to whether what is wanted is to individuate discursive or narrative isotopies, to disambiguate definite descriptions or sentences and produce co-references, to decide what things certain individuals do, or to establish how many different stories the same deed by the same individuals can generate.

What should be clear in any case is that the identification of the topic is a cooperative (pragmatic) movement guiding the reader to individuate the isotopies as semantic features of a text.

# [7]
# MIRRORS

## 7.1. Is the mirror image a sign?

Is the mirror a semiotic phenomenon? Or else, is the image reflected from the mirror surface a sign? These questions may well be nonsense — in that common sense would suggest that mirrors are just mirrors. In any case, putting such questions is not without purpose: it might be somewhat meaningless to discover that the mirror image is a sign, but it would be more interesting to discover that the mirror image is *not* a sign and why. Even though we assume we know everything about the mirror, excluding mirrors from the class of signs might help us better to define a sign (or at least to define what a sign is not).

Of course, we should first establish what we mean by both sign and mirror. But we are immediately faced with the question of whether the two definitions may somehow be linked to one another in a circle; so that we would not be able to decide whether we should begin from the mirror to define a sign, or vice versa. How can we know that, if we begin from a definition of sign, it is not so constructed as to exclude the mirror? It would seem easier to begin from the mirror (which is assumed to be thoroughly, objectively, and unquestionably described by optics). But defining what a mirror is and what it is not may depend on certain previous assumptions — although unspoken — on the nature of semiotic phenomena as different from mirror phenomena.

No phylogenetic argument can be of any use in establishing a priority. Man is a semiotic animal; this is a matter of fact. But saying so does not exclude that man is so thanks to an ancestral experience with mirrors. No doubt, the myth of Narcissus seems to refer to an already speaking animal, but how far can we trust myths? From a phylogenetic viewpoint, the question sounds like that of the chicken and the egg or of the origin of language. Since we lack any good document on the 'dawn' of our species, we had better keep silent.

From an ontogenetic viewpoint, too, we definitely have very poor certainties. We are not sure whether semiosis is at the basis of perception or vice versa (and, therefore, whether semiosis is at the basis of thought or vice versa). Psychoanalytical inquiries on the 'mirror stage' (Lacan 1966) would suggest that perception (or at least the perception of one's own body as an unfragmented unit) and the experience with mirrors go hand in hand. And, therefore, perception — thought — self-consciousness — experience with mirrors — semiosis seem to be the points of a rather inextricable knot, the points of a circle where it would be difficult to spot a starting point.

## 7.2.  The imaginary and the symbolic

Lacan's pages on the 'mirror stage' would seem to solve our problem from the very beginning. The mirror is a threshold-phenomenon marking the boundaries between the *imaginary* and the *symbolic*. When a child is between six and eight months old, at first he mistakes the image for reality, then he realizes that it is just an image, and later still he understands that it is his image. In this 'jubilant' acceptation of the image, the child reconstructs the still scattered fragments of his body as something outside himself — in terms of inverse symmetry, so to speak (a notion we shall take up again later). The experience with mirrors still belongs to the imaginary, just as the experience of the deceptive image of a bunch of flowers created in a spherical mirror described in "Topïcs of the Imaginary" (Lacan 1953:101). The imaginary mastering of one's own body which the experience with mirrors induces is earlier than actual mastering: the final development "is achieved insofar as the subject integrates into the symbolic system and asserts itself there, through the exercise of a true word" (Lacan 1953). By the way, what Lacan defines as the symbolic is actually the semiotic, although he identifies it with verbal language. In the acceptation of the mirror image there is a symbolic matrix into which the ego plunges under a primeval form; only language should give it back its function of a subject *"in the universal"* (Lacan 1966:94). As we shall see, this restitution back "to the universal" should pertain to any semiotic process, although not verbal.

The mirror as the moment when the reflected ego changes to social ego is a "structural crossroads" or, as we were saying before, a threshold phenomenon.

## 7.3.   Getting in through the mirror

However, in the event these conclusions are valid, they only tell us what the mirror is (or, better, what use it is for) at a single moment in the subject's ontogenesis. On the whole, the considerations of the mirror stage do not exclude that, at any further stage in the development of symbolic life, the mirror may be used as a semiotic phenomenon. This is why it is worthwhile considering a different approach, that is, questioning ourselves about the use of mirrors by human adults who produce signs, perceive themselves as subjects, and, above all, are already familiar with mirror images, rather than considering an auroral or primary moment (be it phylo- or ontogenetic). If we consider the problem at this stage, we can avail ourselves of our everyday experience, with a pegging down to phenomena, instead of searching into our ancestors' experience (which cannot be verified) or our infant children's (which we define conjecturally, based on guesswork and external data).

But, once again, the problem is whether to begin from mirrors or from signs.

If there is a circle, we might as well get in from any point whatsoever. Let us then get in through the mirror (without getting stuck inside it, as we shall see), since optics seems to know a lot about mirrors, whereas it is doubtful whether semiotics knows anything about signs. On the whole, optics is an 'exact' science, and so-called exact sciences are supposedly more accurate than so-called nonexact sciences. When questioning ourselves on our experience with mirrors (but from now on we are entitled to speak 'scientifically' of *catoptric* experience), we might at the most wonder to what extent catoptrics is actually exact.

## 7.4.   A phenomenology of the mirror: the mirror does not invert

We initially define a mirror as any polished surface reflecting incident rays of light (therefore excluding so-called mirrors reflecting other kind of waves, such as repeater systems). These surfaces are either plane or curved.

By plane mirror we mean a surface reflecting a virtual image, which is straight, inverted (or symmetrical), specular (the same size of the reflected object), free of so-called chromatic aberrations. By convex mirrors we mean a surface reflecting virtual, straight, inverted, and reduced images.

By concave mirror we mean a surface (a) reflecting virtual, straight, and magnified images, when the object stands between the focus and the observer, and (b) reflecting real, upside-down, magnified, or reduced images depending on the position of the object anywhere in space between infinity and the focal point, which can both be observed by human eyes and be projected on a screen.

We shall not consider parabolic, ellipsoid, spherical, or cylindrical mirrors, because they are not in common use; they do not belong to our everyday experience. Their results will possibly be considered under the general heading of distorting mirrors and catoptric theaters.

Already, when working out these definitions, we should question ourselves on the meaning of terms such as *virtual* and *real*. The real image in concave mirrors is actually unreal in terms of common sense, and is called real not only because the subject perceiving it may mistake it for a physical object but also because it may be projected on a screen, which is impossible with virtual images. As for the virtual image, it is so called because the observer perceives it as if it were inside the mirror, while, of course, the mirror has no 'inside'.

On the other hand, the definition by which a mirror image — as it is commonly said — would have an inverted symmetry is even more whimsical. This belief (that after all the mirror shows the right place of the left) is so deeply rooted that some went so far as to suggest that the mirror has this odd quality of exchanging the right with the left, but not the top with the bottom. Catoptrics, of course, does not allow for this conclusion; if, instead of being used to vertical mirrors, we would more generally be used to mirrors horizontally fixed to the ceiling, as libertines are used to them, we would come to believe that mirrors also tip top with bottom and show us the world upside-down.

But the point is that vertical mirrors themselves do not reverse or invert. A mirror reflects the right side exactly where the right side is, and the same with the left side. It is the observer (so ingenuous even when he is a scientist) who by self-identification imagines he is the man inside the mirror and, looking at himself, realizes he is wearing his watch on his right wrist. But it would be so only if he, the observer I mean, were the one who is inside the mirror (*Je est un autre!*). On the contrary, those who avoid behaving as Alice, and getting into the mirror, do not so deceive themselves. And, in fact, every morning, in the bathroom, each of us does use a mirror without behaving as a spastic. But we are clumsy right when we use lateral opposite mirrors to cut our sideburns and see an image (the reflection of a reflection) having its right side where we feel we have it and vice versa. It means that our brain has got used to using mirrors for what they are, faithfully reflecting what is in front of them, the same way it has got used to turning the retinal image upside-down, which we do actually reverse. But although our brain had millions of years (including the very many before the appearance of *Homo sapiens*) to get used to retinal images, so that for quite a long period man did not even think of this phenomenon, it had only a few thousand years to get used to mirror images. And, although at a perception and motor level, it interprets them correctly, at the level of conceptual consideration, it cannot quite clearly differentiate between the physical phenomenon and the deceptive illusion it encourages, in a sort of spread between perception and judgment. So we use the mirror image correctly, but speak of it wrongly, as if it did what we ourselves are doing with it (that is, reversing it).

If we reduce the phenomenon of mirror reflection to a purely abstract scheme, we realize that it does not imply any phenomena of the dark-chamber kind (Figure 7.1) and that there is no crossing of rays (Figure 7.2). It is only when we anthropomorphize the virtual image that we are puzzled by right and left — that is, only at this point do we start wondering what right and left would be *if* the virtual image were the real object.

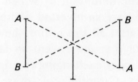

FIGURE 7.1

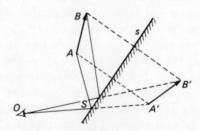

FIGURE 7.2

In front of a mirror we should not speak of inversion but, rather, of absolute *congruence:* the same congruence we observe when we press blotting paper onto a page written with fresh ink. If then I cannot read what is printed on the blotting paper, it depends on my reading habits rather than on the relation of congruence (and, in fact, I can read it by using a mirror, that is, by reversing to a second congruence, as it happens with laterally opposed mirrors in the bathroom). This again means that mankind had more time to learn how 'to read' mirrors than to read blotting paper (except Leonardo). And on blotting paper writing appears reversed with respect to grammatological rules, but, if we consider it as an *actual* imprint, ink signs are exactly where the paper was lying. Men can use mirrors just because they know that there is no man in the mirror and that the man to whom right and left are to refer is the observer and not the (virtual) individual who seems to be looking at the observer.

All this shows us how difficult it would be to speak of mirrors as if we spoke of them before knowing and experiencing them (and we can easily imagine how dismayed the baby is at the fatal stage when he/she does not yet know his/her body). When grown up, we are the way we are just because we are (also) catoptric animals and have developed a double ability to look at ourselves (insofar as it is possible) and the others in both our and their perceptive reality and catoptric virtuality. Of course, we do use mirrors more easily with respect to our body than to someone else's. Just now, while writing, I am facing a mirror reflecting a door with a handle, behind me. Before deciding whether the door handle is on the right or on the left (whose right and left?) or how I should move my arm (backward) in the event I wanted to throw my lighter and hit the handle, I first check *with* and *on* my body. I should move my right hand backward, toward my left shoulder, behind which I see the handle. Done! I almost hit it. Now I know (but I knew it also before trying) that, if I turned around, the handle would be on my right. But I had to reckon with an inverted image, because I was actually aiming (with my eyes) at the virtual image of the door in the mirror. It was *my* problem. Between the mirror and the door (both lacking organs of perception) there was no relation of inversion.

### 7.5. A pragmatics of the mirror

We usually know how to use mirrors correctly. This means that we have introjected the rules of catoptric interaction. It means also that we are to speak of a pragmatics of the mirror. It is no use arguing that, since pragmatics is a branch of semiotics, we cannot speak of it before defining semiotic phenomena. I have said already that we must get into the circle from somewhere. On the other hand, in this connection we may as well use the term 'pragmatics' in a rather broad sense, to cover also perceptive interaction. The problem is that, in order to use a mirror correctly, we should first *know that we are facing a mirror* (which is an essential condition also in Lacan's study, for the mirror not to be a sheer illusion or a hallucinatory experience).

Once we have acknowledged that what we perceive is a mirror image, we always begin from the principle that the mirror 'tells the truth'. And it is so true that it does not even bother to reverse the image (as a printed photograph does to give us an illusion of reality). The mirror does not even allow us this tiny advantage that would make our perception or our judgment easier. A mirror does not 'translate'; it records what struck it just as it is struck. It tells the truth to an inhuman extent, as it is well known by those who—facing a mirror—cannot any longer deceive themselves about their freshness. Our brain interprets retinal data; a mirror does not interpret an object.

But it is just this Olympian, animal, inhuman nature of mirrors that allows us to trust them. We trust mirrors just as, under normal conditions, we trust our organs of perception. Now it is clear why I spoke of pragmatics: with mirrors, we can apply some of the rules which, by social convention and very relatively, are applied to conversational interactions, although in conversation lies are reckoned as breaches. It is not so with mirrors.

## 7.6.  The mirror as a prosthesis and a channel

We trust mirrors just as we trust spectacles and binoculars, since, like spectacles and binoculars, mirrors are prostheses. In a strict sense, a prosthesis is an apparatus replacing a missing organ (an artificial limb, a denture); but, in a broader sense, it is any apparatus extending the range of action of an organ. This is why we can also consider hearing aids, megaphones, stilts, magnifying lenses, periscopes as prostheses.

A prosthesis extends the organ range of action according to the organ mode of action, but it may have either a *magnifying* (like a lens) or a *reducing* (pliers extend our fingers' prehension, but eliminate thermic and tactile sensations) function. In this sense, a mirror is an absolutely neutral prosthesis, and it allows us to catch visual stimuli from where our eye could not reach (in front of our own body, around the corner, in a hole) with the eye's same evidence and force. A mirror may at times work as a reducing prosthesis (curved mirrors or smoked mirrors, where the perception of intensity ratios is privileged over the perception of wave lengths).

Prostheses may be merely *extensive* (like a lens) or *intrusive* (like a periscope or certain specula used by physicians): mirrors may serve both functions (that is, a mirror may be used to extend the eye's reach as if we had a visual organ on our forefingers). Even barbers' *en abîme* mirrors have an intrusive function. The magic of the mirror lies in the fact that their extensiveness-intrusiveness allows us both to have a better look at the world and to look at ourselves as anybody else might; it is a unique experience, and mankind knows of no other similar one.

And, since mirrors are prostheses, they are channels, too. A channel is any material *medium* for the passage of information (the notion of information is here a physical one, that is, information as a passage of stimuli-signals which can be quantitatively measured, not yet connected with semiotic phenomena). Not all channels are prostheses, because they do not all necessarily extend an organ range of action (for example, air is the channel through which sound waves travel), whereas all prostheses are channels or *media*. There may also be a channel of a channel. For instance, if you use a mirror to reflect the rays by which somebody is modulating Morse signals, the mirror is a primary channel conveying light (it may act as a prosthesis if it magnifies the ray power or if, in a system of mirrors reflecting one another, it allows you to catch the rays reflected in an original mirror, which is beyond your eye's reach). But reflected light rays, in their turn, become a secondary channel conveying the features pertaining to the Morse code. In any case, this phenomenon concerning the reflection and channeling of light rays has nothing to do with mirror images.

If we identify mirrors as channels, we can easily dispose of the cases when a mirror image is used as the *symptom* of a presence. For instance, if I look at a mirror located vertically in front of me and diagonally to the plane of observation, I can see human shapes moving in the adjacent room. In this case, too, the mirror acts as a prosthesis, but we might think that — since mirror images are the symptoms of someone's presence elsewhere — it might have semiotic functions. However, any channel when working is a symptom of the existence of a source issuing signals. If this is so, when someone is talking to me, independently of what he is telling me, I can see his act of speaking as a double symptom: that he is not dumb and that he wants to say something, that is, to express an inner state. These cases, when the channel state of activity is a symptom of both the channel efficiency and the existence of a source, are connected to the symptomatic use of the channel rather than to the messages it conveys. When used as a symptom, the mirror tells us something about mirrors and the use we can make of them, but nothing about mirror images.

As a channel-prosthesis, the mirror can be a source of perceptive deception, just as any other prosthesis. I enter a room and seem to see a man coming toward me, and then I realize it is my image reflected in a mirror. This image 'standing for something else', albeit temporarily, might induce us to perceive the shadow of a semiotic phenomenon. But it is a perceptive deception, as I can well have without mirrors, as when I take dross for gold or see things that are not there. Similarly, deceptions can be created by presenting things which are not mirrors as being mirrors. In a film by the Marx Brothers there is a scene where Groucho is looking at himself in a mirror, but the mirror is not a mirror; it is an empty frame behind which Harpo is awkwardly (and with funny effects) trying to imitate Groucho's gestures. This phenomenon of lying *about* mirrors of course has nothing to do with mirror images. No doubt the deceiver's performance has something to do with fiction, with signification, with lying through signs, but all this does not concern the nature of the mirror image. This will come up again (7.12) when we deal with a semiotics of the *mise-en-scène*, which might apply to the use of mirrors as channels.

## 7.7.  Absolute icons

We have said that a catoptric prosthesis extends an organ range of action and supplies the organ with the same stimuli it would receive if it could act right where the prosthesis extends its range. In this sense, the mirror provides me with an *absolute double* of the stimulating field. We might quite naively say that the mirror provides me with an icon of the object — if we define the icon as an image having *all* the properties of its denotatum. But catoptric experience tells me that (if any sign called icon and endowed with these properties exists) a catoptric absolute icon is not an icon but a *double* (see Eco 1975, 3.4.7). At the macroscopic level of my perceptive experience and to the practical purpose it must serve, the sheet of paper I am writing on is the double of the sheet I have just filled. But this is not a good reason to consider the former a sign of the latter. You may argue that the mirror image is not to its object as the former sheet is to the latter. But you should not forget that the mirror image is not a double of its object but, rather, a double of the stimulating field one could have access to if one looked at the object instead of looking at its mirror image. The fact that the mirror image is a most peculiar case of double and has the traits of a unique case explains why mirrors inspired so much literature; this virtual duplication of stimuli (which sometimes works as if there were a duplication of both my body as an object and my body as a subject, splitting and facing itself), this theft of an image, this unceasing temptation to believe I am someone else, makes man's experience with mirrors an absolutely unique one, on the threshold between perception and signification. And it is precisely from this experience of absolute iconism that the dream of a sign having the same characteristics arises. This is why men draw (and produce the signs which are precisely defined as iconic): they draw to achieve without mirrors what mirrors allow them to achieve. But the most realistic drawing does not show all the characteristics of absolute duplication as a mirror does (besides having a different relation of dependence to its object).

Man's experience with mirrors may then *explain* the emergence of a notion like the (semiotic) one of iconism but *is not explained* by it.

However, the mirror as a threshold phenomenon may lend itself to a number of operations making it even more 'threshold'. I can, in fact, reduce the absolute iconism of mirror images, and smoked mirrors are an excellent example of this technique. The mirror almost becomes a reducing prosthesis.

Let us imagine a mirror made of horizontal strips of reflecting material with thin opaque strips in between. The virtual image I see is obviously incomplete. At the level of perceptive reconstruction, the result may nevertheless be excellent, with varying degrees of efficiency depending on the thickness of opaque strips. If we imagine opaque strips of a reasonable thickness, even though the reflected image is not mine (because, of course, I know a lot about my image, and the reconstruction of the *perceptum* may in this case be affected by previous information), I can satisfactorily perceive the reflected object. This, of course, does not exclude that some elements of interpretation (although very slight ones) do come into play. Such interpretation, however, also affects the perception of objects in the world around us. Darkness, the presence of opaque obstacles, fog are all 'noises' in the channel diminishing sensory data and requiring interpretative efforts in order to achieve the (often conjectural) formation of a *perceptum*. If these conjectural and interpretive efforts are to be taken as semiosic, then semiosis creeps into any aspect of our relation to the surrounding world. But, even if we take this for granted, we should not conclude that any aurorally semiosic process is productive and interpretive of signs. If also mirrors impose semiosic processes, one thing remains to be defined, that is, in which sense these processes do not lead to the production, interpretation, and use of signs.

## 7.8.  Mirrors as rigid designators

The mirror has a peculiar characteristic. As long as I look at it, it gives me back my facial features, but if I mailed a mirror which I have long looked at to my beloved, so that she may remember my looks, she could not see me (and would instead see herself).

The self-evident datum I have just highlighted deserves some thought. If we compared mirror images to words, they would be like personal pronouns: like the pronoun /I/, meaning «Umberto Eco» if I pronounce it, and someone else if someone else does so. I may, however, happen to find a message in a bottle reading "I was shipwrecked in the Juan Fernandez islands"; it would be clear to me that someone (someone who is not myself) was shipwrecked. But, if I find a mirror in a bottle, after taking it out with considerable effort, I would always see myself in it, whoever may have sent it as a message. If the mirror 'names' (and this is clearly a metaphor), it only names a concrete object, it names one at a time, and it always names only the object standing in front of it. In other words, whatever a mirror image may be, it is determined in its origins and in its physical existence by an object we shall call the image *referent*.

In an extreme attempt to find one more relation between mirror images and words, we might compare mirror images to proper names. If in a crowded station I would shout *John!* I am likely to see a great many people turning around — which allowed many to say that proper names have a direct relation to their bearers. Yet, if someone looking out of the window would say *Look, there comes John!*, inside the room and without knowing John, I would know that the other saw (or says he saw) a male human being (provided he is making an appropriate use of language). If this is so, then even proper names do not refer directly to an object whose presence determines the proper name utterance. Not only could my comrade lie, and mention John when John is not there, but the linguistic expression *John* first and foremost refers me to a general content. So much so that, if someone would eventually decide to christen his newborn daughter *John,* I would tell him that he is making an inappropriate use of current onomastics, since *John* usually names males.

Therefore, there is a difference between a mirror image and a proper name, in that a mirror image is an *absolute proper name* as it is an absolute icon. In other words, the semiotic dream of proper names being immediately linked to their referent (just like the semiotic dream of an image having all the properties of the object they refer to) arises from a sort of *catoptric nostalgia*. There is actually a theory of proper names as *rigid designators* (Kripke 1972) by which proper names could not be mediated by definite descriptions (like *John is the fellow who* . . .) but could undergo counterfactual exercises (like *Would John still be John, were he not the fellow who . . .?*). An unbroken chain of designations, called a 'causal' chain, links them to an original object they were allocated to by a sort of initial 'baptism'.

Now, it is mirrors which allow us to imagine this kind of situation. Let us assume that along a certain distance, between point A, where the reflected object is located, and point B, where the observer is standing (who under normal conditions cannot see point A), we fit an unbroken series of mirrors at regular intervals and at a suitable inclination, so that by chain reflection, the observer in B may see the object image from A in the nearest mirror.

We would always be in the case of a prosthesis-channel. Of course, we must necessarily assume that there is an odd number of mirrors. Only in this event would the mirror nearer to the observer give him an image of the original object as if it were reflected in the first mirror. With an even number of mirrors, in fact, the image would be 'reversed' twice, and we would not be in the presence of a simple prosthesis but, rather, of the effect of a more complex catoptric apparatus, this having translation functions. In any case, for the problem we are concerned with here, the observer need only know that there is an odd or even number of mirrors, and he will then behave as he does when facing his bathroom mirror or his barber's mirrors. Now, on the grounds of the principles enunciated in our previous pragmatics of the mirror, the observer knows (a) that the final mirror is a mirror and (b) that it is telling the truth; therefore, he also knows (c) that, at that very moment, the reflected object does exist in point A. Through this causal chain, the final mirror image becomes a rigid designator of the object which is the source of stimuli; better still, we know that the final image 'christens', so to say, the initial object in that very moment.

Such catoptric apparatus would be a rigid-designation apparatus. There is no linguistic contrivance which would provide the same guarantee, not even a proper name, because in this event two conditions of absolutely rigid designation would be missing: (1) the original object might well not exist at the moment and also might never have existed; (2) there would be no guarantee that the name corresponds to that object alone and to no other having similar general characteristics.

We therefore come to discover that the semantics of rigid designation is in the end a (pseudo-) semantics of the mirror image and that no linguistic term can be a rigid designator (just as there is no absolute icon). If it cannot be absolute, any rigid designator other than a mirror image, any rigid designator whose rigidity may be undermined in different ways and under different conditions, becomes a *soft or slack designator*. As absolutely rigid designators, mirror images alone cannot be questioned by counterfactuals. In fact, I could never ask myself (without violating the pragmatic principles regulating any relation with mirrors): "If the object whose image I am perceiving had properties other than those of the image I perceive, would it still be the same object?" But this guarantee is provided precisely by the threshold-phenomenon a mirror is. The theory of rigid designators falls a victim of the magic of mirrors.

## 7.9.  On signs

If the mirror has nothing to do with proper names, it has nothing to do with common nouns, either, which always refer (except with regard to their indexical use) to general concepts. But this does not mean that the mirror image is not a sign because semiotic tradition, from Hellenism to the present days, has developed a sign concept which goes beyond the mere concept of verbal sign.

According to the earliest definitions, a sign is *aliquid* which *stat pro aliquo*. The most elementary type of recollectable sign, as theorized by the Stoics, is smoke which stands for fire.

At this point, we should establish whether the mirror image *stands for* the body emanating it as a reflection just as smoke *stands for* the fire which produces it.

A correct understanding of the first and most thorough sign theory ever produced (that is, the Stoics theory) will inevitably lead us to assume that anything may be taken as a sign of anything else provided that it is an *antecedent* revealing a *consequent* — where antecedent and consequent have the value they assume according to the logical ratio of implication p ⊃ q. Thus the consequent might well be the more or less chronologically remote cause of the antecedent — as it is in the case of fire and smoke.

However, this definition (as we have seen in chapter one of this book) is not sufficient to characterize a sign as such. The semiotic requirements are the following:

(1) In order that the antecedent might become a sign of the consequent, the antecedent must be potentially present and perceptible while the consequent is usually absent. For the Stoic *sēmeîon*, the absence of the consequent seems to be strictly necessary: if one sees smoke billowing out of flames, there is no need to consider it a sign of fire. Words and many nonverbal indexical devices can be produced while their referent is present, but their condition for being a sign is that they must be understandable as sign even though their supposed referent is not there. The consequent may be absent whether because it is out the reach of my actual perceptibility or because it does not subsist any longer at the very moment in which I interpret the sign (think, for example, of the tracks of prehistorical animals). As Abelard said, the power of language is given by the fact that the expression *nulla rosa est* (translatable either as *there is no rose* or as *such a thing like a rose has never existed*) is fully comprehensible even though there are no roses.

(2) As a result, the antecedent may be produced even though the consequent does not subsist or has never subsisted. One can produce smoke by means of chemical substances thus pretending that there is (somewhere) fire. Signs can be used *to lie* about the world's state of affairs.

(3) Signs can be used to lie because the antecedent (expression) does not require the consequent as either its necessary or its efficient cause. The antecedent is only *presumed* to be caused by the consequent.

(4) This happens because the antecedent is not primarily related to an actual state of affairs but to a more or less general *content*. In every signification system, the consequent conveyed by the antecedent is only *a class of possible consequents*. Signs can be referred to referents because they are primarily correlated to a content (extensions are functions of the intentions). Even a gestural index, like a finger pointing at something, before being characterized by its contiguity to the object indicated, is characterized by the fact that, in a given gestural convention's system, it

signifies «focus your attention on the possible object in the radius of the digital apex»; in fact, I might indicate something which does not exist, and my (deceived) interlocutor will at first be led into thinking that something must be there. This something is the consequent content of the antecedent-expression /finger pointed at something/.

(5) But the Stoics' semiotics tells us something more. It does not tell us that smoke as a sign is smoke as a material *occurrence*. The Stoics' sign is *incorporeal:* it is the relationship of implication between two propositions ('if there is smoke there must be fire', which could also be translated in terms of a law: 'each time there is smoke there must be fire'). The semiotic relationship is, therefore, a *law* correlating a *type*-antecedent to a *type*-consequent. The sign is not given by the fact that *this* smoke automatically leads me to *that* fire, but that a general class of occurrences recognizable as smoke automatically leads me to the general class of occurrences definable as fire. The relationship exists between *types* rather than between *tokens*. In other words, the interpreter of certain semiotic situations makes them occur as relations between tokens owing to the fact that he *knows* (while the barbarian does not) that — first of all — the same relation holds between types.

(6) The fact that the semiotic relationship occurs between types makes it *independent of the actual channel or medium* in which and by which its corresponding occurrences are produced and conveyed. The smoke-to-fire sign relationship does not change whether or not the smoke is chemically produced or spoken about or portrayed by images. The relationship linking dots and dashes to the letters of the alphabet as codified by Morse code does not change according to whether the dots and dashes are conveyed by electric signals or tapped out by a prisoner against the wall of his cell.

(7) Finally (and here the original Stoic concept is partially developed), the content of an expression *may be interpreted*. If after seeing smoke somebody tells me there is fire, I might ask him what he means by fire, and he might explain this by showing me some fire, or with the image of a flame, or by giving a verbal definition, or by causing me to recollect a sensation of heat, or by reminding me of a past event when I experienced the presence of fire. In the same way, when hearing the name *John* I might ask for the meaning of this name, and the speaker need not necessarily show me John, he only need define him in one way or another (Lucy's husband, the guy you met yesterday, the one portrayed in this miniature, the guy who walks moving his head like this or like that, and so on . . .). Each interpretation not only defines the content of the expression, but also in its own way *provides me with more information* (Peirce, *C. P.* 8.322).

## 7.10.   Why mirrors do not produce signs

In the light of what has been said above, the mirror image does not meet the requirements for a sign. One cannot say that, when discovering through a mirror that someone is standing behind one, one infers a consequent by an antecedent. Since, as we have seen, mirrors are prostheses, this inference is not so different from the many pseudo-inferences one can draw from the use of periscopes or binoculars: if I see something through them, then there must be something. But this inference is not dissimilar from the fundative inference that rules our relationship with our own senses: if I see something, then it means that *there* there is something.

(1a) The mirror image (even when it is taken as an antecedent) is present in the presence of *a referent which cannot be absent*. It never refers to remote consequents. The relationship between object and image is the relationship between two presences, without any possible mediations. The consequent (by virtue of the prosthesis action of the mirror) comes into the radius of the interpreter's perceptibility.

(2a) The image is causally produced by the *object* and cannot be produced in the absence of the object itself.

(3a) Thus, as we have already seen, the mirror image *cannot be used to lie*. We can lie *about* mirror images (making phenomena which are not mirror images pass as such), but we cannot lie with and through a mirror image.

(4a) The mirror image *cannot be correlated to a content*, or, rather, it might well be (I look at my image in the mirror to reflect on the generic characteristics of the human body), only by virtue of its necessary relationship to the referent. The signs can refer to a referent because they automatically refer us to a content, whereas the mirror image refers only to one content as it has a primary relationship with the referent.

(5a) Thus the mirror image never establishes a relationship between types but only between tokens, which is another way of distinguishing the imaginary from the symbolic — where the symbolic implies a 'universal' mediation which is in fact the relationship between types.

(6a) It goes without saying that the mirror image *is not independent of the medium or channel* in which it is formed and by which it is conveyed. It is embodied by one, and only one, channel, the mirror.

(7a) In the end, the mirror image *cannot be interpreted*. At most, the object to which it refers can be interpreted (in terms of different types of inferences, definitions, and descriptions which are increasingly analytical), or, rather, the stimulating field from which the double is produced. The image as such can only be reflected as such by a second (third, fourth . . .) mirror. On the other hand, if the *interpretability* is an inherent feature of the content, an image without content cannot by definition be interpreted (at least in the sense which we have given to the concept of interpretability).

### 7.11.  Freaks: distorting mirrors

Mirror images are not signs and signs are not mirror images. And yet there are cases when mirrors are used to produce processes which can be defined as semiotic.

The first peculiar case is that of distorting mirrors, whose amazing effects were already observed by Arab physicists and in *Le Roman de la Rose*. A strange prosthesis, the distorting mirror amplifies but distorts the organ's function, as a hearing aid which transforms all conversation into a pop song. Therefore, a prosthesis with hallucinatory functions. If we take hallucinatory substances, we continue to perceive shapes, colors, sounds, and smells, but in an altered form. The sensory organs function abnormally. And yet we know that these are our sensory organs, which we usually trust. If we are not aware that we are drugged, we trust them, with the most unforeseeable effects; if, on the other hand, we are aware, in that we are still able to control our reactions, we force ourselves to interpret and translate the sensorial data to reconstruct 'correct' perceptions (or, rather, analogous to the perceptions of most human beings). The same thing occurs with the distorting mirror. If we know neither that it is a mirror nor that it is distorting, we will therefore find ourselves in a situation of normal perceptive deceit. It is just a question of noise on the channel. At times this noise is not perceived as such, and if while speaking to someone on the telephone the line is disturbed, we are bound to assume that the noises are the mutterings, the coughing, or the hoarseness of the person we are talking to. But in this case we are wrongly interpreting sensations, and once again we are taking dross for gold.

The case where we know that we are in front of a distorting mirror, as, for instance, at a fun fair, tends to be more interesting.

Our attitude is therefore double: on the one hand, we find it amusing; that is, we enjoy the hallucinatory characteristics of the medium. We therefore decide (for the sake of playing) to accept that we have three eyes or an enormous stomach or very short legs, just as we accept a fairy tale. In reality, we give ourselves a sort of pragmatic holiday: we accept that the mirror, which usually tells the truth, is lying. But the fact that our disbelief is suspended does not concern the image as much as the distorting prosthesis. The game is a complex one: on the one hand, I behave as if I were standing in front of a plane mirror telling the truth, and I find that it gives back an 'unreal' image (that which I am not). If I accept this image, I am helping, one could say, the mirror to lie. The pleasure that this game gives me is not of a totally semiotic nature but of an aesthetic nature. I do the same with other prostheses if, for example, I observe the world through colored lenses. But this game is not so different from the one I play when in the midst of an incredible hum of voices: I place the palms of my hands over my ears, lifting my hands off and replacing them rhythmically in order to hear an 'unreal' noise.

However, at the same time (or immediately afterward), another attitude comes into play: since I know that I am standing in front of the mirror, I imagine that in one way or another it always tells the truth because it reflects (even if poorly) incident rays emanating from my body. (Naturally, the same applies if I look at someone else's body in the distorting mirror; however, there is no doubt that the whole business becomes psychologically more interesting, from a narcissistic point of view, if that body is mine.)

Under these circumstances I interpret the data given back to me by the mirror, in the same way in which, with regard to refractory phenomena, even if I continue to see the stick which is broken in half by the water, I nonetheless interpret these data by continuing to accept this stick as unbroken. Interpretive rules to decode the optical illusions exist (if not at a perceptive level, at least at a level of intellectual judgment). In front of the distorting mirror, I put a few projective rules to the test, so that a given length or width of the virtual image must proportionally correspond to different lengths or widths of the reflected object. I proceed as if I had to interpret a type of cartographic projection in terms of another. These projective rules are no different from the ones I apply in order to recognize, in a stylized or grotesque drawing, the characteristics of the object or the class of type-objects to which it refers. In this sense the experience of the distorted image constitutes a further threshold phenomenon which shifts the boundaries between catoptrics and semiosis. If the distorted image were not also parasitic with respect to its referent, we would have to admit that it has many semiotic characteristics, even if rather vague, imprecise, and erratic. For example, in this relationship (which is *always* a token-to-token one), I am forced to see myself as another (as a dwarf, a giant, a monster): it is like the beginning of a generalization process, the negligence of the referent to fantasize on the content — even if in terms of a continually repressed temptation controlled by a consciousness of the singularity of the phenomenon, a cold reasoning on a hallucinatory situation. There is that extra knowledge concerning what I am or could be, the dawn of a counterfactual exercise — the beginning of semiosis.

Perhaps, in accordance with this possibility, we relegate the distorting mirrors to enchanted castles, so as not to question the frontier between catoptrics and semiosis which we have instinctively demarcated so well.

Finally, undoubtedly the image reflected by the distorting mirror is an indication of the fact that the mirror as a channel is in fact a distorting one. Just as the image of the broken stick tells me that (as if I didn't already know) the stick is immersed in water. We have already described these symptomatic uses of the image, where the image does not give us information about the object, but about the nature of the channel. In these cases it is my perceptive surprise which becomes the symptom of the channel anomalies (how can I see a broken stick and my face with three eyes when I know that 'it is not the case'?), so that the semiosis effort actually is between the perceptive surprise (equivalent in this case to an anomalous thermic sensation) and the channel, not between the image and the object.

### 7.12.  Procatoptric staging

Let us consider a more disquieting event. I am in a room, in front of me is a vertical mirror, located at a slant with respect to the rays emanating from by body. Actually, I do not see myself, but somebody in the adjoining room, who acts without knowing someone is looking at him. The case is similar to the sheriff in Westerns who sees the bandit coming in behind him in the mirror over the counter in front of him. These cases are not perplexing; we said already that the mirror is a prosthesis and at times has the same intrusive action as a periscope.

But let us now imagine that in the adjoining room there is a subject S1 who knows that S2 is spying on him in the mirror, but assuming (correctly) that S2 thinks that S1 does not know S2 is seeing him do so. Now, S1 wishes to make S2 believe that S2 (thinking he is unseen) is doing something commendable and behaves in a way S2 is to consider as spontaneous although S1 behaves so only and exclusively for (or against) S2. S1 is therefore staging an almost theatrical performance, the difference being that the audience should mistake theater for reality. Then, S1 is using the mirror image to lie. Is there anything semiosic in such a situation?

Everything is semiosic in it, and yet nothing concerning the mirror image as such. Even in verbal language I can utter a true statement in order to make my listener believe something else (about my ideas, my feelings, and so on). The same happens in this case. The mirror image still retains each and every characteristic of dull faithfullness it would have in the event S1 were behaving earnestly; it reflects exactly what S1 is doing. It is just that what S1 is doing is a *mise-en-scène*, and therefore a semiosic contrivance.

There is a profilmic staging (Bettetini 1975). Our beliefs about the faithfulness of the camera usually have nothing to do our beliefs about the 'truth' of the scene that the camera is going to shoot. When a movie shows a fairy with seven dwarfs in a flying coach, one knows that such a situation is fictional even though one trusts the faithfulness of the recording apparatuses shooting it. Only children take the *mise-en-scène* for reality as well, but this lack of maturity concerns their competence about a semiotics of *mise-en-scène*, quite apart from their possible lack of competence about a semiotics of filming.

Similarly, there is a procatoptric staging which can create deceptive situations. But, in this case, any semiotic consideration should shift from mirror images to staging, the mirror images being mere channels of procatoptric messages. These considerations also suggest that, besides procatoptric staging, there may also be a grammar of the shot and a specific syntax of catoptric editing. S1 may incline the mirror so that S2 can only see some aspects of the scene taking place in the adjoining room (independently of whether it is real or staged). Mirrors are always 'framing' devices, and inclining them in a certain way is a way to exploit this specific quality of them. Once again, however, this semiosic contrivance does not concern mirror images (which as usual depict things just as the mirror 'sees' them) but a manipulation of the channel.

Let us now imagine that S1 has a remote control to incline the mirror as he likes, so as to show S2 different corners of the adjoining room, at a few seconds' interval. If, at one angle, the mirror shows a certain object and, at another, someone staring blankly in front of him, S1 might create catoptric images similar to what in film editing is called the Kuleshov effect. According to the 'editing' he works out, S1 may make S2 believe that the man sitting in the adjoining room is looking at various objects in anger, lust, or surprise. A swift play of inclination and the mirror might make S2 lose the sense of actual space relations between objects. In this case, moving mirrors might create a true semiosic situation, a tale, a fiction, a doxastic *concoction*.

If we use mirrors as channels, staging, shot, and editing are made possible. They are all semiosic contrivances which yield most when used in connection with non-mirror images. What would remain unchanged is the asemiosic nature of mirror images, which are always causally related to their referents. S2 might be inclined to universalizing processes, almost forgetting he is observing mirror images, thus living a type-story rather than a token-story.

But the very nature of this story's being connected to the mirror would make it forever related to its causative referent, would still keep it half way between semiosis and catoptrics, between the symbolic and the imaginary.

## 7.13.   Rainbows and Fata Morganas

Rainbows are phenomena of partial reflection, although combined with refraction and dispersion of sunlight passing through tiny drops of water in the lower layers of the atmosphere. However, their image is never perceived as mirror image. A rainbow can be employed semiosically in two cases only. It can be seen as a wonder, a sign given by the gods, but to the same extent as storms, tidal waves, eclipses, and the flight of birds. From time immemorial, mankind has rendered a number of physical phenomena semiosic, although not in view of their specific catoptric nature.

However, a rainbow can be read and used as a symptom (of the end of a storm). Under this respect, it may even work without its conjectured referent, since rainbows occur in waterfall gorges, too. In any case, even when correctly used as a symptom of the presence of water drops suspended in the atmosphere, it indicates an anomalous condition of the channel, rather than an actual object.

As to Fata Morganas and the like, they are never perceived by a naive observer as mirror phenomena: they are, in fact, instances of perceptive deceptions. In contrast, to a critical eye they may look like the symptom of either a given condition of the atmospheric channel or the presence of a distant object. On these grounds, they may even be used as mirror images of that object and, thus, as prostheses.

## 7.14.   Catoptric theaters

Precisely through phenomena like Fata Morganas, we are led to deal with other plays of mirrors known across the centuries as *Theatrum catoptricum, Theatron polydicticum, Theatrum protei, Speculum heterodictum, Multividium, Speculum multiplex, Tabula scalata,* and so on (see Baltrusaitis 1978). All such contrivances can be grouped into three main classes:

(a) Mirrors multiply and alter the virtual images of objects, which, somehow staged, are recognized by the observer as being reflected in a mirror.

(b) Starting from a staged object, a combined play of different curved mirrors creates real images the observer is supposed to ascribe to a wonder.

(c) Suitably arranged plane mirrors produce, on a mirror surface, the image of several superimposed, juxtaposed, and amalgamated objects, so that the observer, unaware of the catoptric play, gets the impression of prodigious apparitions.

Now, in the first case, the observer is aware of the catoptric nature of the play, so he is in no different position from one who personally controls a set of mirrors facing one another at different angles. He may enjoy the manipulation of the channels from an aesthetic point of view. When he watches the staging of a play with a pair of binoculars, the latter are meant to improve his perception of such a staging. In contrast, in this case, the staging itself is meant to improve the aesthetic perception of the possibilities offered by the prosthesis-channel. Any event enjoyed aesthetically involves self-reflectiveness: one's attention focuses not only on the form of the messages but also on the way the various channels are used. Likewise, the performance of an orchestra is appreciated not only in view of the melody (which, as such, is independent of the channel) but also because of the way the resources of an instrument are exploited.

In cases (b) and (c), we are back to situations similar to Fata Morganas, and optical illusions in general. Mirrors are once again used as channels, but the observer cannot focus his attention on them, being unaware of their presence. At the most, he aesthetically enjoys a staging whose nature he ignores. And in case he thinks he is facing a wonder, his position is the same as that of an observer who, seeing himself in a mirror, believes he is in front of an actual intruder. Sheer perceptive deception, rather than a mirror image experienced as such. In light of the typology of the modes of sign production (see Eco 1976, 3.6.6), such perceptive deceptions can be described as the result of *programmed stimuli*. As a matter of fact, they are based on a staging which is a semiosic phenomenon (so much so that it could be channeled otherwise; besides, mirror theaters are no longer used since different methods of projecting images have become available), but the mirror images employed are true and asemiosic in themselves.

## 7.15.  Mirrors that 'freeze' images

Let us continue with our phenomenological experiment, imagining magic mirrors (that is, really magic and not simply used to give an impression of magic).

Assume we have a 'freezing' mirror: the reflected image 'freezes' on its surface, even when the object disappears. Eventually, we have established a relationship of absence between antecedent and consequent. However, we have not eliminated the causal connection between original referent and image. We have moved further, but just a little. A photographic plate is in fact a freezing mirror. Needless to say, we assume the existence of a plate capable of reproducing an image with a very high definition (wavelength, intensity relation, and outlines), and, after all, we have decided to accept even the images reflected in mirrors that are either broken or crossed by opaque strips.

What makes a picture similar to a mirror image? A pragmatic assumption whereby a dark room should be as truthful as a mirror and, at any rate, testify to the presence of an imprinter (present in the case of mirrors, past in that of photography). The difference lies in the fact that the exposed plate is indeed an *imprint* or a *trace*.

A trace differs under certain respects from a mirror image, even disregarding image reversal on the plate, its further reversal on the printed picture, and the recovery of its inverse symmetry, that is, the actual inversion of the congruence characterizing mirror images.

The main point is that imprints are motivated but *heteromaterial* (Eco 1976, 3.6): the plate *turns light rays into different matter*. We no longer perceive light rays, but pure intensity relations as well as pigmentation relations. Thus there has been a projection from matter to matter. The channel tends to lose its importance, the picture can be transferred on different materials, while relations remain unchanged. The image is not independent of its channel as the Morse code is of the material employed for its standard signals. However, some kind of liberation is foreshadowed.

Probably because of the above phenomenon, the 'photograph stage' comes much later than the 'mirror stage' in the subject's ontogenesis. A baby has no problems in recognizing his image reflected in a mirror, whereas a child up to five years of age finds it very difficult (and requires some sort of training) to identify photographed objects. Indeed, he will perceive images as expressions referring to a generic content and, only through this connection with the universal, will he refer to the improper subject. He sees the picture of a woman $X$, considers it the picture of a type-woman, applies it to a token-woman $Y$ and finally states that it is a picture of his mother. He actually fails to *refer* that proper-improper name, that *slack designator* represented by a photographic image. We are witnessing a semiosic phenomenon.

Our pragmatics of photography reflects the effects of those early mistakes. While testifying that the plate has been exposed to something (and, in view of that, photographic images can be used as evidence), it nevertheless arouses the suspicion that something has not been there at all. We know that, through staging, optical tricks, emulsion, solarization, and the like, someone could have produced the image of something that did not exist, had not existed, and will never exist. A photograph can lie. We realize that, even when we assume, naively, if not under the influence of a fideistic attitude, that it does not. The objective referent is conjectured and yet, at every moment, it risks dissolving in pure content. Is a photograph the photograph of a man or the photograph of *that* man? It depends on how we use it (see Goodman's remarks, 1968). Occasionally, on the basis of a surreptitious reference to general (universal) content, we take the photograph of $X$ for that of $Y$. It is not just an error of perception, that is, as if we saw in a mirror the image of $X$ coming in and thought it was $Y$. In fact, there is more to it: in any imprint, however well defined, as that of an exposed plate, *generic characters ultimately prevail over specific ones.*

Except for catoptric theaters, the choice of the shot in the mirror is left to me, even when I am spying on someone: I need only move. Incidentally, if I see a half-length image of myself in a mirror, I need only get closer and look *inside,* downward, to see, within limits, that portion of my body the previous image did not show. The object is there, to produce the image, even where I did not see it at first. In contrast, with photographs, the shot is strictly set. I will never get the chance of seeing those legs if they are not in the image from the start: I just have to assume their existence (and still it could be the photograph of a *cul-de-jatte*). Again, the legs I presuppose are not one's legs, but just one's two-footedness. The impression of actual reference immediately faces into clusters of content. A photograph is already a semiosic phenomenon.

Second magic experiment: the frozen image *moves*. Motion pictures, obviously, to which all the remarks made on photography apply, plus the actual grammar of editing, with all the deceptive and generalizing effects it involves. Imprints, but moving ones.

Third experiment: the imprint has a very low definition, the mirror looks like an image freezer, and, on top of that, there is no longer a guarantee of the existence of a mirror and of a referent for the image. What I see is not only staging, shot, a selected visual angle, but also the result of the work done on the surface so that the latter seems to reflect the rays coming from an object: it is, in fact, a painting. In this case, all the requirements of semiosic phenomena are met; the physics of production combines with the pragmatics of interpretation in an utterly different way from that of the mirror image.

Our three imaginary experiments have led us to imagine phenomena no longer related to mirrors. Despite that, when dealing with such phenomena, we can never totally abandon the memory of the mirror images of which they are monkeys (the same as art is always *simia naturae*).

However, it is worth reconsidering for a moment our experiments involving a sequence of mirrors placed at regular intervals along a row of hills. Let us assume we replace the sequence of mirrors with other devices turning the light rays coming from the initial object into electric signals which are then transformed into optical signals by a final device. The resulting image would have the same characteristics as imprints such as photographs and motion pictures; in other words, they would enjoy a lower definition than the mirror image (anyway, we decided to consider such an inconvenience as only temporary), they would be heteromaterial and retranslated (reinverted). And yet, like the chain of mirrors, such a system would seem to involve a rigid designation: the image would be determined by the present referent which causes it, and the relation would be from occurrence to occurrence.

Obviously, such a system, where a schematic model of TV transmission can be detected, would only have this characteristic in case of *live* emission. As to the pragmatic attitude, a recorded TV broadcast does not differ from a film show, except for image definition and type of sensory stimulus. Only live TV broadcasts would share with mirrors their absolute relation with the referent.

The point is (and this may also apply to the set of mirrors reflecting a distant image) that just the space interval between referent and image arouses, more or less consciously, a suspicion of potential absence. The object should be there, but it may even not be. In addition, a further basic element should be taken into account: recorder emissions give rise to distrust in the audience as to the truthfulness of live emissions. From a pragmatic point of view, TV images share the advantages of mirror images as well as the disadvantages of the other photographic and motion-picture imprints. It is occurrence, acting as a parasite to the referent, but not necessarily. Who can be sure? And how many and what manipulationns may have taken place along the channel? And what is the role played, not only by the shot, but also by the editing, which influences live broadcasts, too, and through which the camera decides which aspects of the real referent to explore and the mixing may produce Kuleshov effects at any moment?

However, such comparisons between photosensitive imprints and mirror images tell us at least something which is highly important for the semiotics of photographic, motion-picture, and television images. The latter lie within the boundaries of semiotics, but certainly not within those of linguistics. Each imprint is a projection working as a toposensitive whole, not as a sequence of discrete elements replicable by *ratio facilis* (Eco 1976, 3.4.9). The way all imprints (which are actual signs) can be interpreted is similar to the way we interpret a distorted or low-defined mirror image (which, on the contrary, is not a sign). The process develops by projective relations, a given dimension must correspond to the same dimension in the image, if not in the object-occurrence (referent), at least in the object-type (content) the image 'tells' me about.

The actual grammatical categories come into play only in connection with shooting and editing. Imprints are not mirror images, but we read them *almost as if* they were. At a certain level of analysis — when, for instance, one is concerned only with iconographic conventions — one is entitled to look at photographic imprints as if they were real mirror images, that is, the immediate result of a reflection *tout court*, and their semiotic strategies will be investigated only at the highest manipulatory levels (staging, framing, and so on). In other cases, it would be, on the contrary, indispensable to cast in doubt their presumed 'innocence', to discuss their cultural origin, the non-naturality of their supposed causal relation with the referent.

## 7.16.   The *experimentum crucis*

However strong illusions, ambiguities, confusions 'on the threshold', and the temptation to rank together mirror images and imprints may be, the *experimentum crucis* will dispel any doubt: just reproduce a mirror in a photograph, in a motion picture or television shot, or in a painting. These images of mirror images do not work as mirror images. There is no in print or icon of a mirror other than a mirror. The latter, in the world of signs, becomes the shadow of its former self: derision, caricature, memory. You can make a portrait, either a photograph or a painting, and assert that it is 'realistic', truer than the original. With mirrors there is no truer image than the original's. A catoptric element, capable of reflecting a semiosic element existing independently of it (without modifying it), cannot, in turn, be reflected by it. The semiosic element can only generalize it, make it a genus, a scheme, a concept, pure content.

These two universes, of which the former is threshold to the latter, have no connecting points, the extreme cases represented by distorting mirrors being in fact 'catastrophe points'. There comes a time when one has to make up one's mind and choose which side one is on. The catoptric universe is a reality which can give the impression of virtuality, whereas the semiosic universe is a virtuality which can give the impression of reality.

# References

Quotations of classical or medieval authors refer to the current available editions. In particular, for Aristotle and Sextus Empiricus: Loeb Classical Library (London-Cambridge); for Augustine and Boethius: *Corpus Scriptorum Ecclesiasticorum Latinorum* (Vienna-Leipzig); for Abelard: *Editio Super Porphyrium: Scritti di Logica*, edited by M. Dal Pra (Florence: Nuova Italia, 1969); for Porphyry: *Commentaria in Aristotelem Graeca* (English translation, Porphyry the Poenician, *Isagoge* [Toronto: Pontifical Institute, 1975]); for Aquinas: the Marietti edition (Turin). The quotations in English without reference to a specific version are mine.

Balme, D. M.
  1975  Aristotle's Use of Differentiae in Zoology. In *Articles on Aristotle*, vol. 1, *Science*, edited by J. Barnes et al. London: Duckworth.
Baltrusaitis, J.
  1978  *Le Miroir*. Paris: Elmayan-Seuil.
Bambrough, R.
  1961  Universals and Family Resemblances. In *Proceedings of the Aristotelian Society* 50. (Also in *Universals and Particulars*, edited by M. L. Loux. Notre Dame, Ind.: University Press, 1970.)
Barthes, R.
  1967  *Système de la mode*. Paris: Seuil.
  1970  *S/Z*. Paris: Seuil. (English translation by R. Miller, *S/Z*. New York: Hill and Wang, 1975.)
Bergmann, M.
  1979  Metaphor and Formal Semantic Theory. *Poetics* 8.
Bettetini, G. F.
  1975  *Produzione del senso e messa in scena*. Milan: Bompiani.
Bierwisch, M.
  1970  Semantics. In *New Horizons in Linguistics*, edited by J. Lyons. Harmondsworth: Penguin.
  1971  On Classifying Semantic Features. In *Semantics*, edited by D. D. Steinberg and L. A. Jakobovits. London: Cambridge University Press.
Bierwisch, M., and Kiefer, F.
  1970  Remarks on Definitions in Natural Languages. In *Studies in Syntax and Semantics*, edited by F. Kiefer. Dordrecht: Reidel.
Black, M.
  1955  Metaphor. In *Proceedings of the Aristotelian Society*, n.s., 55.
Bonfantini, M. A., and Proni, G.
  1983  To Guess or Not to Guess. In *The Sign of Three: Dupin, Holmes, Peirce*, edited by U. Eco and T. A. Sebeok. Bloomington: Indiana University Press.
Bonsiepe, G.
  1965  Visuell/Verbale Rhetorik. *Ulm* 14–16.
Borges, J. L.
  1953  *Historia de la eternidad*. Buenos Aires: Emecé.

Brooke-Rose, C.
   1958  *A Grammar of Metaphor*. London: Secker and Warburg.
Buyssens, E.
   1943  *Le langage et le discours*. Brussels: Office de Publicité.
Carnap, R.
   1947  *Meaning and Necessity*. Chicago: University of Chicago Press.
   1955  Meaning and Synonymy in Natural Languages. *Philosophical Studies* 7.
Cassirer, E.
   1923  *Philosophie der Symbolischen Formen*. Leipzig: Bruno Cassirer. (English
         translation by R. Mannheim, *The Philosophy of Symbolic Forms*, vol. 1.
         New Haven: Yale.)
Charniak, E.
   1975  A Partial Taxonomy of Knowledge about Actions. Working Paper 13.
         Castagnola: Institute for Semantic and Cognitive Studies.
   1980  Ms. Malaprop: A Language Comprehension Program. In *Frame Concep-
         tions and Text-Understanding*, edited by D. Metzing. Berlin: De Gruyter.
Cherry, C.
   1957  *On Human Communication*. New York: Wiley.
Compagnon, A.
   1979  *La seconde main*. Paris: Seuil.
Cooper, D. E.
   1974  *Presupposition*. The Hague: Mouton.
Creuzer, G. F.
   1810–12  *Symbolik und Mythologie der alten Volker*. Leipzig-Darmstadt: Leske.
d'Alembert, J. Le R.
   1751  Discours préliminaire. *Encyclopédie*. Paris: Briasson, David, Le Creton,
         Durand.
Dean Fodor, J.
   1977  *Semantics: Theories of Meaning in Generative Grammar*. New York:
         Crowell.
Deely, J.
   1969  *The Philosophical Dimension of the Origins of Species*. Chicago: Institute for
         Philosophical Research.
   1982  *Introducing Semiotics*. Bloomington: Indiana University Press.
Deleuze, G., and Guattari, F.
   1976  *Rhizome*. Paris: Minuit.
De Lubac, H.
   1959  *Exégèse médiévale*. 4 vols. Paris: Aubier.
De Mauro, T.
   1971  *Senso e significato*. Bari: Adriatica.
Derrida, J.
   1977  Limited Inc. *Glyph* 2.
Di Cesare, D.
   1981  Il problema logico funzionale del linguaggio in Aristotele. In *Logos
         Semantikos*, edited by J. Trabant. Berlin: De Gruyter; Madrid: Gredos.
Doroszewski, W.
   1973  *Elements of Lexicology and Semiotics*. The Hague: Mouton.
Dupré, J.
   1981  Natural Kinds and Biological Taxa. *The Philosophical Review* 90.
Eco, U.
   1968  *La struttura assente*. Milan: Bompiani.
   1976  *A Theory of Semiotics*. Bloomington: Indiana University Press.

References [229]

1979   *The Role of the Reader*. Bloomingon: Indiana University Press.

1983   Horns, Hooves, Insteps: Some Hypotheses on Three Types of Abduction. In *The Sign of Three: Dupin, Holmes, Peirce*, edited by U. Eco and T. A. Sebeok. Bloomington: Indiana University Press.

Fann, K. T.

1970   *Peirce's Theory of Abduction*. The Hague: Nijhoff.

Fillmore, C.

1968   The Case for Case. In *Universals in Linguistic Theory*, edited by E. Bach and R. T. Harms. New York: Holt.

1970   Types of Lexical Information. In *Studies in Syntax and Semantics*, edited by F. Kiefer. Dordrecht: Reidel.

1975   An Alternative to Checklist Theories of Meaning. *BLS* 1.

1976a  Frame Semantics and the Nature of Language. In *Origins and Evolution of Language*, edited by J. Harndard et al. *Annals of the New York Academy of Sciences* 5.

1976b  Topics in Lexical Semantics. In *Current Issues in Linguistics Theory*, edited by R. Cole. Bloomington: Indiana University Press.

1977   The Case for Case Reopened. In *Syntax and Semantics*, vol. 8, edited by P. Cole and J. L. Morgan. New York: Academic Press.

1981   Ideal Reader and Real Readers. Mimeograph. Georgetown University.

Firth, R.

1973   *Symbols Public and Private*. London: Allen and Unwin.

Frede, M.

1978   Principles of Stoic Grammar. In *The Stoics*, edited by J. M. Rist. Berkeley and Los Angeles: University of California Press.

Freud, S.

1899   *Die Traumdeutung*. Leipzig-Wien: Deuticke. (English translation in Freud 1953.)

1905   *Der Witz und seine Beziehung zum Unbewussten*. Leipzig-Vienna: Deuticke. (English translation in Freud 1953.)

1953   *The Standard Edition of the Complete Psychological Works of Sigmund Freud*. London: Hogarth.

Gilson, E.

1947   *Le Thomisme*. Paris: Vrin. (English translation, *The Christian Philosophy of St. Thomas Aquinas*. London: Gollancz, 1961.)

Ginzburg, C.

1983   Morelli, Freud, and Sherlock Holmes: Clues and Scientific Method. In *The Sign of Three: Dupin, Holmes, Peirce*, edited by U. Eco and T. A. Sebeok. Bloomington: Indiana University Press.

Goethe, W.

1797   Über die Gegenstände der bildenden Kunst. *Samtliche Werke*, vol. 33. Stuttgart-Berlin: Cotta, 1902–12.

1809–32  Maximen und Reflexionen. *Werke*. Leipzig: Bibliographisches Institut, 1926.

Goodman, N.

1968   *Languages of Art*. New York: Bobbs-Merrill.

Goux, J.

1973   *Freud, Marx: Economie et symbolique*. Paris: Seuil.

Graeser, A.

1978   The Stoic Theory of Meaning. In *The Stoics*, edited by J. M. Rist. Berkeley and Los Angeles: University of California Press.

Greimas, A. J.
   1966   *Sémantique structurale*. Paris: Larousse.
   1970   *Du sens*. Paris: Seuil.
   1973   Lex actants, lex acteurs et les figures. In *Sémiotique narrative et textuelle*, edited by C. Chabrol. Paris: Larousse.
Greimas, A. J., ed.
   1972   *Essais de sémiotique poétique*. Paris: Larousse.
Greimas, A. J., and Courtés, J.
   1979   *Sémiotique: Dictionnaire raisonné de la théorie du langage*. Paris: Hachette. (English translation by L. Crist and D. Patte, *Semiotics and Language: An Analytical Dictionary*. Bloomington: Indiana University Press, 1982.)
Greimas, A. J., and Rastier, F.
   1968   The Interaction of Semiotic Constraints. *Yale French Studies* 41.
Grice, H. P.
   1957   Meaning. *Philosophical Review* 46.
   1967   Logic and Conversation. In *Syntax and Semantics*, vol. 3, edited by R. Cole and J. L. Morgan. New York: Academic Press, 1975.
   1968   Utterer's Meaning, Sentence-Meaning and Word-Meaning. *Foundations of Language* 4.
Groupe μ
   1970   *Rhétorique générale*. Paris: Larousse. (English translation by P. B. Burrell and E. M. Slotkin, *A General Rhetoric*. Baltimore and London: Johns Hopkins University Press, 1981.)
Guenthner, E.
   1975   On the Semantic of Metaphor. *Poetics* 4.
Haiman, J.
   1980   Dictionaries and Encyclopedia. *Lingua* 50.
Harman, G.
   1977   Semiotics and the Cinema. *Quarterly Review of Film Studies* 2. (Also in *Film Theory and Criticism*, edited by G. Mast and M. Cohen. New York: Oxford University Press, 1979.)
   1979   Eco-location. In *Film Theory and Criticism*, edited by G. Mast and M. Cohen. New York: Oxford University Press.
Hegel, G. W. F.
   1817–29   *Ästhetik*. Berlin: Aufbau, 1955. (English translation by F. P. D. Osmaston, *The Philosophy of Fine Arts*. London: Bell, 1920.
Henry, A.
   1971   *Métonymie et métaphore*. Paris: Klincksieck.
Hjelmslev, L.
   1943   *Omkring sprogteoriens grundlaeggelse*. Kφbenhavn: Munksgaard. (English translation by F. J. Whitfield, *Prolegomena to a Theory of Language*. Madison: University of Wisconsin, 1961.)
   1957   Pour une sémantique structurale. In *Essais Linguistiques*. Copenhagen: Nordisk Spro-og Kulturferlag, 1959.
Holenstein, E.
   1974   *Jakobson*. Paris: Seghers.
Jakobson, R.
   1932   Musikwissenschaft und Linguistik. *Prager Presse* (7 December).
   1949   On the Identification of Phonemic Entities. *Travaux du Cercle Linguistique de Copenhague* 5.
   1954   Two Aspects of Language and Two Types of Aphasic Disturbance. In

References                                                              [231]

R. Jakobson and M. Halle, *Fundamentals of Language*. The Hague: Mouton, 1956.

1961    Linguistics and Communication Theory. In *Structure of Language and Its Mathematical Aspects*, edited by R. Jakobson. *Proceedings of Symposia in Applied Mathematics* 12.

1968    Language in Relation to Other Communication Systems. *Linguaggi nella società e nella tecnica*. Milan: Comunità, 1970.

1970    Linguistics. *Main Trends of Research in the Social and Human Sciences* I. The Hague: Mouton.

1974    *Coup d'oeil sur le développement de la sémiotique*. Bloomington: Indiana University Publications, 1975. (English translation in Jakobson 1980.)

1980    *The Framework of Language*. Michigan Studies in the Humanities.

Jakobson, R., and Halle, M.

1956    *Fundamentals of Language*. The Hague: Mouton.

Jung, C. G.

1934    Über die Archetypen des kollektiven Unbewussten. In *Von den Wurzeln des Bewusstseins Studien über des Archetypus*. 2d ed. Zurich: Rascher, 1954. (English translation by R. F. C. Hull, Archetypes and the Collective Unconscious, in *Collected Works*, vol. 9. New York: Bollingen.)

Katz, J. J.

1972    *Semantic Theory*. Harper.

1977    *Propositional Structure and Illocutionary Force*. New York: Crowell.

1979    The Neoclassical Theory of Meaning. In *Contemporary Perspectives in the Philosophy of Language*, edited by P. A. French et al. Minneapolis: University of Minnesota Press.

Kerbrat-Orecchioni, C.

1976    Problematique de l'isotopie. *Linguistique et sémiologie* I.

Kripke, S.

1972    Naming and Necessity. In *Semantics of Natural Languages*, edited by D. Davidson and G. Harman. Dordrecht: Reidel.

Kristeva, J.

1969    *Sémeiotiké*. Paris: Seuil.

1974    *La révolution du language Poétique*. Paris: Seuil.

Kuhn, T.

1962    *The Structure of Scientific Revolutions*. Chicago: University of Chicago Press.

Lacan, J.

1953    Le séminaire I. In *Le Séminaire de J. Lacan*. Paris: Seuil, 1975.

1966    *Ecrits*. Paris: Seuil.

Lakoff, G.

1980    Getting the Whole Picture. *BLS* 6.

Lakoff, G., and Johnson, M.

1980    *Metaphors We Live By*. Chicago: University of Chicago Press.

Lalande, A., ed.

1926    *Vocabulaire technique et critique de la philosophie*. Paris: P. U. F.

Lausberg, H.

1960    *Handbuch der literarischen Rhetorik*. Munich: Hüber.

Leech, G.

1974    *Semantics*. Harmondsworth: Penguin.

Levin, S.

1977    *The Semantics of Metaphor*. Baltimore: Johns Hopkins University Press.

Lévi-Strauss, C.
  1945  L'Analyse structurale en linguistique et anthropologie. *Word* 1,2. (Also in *Structural Anthropology*. New York: Basic Books, 1963.)
  1947  *Les structures élémentaires de la parenté*. Paris: P. U. F. (English translation, *The Elementary Structures of Kinship*. Boston: Beacon, 1969.)
  1950  Introduction à l'oeuvre de Marcel Mauss. In M. Mauss, *Sociologie et anthropologie*. Paris: P. U. F.
  1951  Language and the Analysis of Social Laws. *American Anthropologist* 53. (Also in *Structural Anthropology*. New York: Basic Books, 1963.)
  1958–59  La geste d'Asdival. *Annuaire de l'EPHA* 5. (English translation, "The Story of Asdival." In *The Structural Study of Myth and Totemism*, edited by E. Leach. London: Tavistock, 1967.)
  1960  Discours au Collège de France. *Annuaire de Collège du France* 40.
  1964  *Le cru et le cuit*. Paris: Plon. (English translation, *The Raw and the Cooked*. New York: Harper, 1969.)
  1971  *L'homme nu*. Paris: Plon.
Lieb, H. H.
  1981  Das 'Semiotische Dreieck' bei Ogden un Richards: Eine Neuformulierung des Zeichenmodells von Aristoteles. In *Logos Semantikos*, edited by J. Trabant. Berlin: De Gruyter; Madrid: Gredos.
Lotman, J. M.
  1969  O Metayazyke tipologiceskick opisanij kul'tury. *Trudy po znakovym sistemam* 4.
Lotman, J. M., and Uspenskij, B. A.
  1971  O Semiotičeskom mechanizm kul'tury. *Trudy po znakovym sistemam* 5.
Lyons, J.
  1977  *Semantics*. 2, vols. London: Cambridge University Press.
Malmberg, B.
  1977  *Signes et symboles*. Paris: Picard.
Manetti, G., and Violi, P.
  1977  Grammatica dell'arguzia. *VS* 18 (Special Issue).
McInerny, R.
  1961  *The Logic of Analogy*. The Hague: Nijhoff.
Minsky, M. M.
  1974  A Framework for Representing Knowledge. AI Memo 306 Cambridge: MIT Press.
Moody, E. A.
  1935  *The Logic of William of Ockham*. New York: Sheed and Ward.
Morris, C.
  1938  *Foundations of a Theory of Signs*. Chicago: University of Chicago Press.
Neubauer, F., and Petőfi, J. S.
  1981  Word Semantics, Lexicon System, and Text Interpretation. In *Words, Worlds and Contexts*, edited by H. J. Eikmeyer and H. Rieser. Berlin: De Gruyter.
Nef, F.
  1979  Case Grammar *vs*. Actantial Grammar: Some Remarks on Semantic Roles. In *Text vs. Sentence*, edited by J. S. Petőfi. Hamburg: Buske.
Nerval, G. de
  1853  *Sylvie*. (English translation by R. Aldington, in *Aurelia*. London: Chatto and Windus, 1932.)
Nida, E.
  1975  *Componential Analysis of Meaning*. The Hague: Mouton

References                                             [233]

Peirce, C. S.
1931 – 58   *Collected Papers*. Cambridge: Harvard University Press.

Pelc, J.
1981   Theoretical Foundations of Semiotics. *American Journal of Semiotics* 1.

Petőfi, J. S.
1976a   Lexicology, Encyclopedic Knowledge, Theory of Text. *Cahiers de Lexicologie* 29.
1976b   A Frame for Frames. *Proceedings of the Second Annual Meeting of the Berkeley Linguistic Society*. Berkeley: University of California, Berkeley.

Petőfi, J. S., ed.
1979   *Text vs. Sentence*. 2 vols. Hamburg: Buske.

Popper, K.
1968   *Conjectures and Refutations*. New York: Harper.

Prieto, L.
1966   *Messages et signaux*. Paris: P. U. F.
1975   *Pertinence et pratique*. Paris: Minuit.

Prodi, G.
1977   *Le basi materiali della significazione*. Milan: Bompiani.
1982   *La Storia Naturale della Logica*. Milan: Bompiani.

Putnam, H.
1975   *Mind, Language and Reality*, vol. 2. London: Cambridge University Press.

Quine, W. van O.
1951   Two Dogmas of Empiricism. *Philosophical Review* 50.
1969   Natural Kinds. In *Ontological Relativity and Other Essays*. New York: Columbia.

Rey, A.
1970   *La lexicologie*. Paris: Klincksieck.
1973   *Théories du signe et du sens*. Paris: Klincksieck.

Rey-Debove, J.
1971   *Etude linguistique et sémiotique des dictionnaires français contemporains*. The Hague: Mouton.

Ricoeur, P.
1962   Hermeneutique et réflection. In *Demitizzazione e immagine*, edited by E. Castelli. Padua: Cedam.
1975   *La métaphore vive*. Paris: Seuil. (English translation, *The Rule of Metaphor*. Toronto: University Press, 1979.)

Rosensthiel, P.
1971   Labyrinthologie mathématique (1). *Mathématique et Sciences Humaines* 9.
1980   Les mots du labyrinthe. *Cartes et figures de la terre*. Paris: Centre Culturel Pompidou.

Rosenstiehl, P.; Fiksel, J. R.; and Holliger, A.
1972   Intelligent Graphs: Networks of Finite Automata Capable of Solving Graph Problems." In *Graph Theory and Computing*. New York: Academic Press.

Rossi-Landi, F.
1974   Linguistics and Economics. In *Current Trends in Linguistics*, vol. 12, edited by T. A. Sebeok. The Hague: Mouton.

Russell, B.
1940   The Object-Language. In *An Inquiry into Meaning and Truth*. London: Allen and Unwin, 1950.

Saussure, F. de
 1906– 11   *Cours de linguistique générale*. Paris: Payot, 1916.
Schank, R.
 1975   *Conceptual Information Processing*. Amsterdam: North Holland.
 1979   Interestingness: Controlling Inferences. *Artificial Intelligence* 12.
Schank, R., and Abelson, R. P.
 1977   *Scripts, Plans, Goals and Understanding*. Hillsdale, N. J.: Erlbaum.
Schank, R., and Riesbeck, C. K.
 1981   *Inside Computer Understanding*. Hillsdale, N. J.: Erlbaum.
Schmidt, S.
 1973   *Texttheorie*. Munich: Fink.
Scholem, G.
 1960   *Zur Kabbala und ihrer Symbolik*. Zurich: Rhein. (English translation by
        Ralph Mannheim, *On the Kabbalah and Its Symbolism*. New York: Schoc-
        ken, 1965.)
Schwartz, S. P., ed.
 1977   *Naming, Necessity and Natural Kinds*. Ithaca: Cornell University Press.
Scruton, R.
 1980   Possible Worlds and Premature Sciences. *The London Review of Books* (7
        February).
Searle, J. R.
 1971   Introduction to *The Philosophy of Language*, edited by J. R. Searle. Lon-
        don: Oxford University Press.
 1979   *Expression and Meaning*. London: Cambridge University Press.
Sebeok, T. A.
 1976   *Contributions to the Doctrine of Signs*. Bloomington: Indiana University.
Sebeok, T. A., and Sebeok-Umiker, J.
 1979   You Know My Method: A Juxtaposition of Charles S. Peirce and Sher-
        lock Holmes. *Semiotica* 26. (Also in *The Sign of Three: Dupin, Holmes,
        Peirce*, edited by U. Eco and T. A. Sebeok. Bloomington: Indiana Uni-
        versity Press, 1983.)
Shannon, C. E.
 1948   The Mathematical Theory of Communication. *Bell System Technical
        Journal* (July-October). (Also in C. Shannon and W. Weaver, *The Math-
        ematical Theory of Communication*. Urbana: University of Illinois Press,
        1949.)
Shibles, W. A.
 1971   *Metaphor: An Annotated Bibliography and History*. Whitewater, Wis.:
        Language Press.
Speciale, E.
 1978   *La teoria della metafora in E. Tesauro*. Doctoral thesis, University of
        Bologna.
Stump, E.
 1978   Differentia and the Porphyrian Tree. In *Boethius's De Topicis Differentiis*.
        Ithaca: Cornell University Press.
Thagard, P. R.
 1978   Semiotic and Hypothetic Inference in C. S. Peirce. *VS* 19– 20.
Tesauro, E.
 1655   *Il cannocchiale aristotelico*. 2d ed. Venice: Baglioni.
Todorov, T.
 1977   *Théories du symbole*. Paris: Seuil.
 1978   *Symbolisme et interprétation*. Paris: Seuil.

References                                                                [235]

van Dijk, T. A.
  1972  Aspects d'une théorie générative du texte poétique. In *Essais de sémiotique poétique*, edited by A. J. Greimas. Paris: Larousse.
  1975  Formal Semantics and Metaphorical Discourse. *Poetics* 4.
  1977  *Text and Context*. New York: Longman.
Vico, G.
  1744  *La scienza nuova giusta l'edizione del 1744*. Bari: Laterza, 1967. (English translation by T. G. Bergin and M. Fisch, *The New Science of Giambattista Vico*. Ithaca: Cornell University Press, 1968.)
Weinreich, U.
  1980  *On Semantics*. Philadelphia: University of Pennsylvania Press.
Weinrich, H.
  1976  Streit und Metaphoren. In *Sprache in Texten*. Stuttgart: Kleitt
Wierzbicka, A.
  1972  *Semantic Primitives*. Frankfurt: Athenäum.
Wilson, N. L.
  1967  Linguistics Butter and Philosophical Parsnips. *Journal of Philosophy* 64.
Winston, P. H.
  1977  *Artificial Intelligence*. Reading, Mass.: Addison-Wesley.

# Index of Authors

# Index of Subjects